IMPERIALISM AND GLOBAL POLITICAL ECONOMY

To Sam, again, with love

Imperialism and Global Political Economy

Alex Callinicos

polity

First published in 2009 by Polity Press

Reprinted 2009 (twice), 2010

Polity Press
65 Bridge Street
Cambridge CB2 1UR, UK

Polity Press
350 Main Street
Malden, MA 02148, USA

ISBN-13: 978-0-7456-4045-7
ISBN-13: 978-0-7456-4046-4(pb)

A catalogue record for this book is available from the British Library.

Typeset in 10.5 on 12 pt Sabon
by SNP Best-set Typesetter Ltd, Hong Kong
Printed and bound in Great Britain by the MPG Books Group

The publisher has used its best endeavours to ensure that the URLs for external websites referred to in this book are correct and active at the time of going to press. However, the publisher has no responsibility for the websites and can make no guarantee that a site will remain live or that the content is or will remain appropriate.

Every effort has been made to trace all copyright holders, but if any have been inadvertently overlooked the publishers will be pleased to include any necessary credits in any subsequent reprint or edition.

For further information on Polity, visit our website: www.politybooks.com

CONTENTS

CONTENTS

TABLES

PREFACE AND ACKNOWLEDGEMENTS

Imperialism, to many people's surprise, survived the Cold War. More to the point, it has also survived the presidency of George W. Bush. So it is an important subject. I have been fortunate enough to write about it during what can only be considered a great renaissance of the Marxist theory of imperialism. This has allowed me to develop my own ideas in dialogue – and sometimes in confrontation – with many of the leading contributors to this revival. Thanks to a variety of social forums, congresses and conferences, mostly generated by the contemporary movements against neoliberal globalization and imperial war, I have been able to debate with, and learn from, Gilbert Achcar, Samir Amin, Giovanni Arrighi, Daniel Bensaïd, Bob Brenner, Frank Deppe, Peter Gowan, Michael Hardt, David Harvey, David McNally, Toni Negri, Leo Panitch and Claude Serfati.

I have also benefitted from being allowed to present the thought that forms the subject of chapter 2 of this book – that there is a necessary relationship between capitalism and the international state system – in various forums, including the *Cambridge Review of International Affairs*. I am grateful to the editors of this journal, and particularly to Alex Anievas, who has both orchestrated and contributed to a much more extensive debate about Marxism, the international, and uneven and combined development in the pages of *CRIA*. It has also helped to have had the opportunity to present my ideas to seminars at Birmingham, Cambridge, London Metropolitan, and Nottingham universities, and at Goldsmiths College, to the Historical Sociology Group of the British International Studies Association, and to the 7th International Relations Conference of the Middle East Technical University in Ankara. My thanks to all involved, and perhaps especially to Gonso Pozo-Martin for his searching criticisms both in print and in discussion.

Sam Ashman, Chris Harman, Nigel Harris, Justin Rosenberg, Andrew Wright and an anonymous reviewer all read this book in draft and made very helpful comments. Both Sam and Andrew are engaged in research of their own, some of whose findings overlap with my arguments; I am very grateful to the intellectual support their work has given me. My correspondence and conversations with Justin have provided enormous stimulus and pleasure. Chris and Nigel wrote at once the most detailed and much the rudest comments, showing that old comrades may diverge politically without losing the robust intellectual training all three of us received from the late Tony Cliff. I particularly appreciate Nigel's patience and kindness in sticking with a train of thought that he regards as thoroughly misguided.

At Polity David Held suggested that I write a short book about imperialism and has taken this much longer one on the chin. I am grateful to him and also to Clare Ansell, Helen Gray and Sarah Lambert for guiding the book to publication.

My biggest debt, however, is to Sam Ashman. We have talked non-stop about many of the topics that I have ended up writing about in this book. My debt to her is enormous, not just intellectually, but also for the support she has provided in what have proved to be quite stressful times. It is in token of what I owe that I am dedicating this book to her.

INTRODUCTION: EMPIRE OF THEORY, THEORIES OF EMPIRE

Empire is back with a vengeance.[1] This is largely because the thing imperialism has increasingly obtruded itself on us all over the past few years, till now all the blood and clamour, the colonial expeditions and the grand financial and commercial manoeuvres are quite inescapable and undeniable. But, as historians have noted, empires have often disavowed themselves, and here there was a marked discursive shift in the United States, most notably during the administrations of George W. Bush. The journalist Ron Suskind reports a remarkable conversation with 'a senior adviser to Bush' during the summer of 2002, when the drums of war against Iraq were beating ever louder:

> The aide said that guys like me were 'in what we call the reality-based community' which he defined as people who 'believe that solutions emerge from your judicious study of discernible reality'. I nodded and murmured something about enlightenment principles and empiricism. He cut me off. 'That's not the way the world really works anymore,' he continued. 'We're an empire now, and when we act, we create our own reality. And while you're studying that reality – judiciously, as you will – we'll act again, creating other new realities, which you can study too, and that's how things will sort out. We're history's actors . . . and you, all of you, will be left to just study what we do.[2]

These remarks reverberate with a hubris that was soon enough to meet its nemesis at the hands of the armed resistance to the occupation of Iraq by the US and its allies. But the willingness to conceive America explicitly as an empire is by no means confined to the right-wing nationalists and neoconservatives who drove US global policy under the younger Bush. In the 1990s, Zbigniew Brzezinski, National Security Adviser to President Jimmy Carter, an influential figure in

1

Bill Clinton's administrations, and a ferocious critic of the Iraq adventure, was also willing to view the world in explicitly imperial terms:

> America's global supremacy is reminiscent in some ways of earlier empires, notwithstanding their more confined regional scope. These empires based their power on a hierarchy of vassals, tributaries, protectorates, and colonies, with those on the outside generally viewed as barbarians. To some degree, this anachronistic terminology is not inappropriate for some of the states currently within the American orbit.[3]

But the willingness to perceive the present through the grid of empire is also a marked feature of the contemporary academy. The energetic and ambitious Tory economic historian, Niall Ferguson, has now devoted two books to the theme of what he calls 'Anglobalization'. The first celebrates the British Empire as 'an agency for imposing free markets, the rule of law, investor protection and relatively uncorrupt government on roughly a quarter of the globe'.[4] The second reiterates the case for 'liberal empire' (which Ferguson describes as 'the political counterpart to economic globalization'), namely that the 'only hope' for the 'failed states' of the world 'would seem to be intervention by a foreign power capable of constructing the basic institutional foundations that are indispensable for economic development'. Ferguson considers the US to be the sole candidate for resuming the burden once borne by Britain of 'imperial globalization', even though he has doubts whether American political culture has the resources necessary to sustain such a role.[5]

Ferguson is by no means alone in articulating the nostalgia for the British hegemony, deeply embedded in the unconscious of the Anglo-American ruling classes, that often merges with more current preoccupations. How else can we explain that Peter Clarke, a clever, middle-of-the-road historian of the modern British centre-left (subject and object mirroring each other in a satisfactorily Hegelian way), should in retirement mimic Gibbon with a grand tome entitled *The Last Thousand Days of the British Empire*? But the high-profile monographs of Clarke and Ferguson are the tip of a much larger academic iceberg. In recent years: the English-speaking humanities have experienced a remarkable explosion of scholarship devoted primarily to the study of the European colonial empires and their aftermath, which has rescued colonial studies from what Frederick Cooper has called 'the doldrums of imperial history' and transformed them into a cutting-edge form of interdisciplinarity in the contemporary academy.[6]

0.1 Marxism and imperialism

So empire and imperialism have become an acceptable topic again. But this begs the question of how they are to be understood. Imperialism can be defined very broadly or very narrowly. Thus historians and sociologists conceive it as a specific form of political domination. Michael Doyle, for example, succinctly defines empire as 'effective control, whether formal or informal, of a subordinated society by an imperial society'.[7] Cooper offers a looser 'family description' that seeks to emphasize that the differences between dominant and dominated are reproduced and institutionalized by this kind of 'political unit that is large, expansionist (or with memories of an expansionist past), and which produces differentiation and inequality among people it incorporates.'[8] Such broad definitions are of transhistorical scope, designed to cover ancient Rome and China, the Ottomans and the Mughals, as well as more modern candidates. By contrast, imperialism is also sometimes equated with a very specific historical episode, namely the policy pursued during the nineteenth century by the European Great Powers, and later by the United States and Japan, of formally subordinating most of the rest of the world to their rule.

The classical Marxist conception of imperialism, formulated above all by Lenin, is more specific than the broad definition, more general than the narrow one. Imperialism is neither a transhistorical political form nor a state policy, but 'a special stage in the development of capitalism'.[9] Oddly enough, despite the rise of colonial studies and postcolonial theory, for quite a long patch of my own intellectual life, particularly during the 1980s and 1990s, this approach to imperialism was not an academically respectable one. As Fred Halliday has complained, the debate on globalization that became obsessive in the social sciences in the latter decade suffered from 'the absence, or suppression, within orthodox discussion of the two analytic terms central to the analysis of this process' – namely capitalism and imperialism.[10] Even on the Marxist left, the theory of imperialism suffered the indignity of being ignored or relegated to the past. 'Whatever happened to imperialism?' asked the Indian Marxist economist Pratap Patnaik in 1990:

An outsider cannot help noticing a remarkable transformation in the Marxist discourse in America over the last decade or more, namely,

3

hardly any body talks of imperialism any more. I left Cambridge, England, in 1974, where I was teaching Economics, and have returned to the West, this time to the USA, after a lapse of 15 years. When I left, imperialism perhaps occupied the most prominent place in any Marxist discussion, and nowhere was more being written and talked about on this subject than in the USA, so much so that many European Marxists accused American Marxism of being tainted with Third Worldism . . . That is obviously not the case today. Younger Marxists look bemused when the term is mentioned. Burning issues of the day, such as Eastern Europe, or Perestroika, are discussed, but without any reference to imperialism. Radical indignation over the invasion of Panama, or the wars promoted in Nicaragua and El Salvador, does not jell into theoretical propositions about imperialism, and the topic has disappeared from Marxist journals, especially those of a later vintage.[11]

The most influential example of this intellectual shift was offered by Bill Warren in his posthumous *Imperialism – Pioneer of Capitalism* (1980), which portrayed colonialism as an essentially progressive force, drawing the societies of the South into the dynamism and liberty that a global capitalist system with a long future ahead of it offered. If you think this sounds a bit like George W. Bush you wouldn't be wrong. And maybe this helps to explain the anomaly that the quarter of the contemporary political world where resistance to acknowledging the reality of contemporary imperialism is strongest is among some intellectuals from a left-wing background. A prominent British example is Norman Geras, a Marxist philosopher with impressive achievements to his name, but who has in recent years been vehement in his support for the wars in Afghanistan and Iraq and in his denunciation of the movements that have opposed them. The main intellectual error that he argues lies behind this is what he calls the 'anti-imperialism' of 'most of the socialist left'. He states:

> even if more advanced models of theoretical explanation are now available to the left, it nonetheless seems to suffice in any given international conflict to know that on one side is the United States, and that the United States is a capitalist power that always has designs on the natural and human resources of the rest of the world. If you know this, everything else falls instantly into place; all other levels of analysis, all other considerations, are superfluous. They can either be ignored altogether, or they can be conceded in passing, but as merely secondary and hence ignorable in practice. The political alignments are always defined by the primary determinant – imperialism.[12]

4

The implication of this diagnosis is that a reductive obsession with American imperialism morally and politically blinds much of the left to the existence of evils unassimilable to this 'primary determinant' – for example, the Taliban in Afghanistan and Saddam Hussein in Iraq. But of course the contemporary anti-war movement never denied that these and other regimes like them were real evils (though they also pointed to the role played by the US in allowing these regimes to come into existence and to flourish). Their – our – main point, however, was that unleashing the military might of the United States on these countries was not the best way of removing these evils – and indeed was much more likely to bring in its wake even greater evils. I think it is clear whose judgement has turned out to be right. Maybe anti-anti-imperialism is a source of its own forms of moral and political blindness. To misquote Oscar Wilde, a map of the world that does not find a place for imperialism is, alas, of little use to us.

In criticizing Geras, I don't want to suggest that traditional Marxist thinking about imperialism (or indeed about anything else) is beyond reproach. On the contrary. In part, writers such as Warren were reacting to a rather caricatural view of imperialism that owed more to influential Third Worldist writers of the 1960s and 1970s, such as Andre Gunder Frank or Samir Amin, than it did to Lenin or Nikolai Bukharin or Rosa Luxemburg. On this conception, imperialism is about the systematic economic and political domination of the global South by the rich countries of the North, a condition that bred what Frank called 'the development of underdevelopment', preventing any economic progress in the countries of the 'periphery'.

One has only to utter the word 'China' to indicate what's wrong with the Third Worldist understanding of imperialism – though twenty years ago, 'South Korea' would have done just as well.[13] But to recognize that the global domination of capitalism does not prevent significant processes of industrialization in parts of the South cannot expunge from the historical record the real human disasters wrought as a result of this domination – what Kenneth Pomeranz has called the 'great divergence' that transformed China and India, a few centuries ago the most advanced economies of the world, into vast pools of poverty and misery, the great famines under British rule of India remorselessly diagnosed by Mike Davis in his book *Late Colonial Holocausts* (the last of which devastated Bengal in 1943, killing up to 3 million people, on the edge of Peter Clarke's 'last thousand days', though he barely registers it), the massacres that accompanied the colonial empires to their grave.[14]

5

Now, of course, the words 'India' and 'China' have turned into different kind of clichés – metonyms for the liberty and prosperity that capitalist globalization and information technology are bringing to what we used to call the South, according to Thomas Friedman in his magnificently absurd potboiler *The World is Flat*, evening out the differences between rich and poor countries. And yet the figures for global poverty and inequality remain an obscenity. One statistic must suffice here. In 2005, the year when the Group of Eight met in Gleneagles and solemnly promised to rescue Africa from its fate, 10.1 million children died. And the colonial massacres continue, even though there are hardly any formal colonies any more – just 'failed states' subjected to the benevolent guardianship of the United Nations and NATO and the martial power of the Pentagon.

0.2 The need for theory

So imperialism has rightly become a topic again. This has been reflected in a revival in specifically Marxist discussion of imperialism, symbolized by the immense success of Michael Hardt's and Toni Negri's book *Empire* (even though it is highly critical of the classical Marxist approach). But registering this revival leaves the question of how to talk about imperialism. Hence the duality of the title of this introduction. Understanding imperialism requires close empirical study since it concerns a historical phenomenon that has complex characteristics and is subject to change. But it also demands theoretical reflection on what makes the imperialism we encounter today historically distinctive.

This seems rather more controversial. One reason why empire and imperialism are, once again, on the agenda is that they connect with preoccupations internal to the academy. If one thinks (as I do) of postmodernism as a sort of virus, then one way in which it survived the growing boredom and incredulity created by its arguments was by transmuting itself into postcolonial theory. Characteristic poststructuralist themes of instability, undecidability, dissemination, contamination, hybridity were given a more definite political and historical content by being reframed in the context of the long encounter between colonizer and colonized. This didn't, in my view, make the underlying philosophical ideas any more plausible, but it would be silly to deny that postcolonialism opened fruitful lines of enquiry. Indeed, one consolation for someone – such as I – lacking enthusiasm for the preoccupation with cultural themes that allowed many historians to retreat back into the cosy empiricist shell from which they had been prodded by the great ideological dramas of the 1960s and 1970s is that postcolonialism has provided a political stiffening and a wider horizon for scholars who might otherwise have been lost forever in the archives.[15]

Linda Colley's brilliant book *Captives* is a particularly distinguished example of what historical writing organized around the theme of empire can achieve. Colley uses the modes in which would-be colonizers could find themselves subjected to the Other – as Barbary slaves or Native American war booty – to construct a highly differentiated account that is, interestingly, sensitive to the contrasting social trajectories that are imposed by class position even in captivity. This is in striking counterpoint to Colley's earlier *Britons*, which sought to deliver the quietus to Edward Thompson's *The Making of the English Working Class* by seeking to demonstrate the hold that Church and King, rather than the radical-democratic dissenting tradition, had on the English crowd in the late eighteenth and early nineteenth centuries.

The intellectual fertility of this rediscovery of empire is, then, demonstrable. But empire itself is under-theorized. Take, for example, *After Tamerlane*, a recent book by the Oxford historian John Darwin. As the book's subtitle, *The Global History of Empire*, indicates, Darwin's aim is to reinstate the active role played by non-European empires – for example, the Ottomans, Mughals and Safavids – in the construction of the modern world. Empires may come and go, Darwin suggests, but empire is perennial:

> A glance at world history suggests . . . that, for most of the time, the default position so far as politics went was imperial power. Empires were systems of influence or rule in which ethnic, cultural or ecological boundaries were overlapped or ignored. Their ubiquitous presence arose from the fact that, on a regional scale, as well as a global, the endowments needed to build strong states were very unequally distributed.[16]

As the figures for child deaths I gave earlier indicate, 'endowments' are still 'very unequally distributed'. And indeed Darwin believes empire, or empires, to remain our fate today: 'What we call globalization today might be candidly seen as flowing from a set of recent agreements, some tacit, some formal, between the four great economic "empires" of the contemporary world: America, Europe, Japan, and China.'[17] I agree with this empirical judgement, which is substantially closer to the truth than the most celebrated contemporary radical theory of Empire – Hardt's and Negri's argument that national antagonisms have been dissolved into a decentred transnational network capitalism, a Marxist version of Thomas Friedman's flat world thesis.[18]

In other words, the world in which we live is characterized by enormously unequal distributions of economic power that drastically limit the life chances and well-being of the large majority of the world's population. These inequalities are closely related to the – again highly unequal – distribution of military and political power. The correlation isn't complete. Famously, the United States is, as Colin Powell put it, 'the bully on the block' militarily but it's also the world's biggest debtor. The European Union remains, despite its economic weight and all the current bragging about its 'soft power', a geopolitical pygmy.[19] All the same, the basic relationship between economic strength and military capabilities continues to hold, as is demonstrated by the Pentagon's growing edginess about Beijing's efforts to use its vastly increased productive resources to modernize its armed forces.

But if that is the core of contemporary imperialism – the continuing domination of the globe by a handful of Great Powers – how are we to understand the sources and nature of this domination? Is it enough simply, as Darwin suggests, to treat 'imperial power' as the 'default position' throughout human history? A similar view is to be found even in quite unexpected quarters. The greatest contemporary anti-imperialist, Noam Chomsky, seems to think something like this. Imperial domination, he suggests, is something that tends to arise when power is unequally distributed. His formidable powers of empirical research are deployed relentlessly to illustrate and provide corroboration for a limited number of transhistorical generalizations – for example: 'Revenge knows few limits when the privileged and powerful are subjected to the kind of terror they regularly mete out to their victims.' Or again, the US effort to dominate space militarily 'makes good sense if hegemony, with its short-term benefits to elite interests, is ranked above survival in the scale of operative values, in accord with the historical standard for dominant states and other systems of concentrated power'.[20] Of course, Chomsky doesn't therefore think that empire is inescapable: as a lifelong anarchist, he believes strongly that democratic, cooperative relationships represent the desirable and feasible alternative to the present, profoundly unjust world, but he doesn't seem to regard imperialism as something that needs special explanation. It is just the likely concomitant of systems of domination, the external expression of inegalitarian social relationships.

The trouble with this way of thinking is that – while not exactly wrong – it fails to address the specificity of contemporary imperialism. Take the case of the United States, undeniably the greatest imperial power today. Among its distinctive features are: (1) the fact that the US still usually disavows its imperial status – 'We don't do empire,' as even Donald Rumsfeld said; (2) as apparent support for this disavowal, the fact that other countries are not formally politically subordinated to the US. Washington's global power is exercised through a complex set of more or less institutionalized relationships with sovereign independent states. In a provocative recent essay, Bernard Porter, a distinguished historian of the British Empire, suggests that these features are less distinctive than is frequently thought.[21] Till the late nineteenth century, Victorian Britain was a lot less comfortable about its empire than retrospect suggests. And some of the areas most important to British capitalism – for example, Latin America – were never politically subordinated to the British state, but instead integrated economically through what John Gallagher and Ronald Robinson famously called the 'imperialism of free trade', based on the 'willingness to limit the paramount power to establishing security for trade'.[22]

This phrase very accurately captures a key feature of how the world is presently organized. The imperialism of free trade is exactly what the EU, as well as the US, have been pressing on other countries, particularly since the establishment of the World Trade Organization in the mid-1990s. Boosters of the flat world of globalized capitalism, such as Friedman, are effectively propagandizing for this very aggressive attempt to crack open the markets of the world for the capital and commodities of the North.

But, although Brussels has been a very active partner in this process of forcing trade liberalization through globally, this has been a much longer-term project for Washington. The Imperialism of the Open Door is the name that William Appleman Williams gave to the project on which American economic and political elites converged at the beginning of the twentieth century.[23] Formal colonies can be expensive and difficult to run, as the US discovered when it annexed the Philippines after the Spanish–American War, only to be confronted with a pattern of national resistance, imperial atrocity and domestic opposition that was to be repeated in Vietnam and Iraq. Far better to leave the locals to run themselves, so long as they don't interfere with the free movement of capital and goods, with military power – preferably in the form of offshore aerial and naval bombardment – in the background to deal with anyone who fails to respect the sacred flows of money and commodities.

It is when we confront this updated version of the Victorian imperialism of free trade that we get closer to what makes modern imperialism distinctive. Max Horkheimer wrote in his famous essay 'The Jews and Europe', first published in 1940, that 'those who do not wish to speak of capitalism should be silent about fascism'.[24] I think Horkheimer was right about fascism, but his remark could be applied to imperialism: modern imperialism is *capitalist* imperialism. Of course, this is very far from being news. As I have already noted, the Marxist theory of imperialism has been defined, since its initial formulation before and during the First World War, by the claim that the geopolitical struggles among the Great Powers for global domination were a consequence of changes in the structure of capitalism at the end of the nineteenth century – in particular, the increasing concentration of economic power and its interweaving with the state.

Now this theory has, in my view, great explanatory power. But it became vulnerable to criticism for a variety of reasons. As Mike Kidron pointed out in pioneering essays written in the 1960s, the classical Marxist theory of imperialism sometimes conflated the historically specific with the universal: thus the theory of finance capital that Lenin took over from Rudolf Hilferding extrapolated far too much from characteristics that were distinctive particularly to late nineteenth-century Germany.[25] Furthermore, the treatment of economic crises by the theorists of imperialism was generally problematic. And, quite simply, they were overtaken by how capitalism changed in the course of the twentieth century.

None of these criticisms constitute good reasons to give up the theory of imperialism. But here it is worth saying something about theory itself. 'Theory' as a noun on its own, without either a definite article or a particular subject matter *of* which it is the theory, has become a way of referring to the seduction of English and other domains of the humanities by poststructuralism over the past generation. This is a usage whereby it is perfectly coherent for Terry Eagleton to write a book – rather a good one, in fact – called *After Theory*. But there is a slightly earlier version of the same usage that got lost in the rush after Derrida & Co. 'Theory' with a capital T was the name that, at the height of his fame in the 1960s, Louis Althusser gave to Marxist philosophy, to highlight its role as what he called

10

'the Theory of theoretical practice', the source of a general ontological guarantee to all the particular sciences.[26]

That whole project, megalomaniacal as it evidently was, soon came crashing down, and its collapse helped to legitimize the postmodernist cult of fragmentation and uncertainty. And for postcolonial theorists such as Robert Young, Althusser's conceptual imperialism is somehow complicit with the West's domination of the world.[27] Maybe this is a fair cop in Althusser's case. In contrast with his friend and colleague Jacques Derrida, like him brought up in colonial Algeria, Althusser says nothing about this dimension of his upbringing.

But, directed as a charge against Marxism in general, as Young's accusation is intended to be, it is nonsense. The connection between Marxism and anti-imperialism runs deep, even in Britain. One of the two greatest Marxists born in these islands, James Connolly, died facing a British firing squad for his part in leading the Easter 1916 rising. British Communists such as the historian John Saville worked closely with the Indian independence movement while serving in the British armed forces during the Second World War. For all the distortions it suffered through its subjection to Stalinism, the Communist International gave rise to mass parties in such key outposts of the South as India, Iraq, and South Africa.

And even the Althusserian enterprise contained elements of lasting value, I think. Particularly in the collective book, *Reading Capital*, Althusser and his pupils sought to undertake a rigorous conceptual interrogation of Marx's *Capital* as the starting point of a broader renewal of Marxism intellectually and politically. They weren't the only ones to do this. In Italy this was undertaken by the workerists, and in Germany by the capital-logicians, but, as David Harvey has recalled, on a much broader scale: thousands, maybe tens of thousands, of young radicalized intellectuals who took part in *Capital* reading groups all over the world in the late 1960s and early 1970s, all sought to study Marx's great work as a means of more effectively understanding and overthrowing capitalism itself.[28]

Not surprisingly, given the grandiose ambitions with which it was invested, Althusser's version of this huge intellectual effort was riddled with error and plain old bullshit. But there remained a 'rational kernel', to borrow a metaphor of Marx's of which Althusser made heavy weather. *Capital*, on Althusser's reading, portrayed the capitalist mode of production as a nexus of relationships that imposed themselves imperatively on individual subjects:

11

the structure of the relations of production determines the *places* and *functions* occupied and adopted by the agents of production, who are never anything more than the occupants of these places, insofar as they are the 'supports' (*Träger*) of these functions. The true 'subjects' (in the sense of the constitutive subjects [*sujets constituants*] of the process) are therefore not these occupants or functionaries, are not, despite all appearances, the 'obviousness' of the 'given' of naïve anthropology, 'concrete individuals', 'real men' – but *the definition and distribution of these places and functions. The true 'subjects' are these definers and distributors: the relations of production* (and political and ideological social relations). But since these are 'relations', they cannot be thought within the category *subject*. And if by chance anyone proposes to reduce these relations of production to relations between men, i.e., '*human relations*', he is violating Marx's thought, for so long as we apply a truly critical reading to some of his rare ambiguous formulations, Marx shows in the greatest depth that the *relations* of production (and political and ideological social relations) are irreducible to any anthropological inter-subjectivity – since they only combine agents and objects in a specific structure of the distribution of relations, places and functions, occupied and 'supported' by objects and agents of production.[29]

What's wrong with Althusser's argument here is the idea that individual human subjects are the mere 'supports' of the relations of production. This is his notorious 'anti-humanism', which Edward Thompson memorably denounced in *The Poverty of Theory*. But the idea that what constitutes capitalism as an economic system is the relations of production, which determine the access that persons have to productive resources in a definite way, is of fundamental importance. One might seek to specify the relationality of capital by saying that it involves two closely interconnected dimensions: first, the exploitive relationship between wage-labour and capital, which presupposes the exclusion of workers from direct access to any productive resource other than their own labour-power; and, second, the competitive relations that exist among the individual capitals that together control the bulk of society's productive resources – the capitalist class is a fragmented, internally divided class whose members struggle among themselves, each trying to grab the largest possible share of the profits they jointly extract from workers.

You may think that the relationality of capital is an abstruse philosophical formula of no practical interest or relevance. You would be wrong about this, as is shown by the sad case of Adam Applegarth, former chief executive of the Northern Rock bank. Mr Applegarth had what he thought was a splendid business model. This involved lending money on ever more generous terms to homeowners. These loans were themselves financed by being packaged in obscure ways, in fancy financial instruments called collateralized debt obligations, that were then sold on to investors all over the world. All went fine till the American housing market, which had become increasingly driven by this kind of practice, collapsed in the first half of 2007.

In August 2007, banks everywhere woke up to the fact that not only were they individually carrying a lot of bad debt, but so was everyone else. Even worse, collateralized debt obligations and the like, previously praised as a terrific example of financial 'innovation', made it much harder to work out where the debt was and which lenders were in real trouble. So the banks stopped lending to each other. A critical feature in the relationship, at once competitive and cooperative, among financial capitals just stopped working. Northern Rock, previously one of the masters of the universe, was now in great difficulty because it relied so heavily on short-term borrowing – hence the first run on a British bank since the collapse of Overend, Gurney & Co in 1866. The baffled (though, it transpired, generously compensated) Mr Applegarth received rather a hard lesson in what Hegel might have called the actuality of the relationality of capital.

But, although I think the relationality of capital is a thoroughly operational concept, it does also have philosophical significance. The priority that Althusser gives to relations over subjects runs counter to the dominant trend in contemporary radical thought, which is to privilege subjectivity. Thus, if we take the case of Hardt's and Negri's theory of Empire, though Empire itself is understood as a nexus of institutions, it isn't where the action is. The locus of creative power lies rather in the multitude, the tendentially existing macro-subject whose affirmation of life is increasingly subverting the dominance of capitalism. Alain Badiou's ontology is much more austere, but philosophically he goes even further than Negri, denying relations any being and giving primacy to the rare events – for example, the emergence of Christianity, the French, Russian and Chinese Revolutions, the formulation of set theory – through which crystallizes a new truth that may be embodied in a subject.

This preoccupation with subjectivity may have been a corrective to Althusser's anti-humanism, in which history is conceived as 'a process without a subject'. But Badiou's events, in the absence of an account of their necessarily relational context, are a mystery, while the Hardt-Negri theory of the multitude is little more than wishful thinking. This doesn't mean, as Negri rather crossly suggested when I put these criticisms to him, giving up on the idea that it is possible to resist and to win. On the contrary, understanding that capital is a relation helps us to recognize its fragility, as the case of Northern Rock indicates. But Althusser's insistence on putting relations before subjects seems to me basically right, even if he got subjects badly wrong.[30]

0.3   Imperialism and global political economy today

You may be wondering what this excursus into high theory and low politics has to do with imperialism. But there is a connection. Amid all the political and intellectual disasters of the past generation, one positive result has been the development of a deeper and more scholarly understanding of Marx's *Capital* that is closely associated with the survival (despite all the obloquy heaped on it, particularly in the 1970s), and, more recently, the expansion of a community of serious students of Marxist political economy. This has to be a good thing in itself. Marx's theme was capitalism, and today we confront a particularly unconstrained capitalism whose apparently baffling behaviour, above all in the global economic crisis that began with the credit squeeze in the summer of 2007, needs decoding.

I'm not saying that *Capital* provides the ultimate code book. Closer study of the text and better knowledge of the complex set of manuscripts from which Marx and his heroic literary executor Engels constructed it have made clear the ellipses and tensions that it contains. Real Marxist political economy has to go beyond Marx and not just repeat him. But then this was true of earlier generations. Rosa Luxemburg, for example, devotes her *Accumulation of Capital* to a thoroughly wrong-headed critique of the reproduction schemes in *Capital*, Volume II. But the final chapters of her book give an account of how late nineteenth-century imperialism brutally and violently broke down the resistance of pre-capitalist societies to the dominance of capital, in a way that many contemporary critics of neoliberalism have found speaks directly to the processes of privatization and marketization witnessed today North as well as South.

The Marxist theorist who has most influentially highlighted these processes is David Harvey. He calls them instances of 'accumulation by dispossession' – the plunder of resources to enable the profitable expansion of capital. He develops this idea in the context of a broader restatement of the theory of imperialism. Quite independently, I came up with a very similar formulation (though one that lacked the bold and rich interpretation of the history of modern capitalism that

Harvey develops in *The New Imperialism*). Both versions were published in 2003, the year of the invasion of Iraq, which amply demonstrated the need to understand contemporary imperialism. I shall give mine, though I don't think there is any substantive difference between the two theories.[31]

The thought is, then, that capitalist imperialism is constituted by the intersection of two forms of competition, namely economic and geopolitical. Economic competition we have already encountered as one of the two interconnected relations constitutive of capital. Geopolitical competition compromises the rivalries among states over security, territory, influence, and the like. Let me mention what seem to me three merits of this way of conceptualizing imperialism. First, it is historically open. Geopolitical competition plainly antedates capitalism: the Greek city-states and the absolute monarchs of early modern Europe pursued it with great gusto. The historical moment of capitalist imperialism is when the interstate rivalries become integrated into the larger processes of capital accumulation – something that happens as the selective advantage of having a capitalist economic base imposes itself on states, but which takes several centuries – starting with the Dutch Revolt, but becoming inescapable in the late nineteenth century.

Secondly, it is a non-reductionist treatment of imperialism. The Marxist theory of imperialism, and indeed of the state more generally, is sometimes caricatured as reducing the motivations behind public policy to direct economic interests. It is tempting to say that the Bush-Cheney administration – memorably described by Mike Davis as the executive committee of the American Petroleum Institute – showed that the caricature is sometimes true. Nevertheless, the idea that imperialism involves the convergence of geopolitical and economic competition opens the door to a much more nuanced approach to the formation of state policy. Even under Bush, the US wasn't driven primarily by the desire to put money in the coffers of Halliburton. Indeed, the preoccupations of Paul Wolfowitz, now disgraced but once the key neocon, involved a much more complex analysis of the potentially destabilizing impact of economic changes – in particular, the expansion of East Asian capitalism – on the global distribution of power. Clobbering Iraq, on this perspective, was about warning off potential 'peer competitors', as well as tightening Washington's grasp on the oil supplies on which all its rivals depend more than it does.

More generally, the simultaneous operation of both economic and geopolitical determinations introduces a degree of indeterminacy into

15

the formation of state policy, one that has the merit of allowing some free play to other dimensions of the social. For example, scope is allowed for ideology – plainly a key topic, given the importance of a Wilsonian conception of a global liberal capitalist order in shaping US foreign policy over the past century. It is here also perhaps that the issues highlighted by the so-called 'neo-Gramscian' school in international relations – the effort by an actual or aspiring hegemonic power culturally and politically to integrate the ruling classes of other states – might find some purchase.

A third merit of Harvey's and my refinement of the Marxist theory of imperialism is that, in focusing on the interrelations of different forms of *competition*, it returns us to the central preoccupation of that theory as it was initially formulated at the beginning of the twentieth century. As a result particularly of the anti-colonial movements of the mid-twentieth century, the idea of imperialism has come to be identified primarily with what we would today call North/South relations. But for the original theorists, writing on the eve of, or during the First World War, 'imperialism' denoted primarily the way in which changes in the structure of capitalism had given rise to intensified economic and strategic rivalries among the Great Powers. Even Rosa Luxemburg, who believed that capitalism could only reproduce itself by incorporating and dominating non-capitalist societies, saw imperialism in these terms. The theory of imperialism is a way of understanding *capitalism* in its heartlands – what is sometimes called the 'core' of the world system.

Now Harvey's and my reconceptualization of imperialism has attracted many criticisms, mainly from other Marxists, many of them working in the field of International Relations.[32] These debates are part of a much wider discussion among Marxists about the implications of the greater transnational economic integration of the past generation for the nature of contemporary capitalism. One major theme has been the contemporary relevance of the classical Marxist theory of imperialism, which, as we shall see in more detail in chapter 1, treated geopolitical competition (understood as inter-imperialist rivalries) as an inevitable consequence of capitalism in its developed form.

One can identify, broadly speaking, three contemporary positions. First, Hardt, Negri and William Robinson all claim that capitalism is now organized both economically and politically along transnational lines: the conclusion straightforwardly follows that geopolitical conflicts among the leading capitalist states are obsolete.[33] The minor premiss of this argument is that the interstate system that has

16

provided the structural context of geopolitical rivalries for the past few centuries, first in Europe, then globally, is neither inherently necessary nor any longer required for capitalist relations of production to function optimally. This claim has been very strongly contested, notably by Ellen Wood.[34] But those who reject it do not share the same view of contemporary imperialism.

A second position, argued most systematically by Leo Panitch and Sam Gindin, but largely shared by Wood, asserts that, while capitalism needs the state system, since the Second World War the US has succeeded in constructing an 'informal empire' that effectively subordinates the other leading capitalist states to an American hegemony that manages their common global interests.[35] This argument implies the same conclusion as is affirmed by Hardt and Negri and Robinson: geopolitical competition is obsolete. Neither the crisis of the 1970s, in which Japanese and West German economic competition with the US played a significant causal role, nor the contretemps over the Iraq War, has significantly dented American primacy, according to Panitch and Gindin. It is probably fair to say that some version of this position is widely supported on the intellectual left: for example, it informs the editorial outlook of *New Left Review*. It has the merit of consistency with the assertion of American national power under Bush Junior (a development highly embarrassing to Hardt and Negri), and it certainly captures the asymmetry of power between the US and all other states in the post-Cold War era.[36]

Both these perspectives are contested by a third group, dubbed by Ray Kiely 'theorists of the new imperialism', most prominently represented by David Harvey, but also including Walden Bello, Peter Gowan, Chris Harman, John Rees, Claude Serfati and myself.[37] Broadly speaking, all these theorists affirm the following:

1   Global capitalism has yet to exit from the era of economic crisis into which it entered in the late 1960s and early 1970s.
2   One important dimension of this crisis is the division of advanced capitalism between three competing centres of economic and political power, the so-called Triad of Western Europe, North America and East Asia.
3   Consequently, despite the real asymmetries of power between the US and the other leading capitalist states, significant conflicts of interest exist among them (and indeed other states such as Russia and China) that are likely, in the context of the continuing 'long downturn', to give rise to geopolitical struggles.

The above classification of current debates isn't exhaustive. The most important contemporary exponent of world systems theory, Giovanni Arrighi, spreads himself with brio across all three positions: he certainly rejects Hardt's and Negri's premisses but accepts their conclusion (that geopolitical rivalries are obsolete), while further affirming that, though the US is currently hegemonic, its dominance has probably entered its 'terminal crisis'.[38] Robert Brenner's position is also, albeit in a different way, inassimilable to this classification, since, though affirming (1) and (2) above, he rejects (3), occupying a position in some ways closer to Hardt and Negri and Robinson, according to which US hegemony, when rationally exercised (as it was not under Bush II), serves the shared interests of the advanced capitalist states in a pacific neoliberal globalization.[39]

My aim in this book is to intervene in these debates, and to clarify my own position within them, through a sustained examination of the Marxist theory of imperialism. The division of this book into two parts reflects a rough-and-ready division between theory and history – rough and ready because neither Marxism as a form of social theory nor the subject under discussion admits of too sharp a distinction between the two. Part I comprises two chapters, the first devoted to a critical examination of the classical Marxist theory of imperialism developed in the early twentieth century; the second to articulating and defending Harvey's and my refinement of this theory, particularly with respect to the problem of the relationship between the capitalist mode of production and the state system.

Part II pursues the theoretical issues formulated in these first chapters by tracing the historical emergence and transformations of modern capitalist imperialism. Chapter 3 undertakes the essential preliminary of clarifying the nature and constitution of capitalism itself – an issue that, as we shall see, plays an important role in differing conceptualizations of imperialism. This allows me to consider some of the issues raised by what Bob Sutcliffe calls 'the second generation of imperialism theory' – the Marxist and *marxisant* dependency and world systems theories influential in the 1960s and 1970s – and also by the more recent school of 'Political Marxism' inspired by Brenner's historical work, but developed mainly by Wood and her pupils.[40] In chapter 4, I explore modern imperialism itself, sketching out the significant changes it has undergone – from the classical imperialism of the colonial era (1870–1945), through what I call the superpower imperialism of the Cold War era (1945–91), to the version that confronts us today, one that is in many respects highly ambiguous. These chapters are not intended as detailed historical narratives: high-resolution accounts of particular episodes or issues are provided as a means of clarifying analytical problems and controversies. Chapter 5 addresses the nature of contemporary imperialism and its future more systematically, seeking to relate it to some of the major features of the contemporary global political economy.

In this respect chapter 5 highlights a feature of the book as a whole: its title, *Imperialism and Global Political Economy*, is in part a *hommage* to Bukharin's classic *Imperialism and World Economy*, but it is also intended to underline that this is intended as a contribution to Marxist political economy. This can be seen at three levels. First, and most fundamentally, the approach to the theory of imperialism pursued here, especially in chapter 2, reflects and seeks to apply my understanding of Marx's explanatory strategy in *Capital*. Secondly, and more concretely, a major preoccupation is to trace the relationship between Marxist understandings of imperialism and explanations of capitalism's crisis tendencies – whether this concerns major historical figures such as Luxemburg, Bukharin, Grossman and Preobrazhensky, or more contemporary debates about capitalism and imperialism today. Finally, and most importantly, since this is not intended primarily as an exercise in philosophical clarification, the test of the theoretical constructions erected in this book lies in their ability to provide a better understanding of the political economy of global capitalism, past and present. Sutcliffe complains that two of the best recent books on imperialism, Harvey's *The New Imperialism* and Wood's *Empire of Capital*, 'like, so much Marxist writing, would, to my mind, have benefited from taking a more serious approach to the existing evidence about the many empirical questions they discuss'.[41] I have tried to bear this stricture in mind, drawing on both historical studies and contemporary empirical evidence.

I have been working on the theory of imperialism for more than two decades. This has been a consequence both of the real-world salience of the thing imperialism and of participation in a collective effort to strengthen the theory. My own understanding has enormously benefited from being located within the International Socialist tradition, which not only based itself on, but also criticized and sought to develop and update the classical Marxist tradition. In earlier generations, I have learned enormously from Tony Cliff, Mike Kidron and Nigel Harris, as well as, among closer contemporaries, from Chris Harman and John Rees: Rees in particular provided much of the political and intellectual drive behind the formulation of the theory of the 'new imperialism' at the end of the Cold War.[42]

Situating my work on imperialism within a version of the revolutionary socialist tradition underlines the importance to it of political concerns – above all, resistance to the increasingly vigorous attempts to reassert American hegemony, from the administrations of Carter and Reagan to those of Clinton and the younger Bush. This doesn't mean of course that one can simply uncritically reaffirm the theory in its original form (or, more accurately, forms, since, as we shall see, it has always been multiple). I have mentioned some criticisms; as we shall also see, there are plenty more, some of them valid. Part of the point of the restatements offered by Harvey and me is to liberate the theory of imperialism from these limitations. Moreover, despite the Marxist intellectual framework informing this book, I have no particular qualms about drawing on other traditions when it seems useful to do so – for example, the Weberian historical sociology of Michael Mann and W. G. Runciman, and the variations on structural realism in mainstream International Relations theory; my suggestion that a Marxist theory of the international might find a place for 'a realist moment' has already caused some anguish.[43]

This insistence that theoretical considerations follow their own logic is not, however, counterposed to political imperatives, but rather seeks to make the pursuit of the latter more effective. Reiterating orthodoxy won't help us understand contemporary trends. Thus the stress on competition, common to both Harvey and me, doesn't imply any claim that the patterns of the first half of the twentieth century are repeating themselves – thank God, since the mutually reinforcing dynamics of economic and geopolitical rivalry that then prevailed produced the two world wars. But anyone who looks around the world can detect underlying, and growing tensions among the Great Powers. Think, for example, of Washington's efforts to isolate and encircle China through alliances with Japan, India and various Central Asian states, and the increasing assertiveness of a Russian state enriched by higher energy prices, which was dramatized by its 2008 war with Georgia. These trends are frightening – as are the more immediate crises provoked by the famous 'war on terrorism' in Iraq, Afghanistan, Pakistan and – potentially – Iran. The replacement of George W. Bush in the White House by Barack Obama, however welcome in other ways, does not mean these conflicts are about to disappear. Naturally, this assessment invites the question of how one might escape from the very great dangers in prospect. One way of addressing this question is to interpret the evidence that the US today is grappling with a crisis of 'imperial overstretch' as signs that American hegemony over the world system is in terminal decline.

These interpretations invite us to look for a potential replacement: China is the usual candidate selected for this role.

But such prognostications imply that the best we can hope for is a change of masters, as the cycle of hegemony turns again and the imperial purple is passed on from one capital to another, from Amsterdam to London and then on to Washington, and some day perhaps to Beijing. Here again we discover a virtue of the Marxist theory of imperialism. For that theory affirms both that 'imperial power' is not 'the default position' and that the problem stems from the system, not from any particular hegemon. Moreover, as the American radicals of the 1960s put it, the theory names the system as capitalism. That still seems right, even if it also indicates the scale of the task that faces us if we are ever to shake off the yoke of empire once and for all.

Part I

THEORY

— 1 —

THE CLASSICAL LEGACY

1.1 Continuing Marx's *Capital*

It seems indisputable that the first third of the twentieth century saw
Marxist political economy achieve a standard of intellectual fertility
and substantive achievement that has set a benchmark for all subsequent efforts. One of the main themes running through the economic
writings of Karl Kautsky, Rudolf Hilferding, Rosa Luxemburg, Otto
Bauer, V.I. Lenin, Leon Trotsky, Nikolai Bukharin, Henryk Grossman and Evgeny Preobrazhensky was the effort to understand imperialism, which they all acknowledged to be a key feature of their
world. Bob Sutcliffe writes: 'The first generation of imperialism theorists represented one of the high points of the application of historical
materialist method to understanding the world of international relations. They wrote in a period of extraordinary fertility. They contributed by not being orthodox and exegetical but by being boldly
revisionist and critical.'[1]

Three key features of this collective, if highly disputatious enterprise are worth stressing. First, it was radically different from contemporary theorizing about imperialism in that it was based outside
the academy. In the preface to his path-breaking work, *Finance
Capital* (1910), Hilferding complains:

> Economic theory, by virtue of the infinite complexity of its subject
> matter, is among the most difficult of scientific enterprises. But the
> Marxist finds himself in a peculiar situation; excluded from the uni-
> versities, which afford the time required for scientific research, he is
> obliged to defer his scientific work to those leisure hours which his
> political struggles may spare him.[2]

Perry Anderson, in drawing his famous contrast between pre-war classical Marxism, geographically located in Central and Eastern Europe, excluded from the academy, organically rooted in the mass working-class movements of the Second and Third Internationals, and focused on substantive economic and political analysis, and postwar Western Marxism, centred on Western Europe and North America, based in the universities, and preoccupied with meta-theory and aesthetics, took Hilferding and his peers as the paradigmatic case of the former tendency.[3] Their engagement in socialist politics is indicated by the violent fate so many suffered – Kautsky dying after fleeing the Nazi *Anschluss* of Austria in 1938, Hilferding tortured to death by the Gestapo in occupied Paris, Luxemburg murdered by the proto-fascist *Freikorps* in revolutionary Berlin, Trotsky, Bukharin and Preobrazhensky all victims of Stalin's tyranny. What the Communist International dubbed the imperialist epoch of wars and revolutions, along with the paradoxical outcome of the Russian Revolution of October 1917, scarred the lives of all these activist intellectuals.

Secondly, these theorists shared an understanding of imperialism as a problem requiring analysis that could provide the basis for political action. This understanding is admirably summarized by Anthony Brewer:

> It is easy to misunderstand the classical Marxist theories of imperialism since the very word has expanded and altered its meaning. Today the word 'imperialism' generally refers to the dominance of more developed over less developed countries. For classical Marxists it meant, primarily, rivalry between major capitalist countries, rivalry expressed in conflict over territory, taking political and military as well as economic forms, and leading ultimately to inter-imperialist war. The dominance of stronger countries over weaker is certainly implicit in this conception, but the focus is on the struggle for dominance, a struggle between the strongest in which less developed countries figure primarily as passive battlegrounds, not as active participants.[4]

But there is a third shared characteristic of Sutcliffe's 'first generation of imperialism theorists': they saw their work as continuing Marx's effort in *Capital* to uncover the dynamics of the capitalist mode of production. They wrote in an intellectual environment in which the posthumous publication of the second and third volumes of *Capital*, in 1885 and 1894 respectively, provoked the first debates on Marx's theory of value, a perennial issue in Marxist political economy.[5] Much more important than these debates, their effort to develop the conceptual apparatus inherited from Marx aimed to analyse the forms taken by capitalist development in the decades since he wrote *Capital* in the 1860s. Thus Hilferding describes *Finance Capital* as 'an attempt to arrive at a scientific understanding of the economic characteristics of the latest phase of capitalist development. In other words, the object is to bring these characteristics within the theoretical system of classical political economy which begins with William Petty and finds its supreme expression in Marx.'[6] Even Luxemburg, the most iconoclastic of the classical theorists of imperialism and the least interested in differentiating within Marx's broad conceptualization of capitalism, calls imperialism 'the final stage of its [capitalism's] historical career'.[7]

This movement between continuing Marx's theoretical enterprise and analytically grasping the specific features of contemporary capitalism requires some consideration of the kind of intellectual project he was undertaking in *Capital*, though this is easier said than done. The growth of scholarly study of Marx's economic writings, facilitated by their publication in the *Marx-Engels Complete Works* (*Marx Engels Gesamtausgabe*, generally known as *MEGA*), has revealed the vast and complex nature of his unfinished effort to write *Capital*, starting with the *Grundrisse* (1857–8), continuing through the *1861–3 Manuscript* (from which *Theories of Surplus-Value* was eventually extracted) and the *1863–5 Manuscript* (the main source used by Friedrich Engels to edit and publish Volumes II and III of *Capital*) to *Capital*, Volume I (1867), together with the *Contribution to the Critique of Political Economy* (1859), the only portions of this mass of texts to appear during Marx's lifetime. Nevertheless, some attempt must be made to identify key features of the scientific approach Marx pursues in *Capital*, since they are of crucial importance to both classical and contemporary theorizations of imperialism.[8]

In the first place, Marx's aim in *Capital* is not to provide an empirical account of the capitalism of his day. He writes in the Preface to the first edition of Volume I that the Britain of the Industrial Revolution serves as 'the main *illustration* of the theoretical developments that I make', but his object is 'the capitalist mode of production, and the relations of production and the forms of intercourse that correspond to it'.[9] In his late return to the drafts of Volumes II and III, he sought to widen the range of illustration by including empirical material on American and Russian agriculture in his analysis of ground-rent, but did not alter his basic strategy of uncovering the structural logic of the capitalist mode of production. In Marx's theory of history the mode of production is a basic type of economic system, combining a particular level of development of the productive forces, that is, of the productive powers of human labour, with a specific set of relations of production, and it is the latter, the form of effective control over the productive forces, that defines the character of the mode of production in question. As I noted in the Introduction, capitalist relations of production are constituted by two dimensions, what Robert Brenner has called 'the "vertical" (market and socio-political) power relations between capitalists and workers', and 'the "horizontal" competition among firms that constitutes the capitalist system's economic mainspring'.[10]

But, secondly, Marx does not start *Capital* with either of these constitutive contradictions, but rather, in the famously difficult (and much revised) first chapter of Volume I, with the commodity. This provides the context for presenting Marx's version of the labour theory of value first rigorously formulated by David Ricardo, according to which commodities exchange in proportion to the socially necessary labour-time required to produce them. But Marx radically changes the function of this theory of value. No longer does it serve, as it did for Ricardo, to provide a theory of price-determination through which to analyse the distributional struggles among the three main classes of the 'commercial society', first conceptualized by Adam Smith as the final and most natural 'mode of subsistence' developed by human beings. Now value theory functions in the first instance to identify what is historically specific to capitalism as a transitory and exploitive mode of production. In particular, Marx conceives value as *abstract social labour* – not a conceptual category invented by the observing analyst to corral the empirical variety of capitalism, but a 'real abstraction', imposed on economic actors by the blind process of competition among the autonomous but interdependent units of production into which any system where commodity production prevails (what Marx calls generalized commodity production) is necessarily fragmented. It is the pressure of competition that compels these units to adopt more advanced productive techniques and hence to reduce their costs below those of their rivals, thereby enforcing upon themselves the law of value – that is, the requirement to minimize the socially necessary labour time involved in producing their output. Already in the *Grundrisse*, at a relatively early stage in the elaboration of Marx's conceptual system, he had recognized the strategically crucial role of the 'horizontal' dimension of competition among the 'many capitals' acting as the individual units of the capitalist mode: 'The influence of individual capitals upon one another has the effect precisely that they must conduct themselves as *capital*; the seemingly independent influence of the individuals, and their

28

chaotic collisions, are precisely the positing of their general law.'[11] One of the most distinctive features of the capitalist mode of production, the accumulation of capital, is 'the effect of a social mechanism', the competitive struggle that presses rival firms to plough their profits back into investments in improved and expanded production.[12]

The most important single application of Marx's value theory is of course his explanation of where these profits come from. He argues in Part 2 of *Capital*, Volume I, that a key difference between capitalism and other kinds of economic system is that labour-power itself is a commodity. Under the capitalism mode, the direct producers are separated from the means of production. But they differ from the exploited classes in earlier forms of class societies – ancient slaves and mediaeval peasants, for example – in that they own and control their own labour-power. In order to gain access to the means of production and thereby the means of subsistence they must sell this, their sole productive asset, to the capitalists who jointly control these means. But the use to which their labour-power is put – labour itself – is the sole way in which new value can be created. The difference between this new value and the value the capitalist must advance, chiefly in the form of wages, to purchase the workers' labour-power – what Marx calls surplus-value – is the source of the profits that capitalists seek both to support themselves and to expand their investments. Thus the capitalist mode, despite the legal and political equality among persons that tends to emerge where it prevails, is a form of class society based on the exploitation of wage-labour.

We shall return to some of the implications of Marx's analysis of this 'vertical' contradiction between capital and wage-labour for an understanding of imperialism in chapter 3. Of more immediate concern here is how Marx's theory of exploitation is related to a third feature of his approach, namely the progressive and non-deductive introduction of ever more concrete determinations. He is highly aware of the complexity of his object. Though he compares his enterprise with that of the founders of classical physics, and stresses the necessity, in constructing any scientific theory, of formulating abstract concepts to identify the fundamental features of its object that may be obscured in or completely absent from what we perceive, Marx believes that the actual operation of the capitalist mode of production presents additional difficulties. These arise from the way in which its real dependence on the circulation of commodities both occults the relations of exploitation and encourages ideologically distorted conceptualizations of economic relations. Already in chapter 1 of *Capital*, Volume I, he outlines his theory of commodity fetishism, according to which the fact that in a system of generalized commodity production the social connection among autonomous but interdependent units of production takes the form of the exchange of their products on the market means that 'the social relations between their private labours *appear as what they are*, i.e. they do not appear as direct social relations between persons in their work, but rather as material relations between persons and social relations between things'.[13]

The italicized phrase 'appear as what they are' indicates that for Marx this tendency to naturalize and fragment social relations is not simply the product of conscious manipulation, but is a necessary consequence of the functioning of capitalist economic relations. This is a particular problem in *Capital*, Volume III, presented by Marx as exposing the unity of capitalist production and circulation (the immediate process of production and the process of circulation are the objects, respectively, of Volumes I and II). Fred Moseley has suggested that this book is best understood as being concerned with the distribution of the total surplus-value created in the production process. Thus Marx successively considers in Volume III the redistribution of surplus-value among competing capitals through the equalization of profit rates (Part 2), the division of this profit among industrial, commercial and interest-bearing capital (Part 4), and the transformation of the surplus-profit arising in agriculture thanks to its relatively low productivity into ground-rent appropriated by landowners (Part 5).[14] Marx himself highlights, at the beginning of Volume III, the significance of this differentiation of capital's forms:

> Our concern is ... to discover and present the concrete forms which grow out of the *process of capital's movement considered as a whole*. In their actual movement, capitals confront one another in certain concrete forms, and in relation to these, both the shape capital assumes in the immediate production process and its shape in the process of circulation appear merely as particular moments. The configurations of capital, as developed in this volume, thus approach step by step the form in which they appear on the surface of society, in the action of the different capitals on one another, ie in competition, and in the everyday consciousness of the agents of production themselves.[15]

But Marx notes that this process of differentiation makes it harder to grasp the underlying relations. Thus he denounces the 'Trinity Formula', according to which profits are not surplus-value but simply the revenue owed to capital as a factor of production, alongside wages for labour and rent for land, as a functionally appropriate conceptualization for economic agents engaged in competition, but one in which the source of profits in exploitation disappears. Thus

> the actual production process, as the unity of the immediate produc-
> tion process and the process of circulation, produces new configura-
> tions in which the threads of the inner connection get more and more
> lost, the relations of production becoming independent of one another
> and the components of value ossifying into independent forms.[16]

Marx's 'method of rising from the abstract to the concrete' is intended precisely to keep hold of the thread of value and exploita-tion amid all the complex configurations thrown up by the capitalist mode in its totality.[17] Gérard Duménil felicitously describes the 'system' of *Capital* as that of 'a dosed abstraction or, if you prefer, of a concretization constructed element by element'.[18] This involves the successive introduction of more complex determinations of the capitalist mode. So Marx begins *Capital*, Volume I, with an analysis in Part 1 of the commodity and money that avoids all consideration of the *differentia specifica* of capitalism, in particular the exploitation of wage-labour and the competitive accumulation of capital. It is only in Part 2 that he starts to focus on these features, first presenting the specificity of capital as its capacity to valorize (or expand) itself, expressed in the general formula of capital, M-C-M' – that is, the peculiarity of capital as an economic form is that a sum of money (M) is exchanged for commodities (C) that in turn are sold for a larger amount of money (M'), thereby allowing the investor who advances the initial capital to realize a profit. It is in order to explain how such a transaction is possible as the basis of a self-standing system of production (as opposed to the perennial forms of mercan-tile capitalism that battened on pre-capitalist modes of production by buying cheap and selling dear) that Marx introduces the further determination that in the capitalist mode labour-power itself is a commodity, thereby permitting the extraction of surplus-value that explains the valorization of capital.

Three crucial features of this method of progressively introducing more complex determinations must be stressed. First, the distinction between the different determinations is analytical, not historical. Thus Engels's celebrated attempt to show that the law of value governs only economies where simple commodity production (small producers controlling the means of production and marketing their own output) prevails, and ceases to operate in the case of the capitalist mode of production, is a grave misinterpretation.[19] Marx understands the capitalist mode as 'a rich totality of determinations and relations' that he analyses as existing simultaneously but does so by introducing them step by step at the appropriate stage in the argument.[20] Secondly, the relationship between each new determination and those preceding it is not a deductive one. The concept of labour-power, for example, is not somehow 'contained' in that of the commodity or money. Jacques Bidet has shown that one of Marx's main achievements across the continual conceptual recastings in successive economic manuscripts was to abandon the attempt he made in the *Grundrisse* 'dialectically' to deduce the concept of capital from that of money and to treat labour-power and related concepts (surplus-value, exploitation, etc.) as a distinct set of determinations irreducible to those they succeed.[21] This marks a definite difference between Marx's method in *Capital* and Hegel's dialectic: both involve a movement from abstract to concrete in which the introduction of new determinations adds further content to the theory, but in Marx, unlike Hegel, these determinations are not implicit in their predecessors, let alone, as in Hegel's teleological system, in the abstract starting point of the entire process. Appropriately, the best description of Marx's procedure is provided by Louis Althusser:

> Far from proceeding by *self-production* of concepts, the thought of Marx proceeded rather by *position* of concepts, inaugurating the exploration (analysis) of the theoretical space opened and closed by this position, then by position of a new concept enlarging the theoretical field, and so on: until the constitution of theoretical fields of extreme complexity.[22]

Thirdly, this process of progressive complication constitutes the entire discourse of *Capital*. The particular point at which a determination is introduced is strategically crucial. Marx criticizes his predecessors, the classical economists, for failing sufficiently to abstract. Thus Ricardo's value theory is compromised by the way in which, in chapter I of *On the Principles of Political Economy and Taxation*, 'all sorts of categories that are still to be arrived at are assumed as *given*, in order to prove their harmony with the law of value'.[23] So he assumes the existence of a general rate of profit, which contradicts the labour-theory of value: once returns on capital are equalized across all sectors, commodities no longer exchange according to the socially necessary labour-time required to produce them, which reflects the production conditions prevailing in specific sectors. In a key passage, Marx explains:

32

Instead of *postulating* this *general rate of profit*, Ricardo should rather
have examined how far its *existence* is in fact consistent with the
determination of value by labour-time, and he would have found that
instead of being consistent with it, *prima facie*, it contradicts it, and
that its existence would have to be explained through a number of
intermediary stages, which is very different from merely including it
under the law of value.[24]

In other words, Ricardo's attempt directly to deduce all the concrete economic determinations of commercial society from the law
of value led him to introduce these determinations from the start,
thereby preventing him from properly explaining them. By contrast,
Marx's approach in *Capital* seeks precisely to account for these
determinations by introducing them in a succession of 'intermediary
stages'. Thus, having analysed the processes of production and circulation in Volumes I and II abstracting from the differences between
and competition among individual capitals, in Volume III, Part 2, he
drops this simplifying assumption, showing how competition and
the mobility of capital across sectors leads to the formation of an
average rate of profit and hence to conversion of values into prices
of production. Though this latter step is the site of the famous 'Transformation Problem', the *pons asinorum* of Marxist value theory,
Marx's procedure is justified by the fact that it was not necessary to
consider the movement and interaction of individual capitals when
analysing the production process and the bulk of the circulation
process. It is only in Volume II, Part 3, when he analyses how the
interweaving of the circuits of individual capitals must meet certain
constraints if the total social capital is to be reproduced on either a
simple or an extended scale, that Marx explicitly thematizes the difference between individual and total social capital. This then sets the
stage for the analysis of competition among 'many capitals' in Volume
III, Part 2, and especially in chapter 10, 'The Equalization of the Rate
of Profit'.[25]

It is important to see that the fact that a determination is introduced relatively late in the discourse of *Capital* does not reduce it to
a mere epiphenomenal expression of, say, the immediate production
process analysed in Volume I. The subject matter of Volume III – the
formation and equalization of the rate of profit, its tendency to fall
and the business cycle, commercial and money capital, rent and
landed property – consists in crucial features of capitalism as a functioning economic system. Thus, in Volume III, Part 5, Marx devotes
nearly 300 pages to the analysis of interest-bearing capital: although

chaotic, incomplete and possibly distorted by Engels's editing, this addresses in a probing manner an aspect of capital that has gained in significance since the 1860s, namely what Marx calls the credit system, but known today as the financial markets. Marx's treatment, here as elsewhere in *Capital*, both pays close (sometimes bewilderingly detailed) attention to the specific mechanisms at work in the credit system and also situates them within the larger operation of the capitalist mode as a whole: thus money capitalists compete among themselves to maximize their individual share of the surplus-value generated in production, and in doing so allow the accumulation process temporarily to overcome its limits, only for these limits brutally to assert themselves in financial crises.[26] Though the ideological representations that arise in the credit system – in particular the belief that money breeds more money without requiring the mediation of the production of surplus-value by wage-labour (M-M') – represent 'the capital relationship' in 'its most superficial and fetishized form', these and similar representations (for example, the Trinity Formula) are functional to the performance of capitalist economic actors in the everyday workings of the system.[27] The precise placing of a determination is thus critical to the explanatory scheme of *Capital*: the introduction at the appropriate point of a specific determination simultaneously explains that determination through its being situated in the larger theory of the capitalist mode, thereby permitting the critique of ideological representations that conceal this situation, and adds further content to that theory.

What is the relevance of this complex and demanding explanatory strategy for the Marxist theory of imperialism? Critically, there is no reason why the introduction of more concrete determinations should stop at the end of *Capital*, Volume III, famously unfinished as it is. Marx himself initially envisaged that his critique of political economy would be 'divided into 6 books: 1. On Capital. 2. Landed Property. 3. Wage Labour. 4. State. 5. International Trade. 6. World Market', though commentators disagree over whether he later abandoned this plan.[28] It is certainly consistent with the procedure he actually followed in *Capital*, in which the more concrete determinations progressively introduced involve analytical distinctions in a whole composed of coexisting elements. But there is an alternative strategy for continuing *Capital*, which is the one largely taken by the classical theorists of imperialism. This is to make Marx's research programme more concrete by building on to it an evolutionary theory of successive stages of capitalist development. Thus Hilferding introduces finance capital by implicitly contrasting it with what comes to be called the 'classical' capitalism of Marx's day, where competition was relatively unrestricted:

> The most characteristic features of 'modern' capitalism are those processes of concentration which, on the other hand, 'eliminate free competition' through the formation of cartels and trusts, and, on the other, bring bank and industrial capital into an ever more intimate relationship. Through this relationship . . . capital assumes the form of finance capital, its supreme and most abstract expression.[29]

Hilferding seeks to substantiate these claims in two main steps. First, in Parts I and II of *Finance Capital*, he extends Marx's analysis of money and the credit system by exploring the implications of the development of the corporation and the stock market, analysing dividends and the profit made by the promoter of a share issue as specific claims on surplus-value. This serves as preliminary to Hilferding's account, in Parts III–V, of the way in which the growing concentration and centralization of capital lead to the formation of monopolies, cartels and trusts – a process that finds its culmination in finance capital, where banking and industrial capital are fused under the dominance of the former, and that leads to the restriction of competition and to changes in the form of economic crises, and in the relationship between the state and capital, notably the replacement of free trade by protective tariffs, alongside the interstate rivalries arising from the increasing export of capital and the ensuing efforts to expand 'national economic territory'.

I consider Hilferding's analysis – enormously influential on the theory of imperialism developed by Lenin and Bukharin – further, in §1.3 below. For the time being I wish rather to emphasize that this strategy for continuing *Capital* by developing a more concrete theory of different phases of capitalist development seems perfectly consistent with Marx's own approach. But that approach also imposes an important constraint on such efforts, namely (to focus on the matter in hand) that the conceptualizations of imperialism be consistent with the more abstract account of the constitutive relations, tendencies and mechanisms of the capitalist mode developed in *Capital*, or, where they depart from that account, that they provide good reasons for doing so. This stipulation may seem like a dogmatic confinement of empirical research, but this is not my intention. In the first place, the classical theories of imperialism that explain it as a specific phase of capitalist development can only claim to be continuations of *Capital* if they observe some such constraint. Moreover, in doing so, far from representing a retreat from empirical enquiry, they offer a way of making Marx's discourse open to refutation: on this basis, these (and indeed contemporary Marxist) accounts of imperialism can play the function of the testable auxiliary hypotheses through which, according to Imre Lakatos, the hard core of a scientific research programme (in this case Marx's general theory of the capitalist mode of production) can be established as progressive or degenerating, according to the degree to which it succeeds, with their aid, in predicting novel facts.[30] And, finally, as we shall see in §1.4 below, a major difficulty with which Bukharin grappled concerned how his theory of imperialism as state capitalism could account for economic crises – one of Marx's major preoccupations in *Capital*.[31]

1.2 Luxemburg's fertile diversion

Nevertheless, I begin my detailed discussion of classical Marxist theories of imperialism with a variant that is concerned less to differentiate among phases of capitalist development than to explain European territorial expansion in the late nineteenth century as a consequence of the limit intrinsic to the capitalist mode of production. I do so for two reasons. First, though the theoretical basis of Rosa Luxemburg's account of imperialism is generally acknowledged to be deeply flawed, her argument that the capitalist process of accumulation is inherently dependent on dominating a non-capitalist 'other' continues to exert a strong hold on the imagination of contemporary anti-imperialists, including leading theorists such as David Harvey and Ellen Wood. Secondly, Luxemburg seems to have been the first major Marxist to regard imperialism as a necessary consequence of capitalist development. Hilferding, by contrast, consistently refers to imperialism, by which he means '[a]rmaments and colonial policy' as a policy that the bourgeoisie tends to adopt as finance capital becomes dominant. Though he says that 'capital can pursue no other policy than that of imperialism', and that socialism is therefore 'the only alternative to imperialism', conceiving imperialism as a 'policy' leaves open the possibility that capitalism may have other options – a possibility that, as we shall see in §§1.4 and 1.5 below, became an important issue for Marxists during and after the First World War.[32] Luxemburg, by contrast, affirms – in a particularly extreme and sometimes sophistically argued way – the proposition subsequently further developed by Lenin and Bukharin that imperialism is inescapable once capitalism attains maturity. Thus she claims that the refusal of Anton Pannekoek, later a leading Left Communist and therefore hardly a shrinking reformist violet, to accept her own theory commits him to believing that 'socialism as the final stage, with imperialism as its predecessor, ceases to be an historical necessity. The one becomes the laudable decision of the working class, the other is simply a vice of the bourgeoisie.'[33]

Luxemburg's argument proceeds at two levels. The first is an iconoclastic critique of the schemes for the reproduction of capital developed by Marx in *Capital*, Volume II, Part 3. These differentiate the capitalist economy into two broad departments of production, I (means of production) and II (means of consumption), and specify the exchanges that must obtain between these departments if capital is to reproduce itself either on a simple basis (i.e., without any accumulation) or in an expanded form; expanded reproduction is more typical under capitalism, where the pressure of competition leads individual capitals to invest in increasing their production and rendering it more efficient. The reproduction schemes provide a basis from which a Marxist theory of effective demand could be developed, since they follow from the premiss that the value created when a commodity is produced must be realized through the sale of that commodity on the market. The schemes thus establish that the continued expansion of capital depends not merely on the creation of value in the production of commodities, but also on the distribution of purchasing power equivalent in aggregate to this value in proportions that secure the material prerequisites of capitalist reproduction through the production of appropriate quantities of means of production and consumption. But Luxemburg argues that the reproduction schemes are inherently flawed. In particular, Marx fails to explain how, in the case of expanded reproduction, that portion of the surplus-value that is invested in the purchase of additional means of production and the employment of extra workers can be realized: on this logic, capitalism suffers from an inherent shortage of effective demand.[34]

The second level of Luxemburg's argument draws the conclusion that this is not simply a fault in Marx's theory but also reveals the limit inherent in the capitalist mode of production: 'the realization of the surplus-value for the purposes of accumulation is an impossible task for a society which consists solely of capitalists and workers'. It can therefore be realized only if the commodities embodying it are sold to 'such organizations or strata whose mode of production is not capitalistic'.[35] Indeed, Luxemburg goes further, arguing that, 'since its first appearance on the stage of history, capitalist production has demonstrated its enormous attraction towards non-capitalist countries. It runs like a red thread throughout its development, grows ever more important, until, in the last twenty-five years in the epoch of imperialism, it appears directly as the determinant and dominant factor in social life.'[36]

This argument leads Luxemburg, in the final part of *The Accumulation of Capital*, to paint a powerful and original portrait of *fin-de-siècle* imperialism. Here again she criticizes Marx, arguing that he is mistaken in *Capital*, Volume I, Part 8, to present the 'so-called primitive accumulation' of capital – the historical process through which the presuppositions of capitalist relations of production were formed in early modern England through, on the one hand, the concentration of wealth in the hands of capital by fraud and plunder on a global scale, and, on the other, the expropriation of the peasantry and the creation of a landless proletariat – as 'incidental, illustrating merely the genesis of capital, its first appearance in the world, . . . travails by which the capitalist mode of production emerges from a feudal society . . . Yet, as we have seen, capitalism in its maturity also depends in all respects on non-capitalist strata and social organizations existing side by side with it.' And, as in the case of primitive accumulation, the relationship is defined, not by peaceful exchange, but by the violent subordination of non-capitalist societies to capitalist imperatives. Thus 'the accumulation of capital, seen as a historical process, employs force as a permanent weapon, not only at its genesis, but further down to the present day.'[37] This involves the systematic destruction of 'natural economy' – non-market social forms – wherever it is to be found, and the incorporation of its productive elements in the world market, as well as the paradigmatic hostility of developed capitalism to simple commodity production, which it treats as a rival for resources and markets.

The comprehensive conquest of the world by the accumulation process, however, highlights the self-defeating logic of capitalism, since its historical tendency is to subvert itself by assimilating and transforming non-capitalist economic forms, thereby driving towards the impossibility of realizing accumulated surplus-value inherent in a pure capitalist society. But this limit-point will never be reached since the disruptive symptoms of its imminence will goad the working class to end their increasing suffering through socialist revolution. Chief among these symptoms is imperialism, 'the political expression of the accumulation of capital in its competitive struggle for what remains still open of the non-capitalist environment' that increasingly 'takes forms which make the final phase of capitalism a period of catastrophe'.[38] Contrary to what is sometimes claimed, however, Luxemburg does not conclude that socialism is inevitable as a result of what she believed to be the inherent tendency of capitalism to economic collapse, anticipated in the era of imperialism by catastrophe (a judgement that she, quite reasonably, felt was confirmed by the advent of the First World War). The disintegration of capitalism could give rise to barbarism rather than socialism. Despite her economic theory, Luxemburg's Marxism is not fatalistic, since she believes that the crises to which capitalism is necessarily driven pose alternatives dependent on human action rather than inevitable outcomes:

> We stand today, as Friedrich Engels prophesied more than a generation ago, before the awful proposition: either the triumph of imperialism and the destruction of all culture, and, as in ancient Rome, depopulation, desolation, degeneration, a vast cemetery; or, the victory of socialism, that is, the conscious struggle of the international proletariat against imperialism, against its methods, against war.[39]

The economic theory itself is at once quite brilliant and thoroughly wrong-headed. No other major Marxist economist has accepted her critique of Marx's reproduction schemes. As M.C. Howard and J.E. King put it, '[o]ver and over again it has been urged against her that capitalists can and must constitute each other's customers, and that demand for that part of the social product which is destined for accumulation comes from capitalists intent upon increasing their employment of constant and variable capital'.[40] Her rebuttal of this objection reveals instructive misunderstandings of Marx's method in *Capital*:

> It cannot be discovered from the assumptions of Marx's diagram for whose sake production is progressively expanded . . . Who, then, realizes the permanently increasing surplus-value? The diagram answers: the capitalists themselves and they alone. – And what do they do with this increasing surplus-value? The diagram replies: They use it for an ever greater expansion of production. These capitalists are thus fanatical supporters of expansion of production for production's sake.[41]

As Bukharin points out in a fine critical essay, this argument is teleological.[42] Brewer elaborates on this objection:

> The essence of capitalism is that it is a decentralized (or anarchic) system. As a system it does not have, nor does it need, a purpose. Individual capitalists, workers, organizations of various sorts, may have purposes, but the system itself cannot. Individual capitalists

accumulate (under favourable conditions) because they are forced by competition, something she understood well enough in other contexts.[43]

Luxemburg's difficulty with the analysis of individual capitals is indeed pervasive. Brewer observes: 'She insisted that the problem of realization must be examined at the level of the aggregate social capital but she treated the aggregate capital as though it were an individual capital which has to sell to others, and buy from others.'[44] Luxemburg's confusion on the subject is indicated by the argument that 'it is quite legitimate to postulate absolute dominance of capital in an analysis of individual capitals, such as is given in *Capital*, Volume I,' but that this assumption must be dropped when dealing with the total social capital in Volumes II and II.[45] Bukharin's objection that '[i]n Marx we find nothing of that sort' is entirely correct: 'The first volume deals with the production of *social* capital, the second with the *circulation* of social capital, the third with the "total process", i.e. the total movement of the *social* capital.' This error leads Luxemburg to hypostasize capital and hence 'she does not understand that the process of realization occurs gradually', through a series of discrete exchanges between individual capitals whose overall, though unplanned, effect is to reproduce capitalism on an extended scale.[46]

The other side to Luxemburg's wholly mistaken critique of Marx is the brilliance of her concrete account of the intrusion of Western capitalism into the rest of the world in the late nineteenth and early twentieth centuries. Both her contemporaries and more recent theorists have sought to distinguish the former, which they reject, from the latter, which they tend to praise very highly. Harvey, for example, writes that '[f]ew would now accept Luxemburg's theory of underconsumption as the explanation of crises,' but agrees that 'capitalism necessarily and always creates its own "other"', and develops her suggestion that the predation and force Marx identifies as essential to the 'so-called primitive accumulation' – what Harvey renames and broadens as 'accumulation by dispossession' – is not confined to an originary moment but accompanies capitalism throughout its history.[47] Luxemburg's analysis of imperialism is indeed powerful, well researched, and in many respects persuasive as an account of trends in her day. She integrates colonial conquest, loans, tariffs and militarism into an analytical whole. But, successful in many ways though this treatment is, it introduces a degree of theoretical tension. Her explanation of capitalism's penetration of non-capitalist societies extends well beyond the impossibility of realizing surplus-value in a pure capitalist society – thus she says that capitalists engage in foreign trade to obtain raw materials and that the industrial reserve army generated by rising productivity in capitalist conditions is insufficient to provide the needed workforce: 'Only the existence of non-capitalist groups and organizations can generate such a supply of additional labour-power for capitalist production.' Whatever we think of these arguments, they undercut Luxemburg's claim, cited *above* in her denunciation of Pannekoek, that imperialism could *only* be explained by what she holds to be the limits inherent in the capitalist reproduction process. And there is a bit of sleight of hand – railway loans to settler colonies in Australia and South Africa and to Argentina, all rapidly developing economies at the end of the nineteenth century, can only rather dubiously be portrayed as illustrations of capital's dependence on a non-capitalist milieu.[48]

These criticisms do not diminish the intellectual and moral grandeur of *The Accumulation of Capital*. The passion with which Luxemburg engages with other economists and with her Marxist critics – particularly in the 'Anti-Critique', written in 1915 while she was imprisoned for opposing the First World War – should not be seen as mere sectarian *parti pris*, but as reflecting the depth of her detestation of an economic system that she saw wreaking destruction on humankind. No one can turn from her writing nurturing the illusion that the problem of imperialism is a purely intellectual one.

1.3   The Lenin-Bukharin synthesis

In one important respect, however, a focus on Luxemburg's version of the theory of imperialism can encourage a misleading take on the larger debate in which she was a leading interlocutor. Ellen Wood typifies what I have in mind here when she writes: 'For all the profound disagreements among the classical Marxist theorists of imperialism, they shared one fundamental premiss: that imperialism had to do with the location of capitalism in a world that was not – and probably never would be – fully, or even predominantly, capitalist.' This reflected the fact that they 'belonged to an age when capitalism, though well advanced in parts of the world, was very far from being a truly global economic system.' Naturally Wood cites Luxemburg to illustrate this claim, and concludes that 'we have yet to see a systematic theory of imperialism designed for a world in which all international relations are internal to capitalism and governed by capitalist imperatives'.[49] I discuss the relationship between capitalism and the 'classical' imperialism of the late nineteenth and early twentieth centuries in §4.2. Here I am concerned with how the Marxists of the day theorized this relationship. Wood is, of course, quite right about Luxemburg, but she is dead wrong to extend this judgement to the generality of the classical Marxist theorists of imperialism.

Thus Bukharin, for example, attacks Luxemburg for defining imperialism as 'the political expression of the accumulation of capital in its competitive struggle for what remains still open of the non-capitalist environment' because it implies that 'a fight for territories that have already become capitalist is not imperialism, which is utterly wrong'.[50] What lies behind this objection is partly a relatively narrow empirical point, but nevertheless an important one for those concerned to oppose imperialism, since a key aim of the German leadership during the First World War was the annexation of economically advanced zones of the Low Countries and northern France, and since France in the aftermath of Germany's defeat took back the highly industrialized area of Alsace Lorraine and (as Bukharin observes) sought to seize the Ruhr, far and away the most important region of continental European capitalism. Preobrazhensky also criticizes Luxemburg for overstating the economic significance of the 'periphery': 'By itself, and in terms of its absolute volume, trade with the colonies plays an incomparably more modest role than trade between the capitalist countries proper.'[51] But underlying these empirical disagreements is a deeper difference, namely that the theorists of imperialism who took their cue from *Finance Capital* saw themselves as seeking to understand the structural changes underway in the most *advanced* capitalisms of their day. The transformations portrayed by Hilferding had indeed taken capitalism to the stage where it is *over*-developed, as Lenin suggests when he surveys the tendencies towards parasitism, stagnation and decay that he holds to be characteristic of imperialism.[52] This doesn't mean that Lenin, for example, ignores the differences between the more and less developed economies of his day – on the contrary, the concept of uneven development that he introduced was intended in part to capture these differences, but Sutcliffe is quite right in saying that 'the relations between developed and underdeveloped countries were scarcely at all at the heart of his concept and theory of imperialism'.[53]

If not these relations, what was central to Lenin's version of the theory of imperialism, much the most influential of any of those produced by a Marxist? His famous definition of imperialism identifies five basic features:

(1) the concentration of production and capital has developed to such a high stage that it has created monopolies which play a decisive role in economic life; (2) the merging of bank capital with industrial capital and the creation, on the basis of this 'finance capital', of a financial oligarchy; (3) the export of capital as opposed to the export of commodities acquires exceptional importance; (4) the formation of international monopolist capitalist associations which share the world among themselves, and (5) the territorial division of the world among the biggest capitalist powers is completed.[54]

The trouble with this definition is that it is a list, which of itself does not allow us to establish the relative importance of the itemized features. This poses difficulties when it comes to assessing, in the light of the historical record, whether these features actually obtained, and, if they did, how universally they did so. Lenin himself was careful to stress 'the conditional and relative value of all definitions in general'. Moreover, *Imperialism* was not intended to be a definitive scientific study but rather, as its subtitle declares, a 'popular outline'. In many ways it can be seen as a critical synthesis of two main theoretical sources, Hilferding's *Finance Capital*, and *Imperialism* (1902), by the radical Liberal economist J.A. Hobson. From these works and the results of his wider studies, Lenin distils a conclusion that to some degree remedies the ambiguity of his list: 'in its economic essence imperialism is monopoly capitalism'. This allows him historically to situate imperialism, to determine 'its place in history, for monopoly that grows out of free competition, and precisely out of free competition, is the transition from the capitalist system to a higher socio-economic order'.[55]

Giovanni Arrighi, in an important study of Lenin and Hobson, makes an interesting comment of the former's refined definition of imperialism:

The first difficulty I encountered was to know what exact significance to attach to Lenin's famous definition of imperialism as 'the monopoly stage of capitalism' – a stage which is at the same time characterized as 'the last' or 'the highest'. This formulation may in fact be interpreted in two quite distinct ways: as a *statement of fact* and as a *postulate of identity*. In the former case, 'imperialism' and 'monopoly stage of capitalism' refer to different ensembles of phenomena which the definition brings into *inter-relationship* without identifying the one with the other ... this reading implies that the definition is submitted to some kind of empirical verification. If it is instead regarded as a postulate of identity, then 'imperialism' or 'monopoly stage of capitalism' designate the *same* ensemble of phenomena and the definition escapes all empirical control.[56]

Arrighi complains that later Marxists tended to turn the definition into an irrefutable postulate, and argues that in *Imperialism* itself 'the empirical and relativist position of its author continually tends to pass into a dogmatic and rigidly deterministic standpoint'.[57] Nevertheless, the basic thrust of Lenin's argument is explanatory, though the explanation presses towards a political conclusion. The First World War brought one critical question into focus for the Marxist left. Did the antagonisms among the Great Powers that had now issued in the carnage of the trenches represent a passing phase in the longer history of capitalism, as Kautsky's theory of ultra-imperialism implied (see §1.5 below), or did they arise from the dynamic of capitalist development, above all from the tendency that Marx had posited in *Capital* towards the progressive centralization and concentration of capital? In opting for the latter answer, Lenin sought both to provide an explanation of the geopolitical rivalries of his day and to show that they could only be ended by socialist revolution. But he did not claim that imperialism was the final stage of capitalism; the original title of his pamphlet, *Imperialism, the Latest Stage of Capitalism*, was changed only after his death.[58]

The explanatory thrust of Lenin's argument is well brought out in a passage where he compares Kautsky unfavourably with 'the *socialliberal* Hobson, who *more correctly* takes into account two "historically concrete" . . . features of modern imperialism: (1) the competition between *several* imperialisms, and (2) the predominance of the financier over the merchant'.[59] In a sense, Lenin here identifies the *explanans* and the *explanandum* of his theory – the object of his explanation and the explanation itself, respectively geopolitical rivalries and the emergence of finance capital. But he also highlights his debt to a non-Marxist theorist, Hobson. It is, therefore, important to consider briefly some elements of Hobson's pioneering interpretation of imperialism. Three features in particular stand out.

First, he thematizes the specificity of modern imperialism in terms that would resonate with his Marxist contemporaries: 'The novelty of recent Imperialism regarded as a policy consists chiefly in its adoption by several nations. The notion of a number of competing empires is essentially modern.'[60] Arrighi elaborates on this assertion, arguing that it reflects a conceptual transformation, since 'the very idea of *empire* was traditionally associated with a *hierarchical order of states guaranteeing universal peace*'.[61] As a historical claim, this seems

44

pretty dubious, given that interstate rivalries among the European powers had spilled over into the competitive construction of colonial empires at least since the Eighty Years War between Habsburg Spain and the United Provinces (1568–1648). Nevertheless, Hobson's characterization of the problem spoke to the sense he shared with the Marxist theorists of imperialism that the interaction between geopolitical competition and territorial expansion had reached a new stage of intensity in the late nineteenth century.

Secondly, Hobson offers an explanation of this new imperialism:

> Aggressive Imperialism, which costs the taxpayer so dear, which is of so little value to the manufacturer and the trader, which is fraught with such grave incalculable peril to the citizen, is a source of great gain to the investor who cannot find at home the profitable use he seeks for his capital, and insists that his Government should help him to profitable and secure investments abroad.[62]

More specifically, 'finance is the governor of the imperial engine':

> If the special interest of the investor is liable to clash with the public interest and to induce a wrecking policy, still more dangerous is the special interest of the financier, the general dealer in investments. In large measure the rank and file of the investors are, for both business and for politics, the cat'spaws of the great financial houses, who use stocks and shares not so much as investments to yield them interest, but as material for speculation in the market . . . These great businesses – banking, broking, bill discounting, loan floating, company promoting – form the central ganglion of international capitalism. United by the strongest bonds of organization, always in closest and quickest touch with one another, situated in the very heart of the business capital of every State, controlled so far as Europe is concerned, chiefly by men of a single and peculiar race, who have behind them many centuries of financial experience, they are in a unique position to manipulate the policy of nations. No great quick direction of capital is possible save by their consent and through their agency. Does any one seriously suppose that a great war could be undertaken by any European State, or a great State loan subscribed, if the house of Rothschild and their connexions set their face against it?[63]

This focus on high finance no doubt has its origins in Hobson's critique of the South African War (1899–1902), in which Britain conquered the Afrikaner republics of the Transvaal and the Orange Free State. As a 'Pro-Boer' opponent of this war, Hobson laid the blame at the door of the great mining finance houses eager to secure their control of the gold of the Witwatersrand.[64] The anti-Semitic spin he puts on his portrayal is quite typical of the critics of the Randlords, but it also betrays a broader racialized ideology that leads Hobson to deny the right to self-determination to 'lower races' and to write: 'A rational stipiculture in the wide social interest might, however, require a repression of the spread of degenerate or unprogressive races, corresponding to the check which a nation might place upon the propagation from bad individual stock.'[65] Hobson's version of Social Darwinism is complex, since it coexists with a highly respectful treatment of the great Asian civilizations and an unflinching description of the exploitation and coercion of colonial labour, but its visibility in his book is a striking indication of the pervasiveness of racial ideology even among progressive critics of Edwardian imperialism. This aspect of Hobson's thought radically differentiates it from the Marxist theorizations of imperialism of his day, from which racial categories are wholly absent. The difference is not simply intellectual or moral, for what revolutionary Marxists such as Lenin sought was not the humanized imperialism advocated by Hobson, but the overthrow of the entire system – a process in which they expected the colonial peoples to emerge as historical subjects by rebelling against their oppression.

Thirdly, Hobson, in locating the problem at the level of high finance, Jewish and otherwise, argues that its source lies not in capitalism itself, but in the tendency of advanced economies to save more income than can be profitably invested at home, which therefore gives rise to pressure to seek outlets abroad through foreign loans and other forms of foreign investment liable to bring in their wake territorial expansion to secure their repayment. The 'economic taproot' of imperialism thus lies in a distribution of income to the benefit of propertied classes with a high propensity to save:

> The fallacy of the supposed inevitability of imperial expansion as a necessary outlet for progressive industry is now manifest. It is not industrial progress that demands the opening up of new markets and areas of investment, but mal-distribution of consuming power which prevents the absorption of commodities and capital within the country. The over-saving which is the economic root of Imperialism is found by analysis to consist of rents, monopoly profits, and other unearned or excessive elements of income, which, not being earned by labour of head or hand, have no legitimate *raison d'être*. Having no natural relation to effort of production, they impel their recipients to no corresponding satisfaction of consumption: they form a surplus wealth, which, having no proper place in the normal economy of production

46

and consumption, tends to accumulate as excessive savings. Let any turn in the tide of politico-economic forces divert from these owners their excess of income and make it flow, either to the workers in higher wages, or to the community in taxes, so that it will be spent instead of being saved, serving in either of these ways to swell the tide of consumption – there will be no need to fight for foreign markets or foreign areas of investment.[66]

This pioneering diagnosis of capitalism's problems as lying in a shortage of effective demand anticipates Maynard Keynes's *General Theory of Employment Interest and Money* and resonates with Luxemburg's argument that difficulties of realization drive imperial expansion. But, unlike Luxemburg and like Keynes, Hobson concludes that remedy lies in social reform, not revolution:

> The struggle for markets, the greater eagerness of producers to sell than of consumers to buy, is the crowning proof of a false economy of distribution. Imperialism is the fruit of this false economy; 'social reform' is its remedy. The primary purpose of 'social reform', using the term in its economic signification, to raise the wholesome standard of private and public consumption for a nation, so as to enable the nation to live up to its highest standard of production.[67]

Adapting Hobson's theory therefore poses problems for Lenin, who, like Luxemburg, sees socialist revolution as the way out of imperialism. He takes over Hobson's under-consumptionist explanation of foreign investment: 'The need to export capital arises from the fact that in a few countries capitalism has become "overripe" and (owing to the backward state of agriculture and the poverty of the masses) capital cannot find a field for "profitable" investment.'[68] I return to the problem that the explanation of capitalist economic crises posed to the theorists of imperialism in the next section; for the moment, I want to highlight the discrepancy between the differing conceptions of finance that Lenin took from his two theoretical sources.

Arrighi observes:

> In Hobson's view, then, high finance presents two main characteristics. In the first place, it is a *supranational* entity lying outside the plane defined by the expansion of the nation-state. Secondly, while not belonging to this plane, it nevertheless influences it in a critical manner. *For in so far as it is a speculative intermediary on the monetary market,* high finance tends to transform the excess liquidity present on the

47

market into demand for new investment opportunities, that is, principally for state loans and territorial expansion.[69]

This conception is very different from Hilferding's theory of finance capital, which he understands as arising from an essentially *national* process of (as he would later put it) economic 'organization', driven by the increasing centralization and concentration of capital. To quote Arrighi again:

Hobson's theory referred especially to late nineteenth century England. Even though, as Lenin put it, this was the country 'richest in colonies, in finance capital, and in imperialist experience', it was also the nation where concentration of the productive apparatus had fallen furthest behind the levels attained on the European continent, particularly in Germany, which was at the centre of Hilferding's analysis . . . This explains why, in the latter's account, capitalist concentration plays such a decisive role in furthering the rise of monopoly capital and imperialism, whereas this phenomenon is virtually absent from Hobson's account.[70]

This dissonance between Hilferding's and Hobson's conceptualizations of finance poses two problems. The first arises from the lack of empirical fit between Hilferding's version and the economic structure of the main global power in the era of classical imperialism, namely Britain. I return in §2.1 and chapter 4 to this problem, and the analytical issue it poses, namely whether conceiving imperialism as a phase (or phases) of capitalist development requires the treatment of one variant of capitalism as the paradigm case of imperialism. The assumption that it does constitutes one of the major limitations of Lenin's *Imperialism*. But, secondly, there is the more straightforward incoherence that arises from Lenin's reliance on two different conceptions of finance – one supranational; the other national. Hobson's influence is to be seen in one of the weakest elements of Lenin's book, the portrayal of imperialism as an increasingly parasitic phenomenon that expressed the transformation of the European powers into 'rentier states':

Hence the extraordinary growth of a class, or rather, of a stratum of rentiers, i.e., people who live by 'clipping coupons', who take no part in any enterprise whatever, whose profession is idleness. The export of capital, one of the most essential economic bases of imperialism, still more completely isolates the rentiers from production, and sets the seal of parasitism on the whole country that lives by exploiting the labour of several overseas countries and colonies.[71]

Passages such as this do point towards the more recent understanding of imperialism as about the relationship between (to put it in contemporary terms) North and South. So too does Lenin's particular variation on the theme of parasitism, the theory of the labour aristocracy. As so often in Lenin's work, he was trying to address a political problem, namely how to explain the collapse of the Second International at the outbreak of the First World War, when most of its constituent parties rallied to the support of their own nation-state in the general conflagration. Eager to revive an authentically revolutionary socialist internationalism, Lenin sought to explain this division as the result of the emergence within the Western working class of a privileged layer, the labour aristocracy, whose support for imperialism reflected the fact that their relatively high wages included a portion of the super-profits extracted by monopoly capital from the colonial and semi-colonial world.

Hobson partially anticipated this analysis when he considered the consequences of the successful establishment of an imperialist condominium of China:

> This would drive the logic of Imperialism far towards realization; its inherent necessary tendencies towards unchecked oligarchy in politics, and parasitism in industry, would be plainly exhibited in the condition of the 'imperialist' nations. The greater part of Western Europe might then assume the appearance and character already exhibited by tracts of country in the South of England, in the Riviera, and the tourist-ridden or residential parts of Italy and Switzerland, little clusters of wealthy aristocrats drawing dividends and pensions from the Far East, with a somewhat larger group of professional retainers and tradesmen and a large body of personal servants and workers in the transport trade and in the final stages of production of the more perishable goods: all the main arterial industries would have disappeared, the staple foods and manufactures flowing in as tribute from Asia and Africa.[72]

Lenin develops this thought further in a discussion of Hobson's argument here: 'Imperialism, which means the partitioning of the world, and the exploitation of other countries besides China, which means high monopoly profits from a handful of very rich countries, makes it economically possible to bribe the upper strata of the proletariat, and thereby fosters, gives shape to, and strengthens opportunism.'[73] There are two problems with this thesis. The first is that, whatever is of lasting value in Lenin's *Imperialism*, the theory of the labour aristocracy is untenable on both theoretical and empirical grounds.

49

Thus Lenin doesn't identify any economic mechanism that could direct the material benefits deriving from overseas trade and investment to specific groups of workers. Moreover, the theory completely fails as an explanation of the division of the international workers' movement between reformist Social Democrats and revolutionary Communists during and after the First World War: right across Europe, in Petrograd, Berlin, Turin, Sheffield and Glasgow, it was the skilled, well-organized, relatively well-paid metalworkers who drove labour resistance to the war and rallied to the Bolsheviks and their supporters elsewhere in the new Communist parties.[74]

The second difficulty is that Hobson frames his prediction of a parasitic West battening off the rest of the world in an argument that the *differentia specifica* of modern imperialism – economic and territorial expansion by rival empires – may prove to be a passing phase. Thus a joint exploitation of China may anticipate a broader weakening of interstate antagonisms since 'the modern science of militarism renders wars between "civilized" Powers too costly, and the rapid growth of effective internationalism in the financial and great industrial magnates, who seem destined more and more to control national politics, may in the future render such wars impossible'.[75] This thesis anticipates Kautsky's theory of ultra-imperialism, which Lenin was determined to reject since, apart from anything else, it would undercut the politics of revolutionary internationalism, central to which is the idea that the only way to get rid of imperialism and war is to overthrow capitalism. Hobson's version of ultra-imperialism depends on his conception of high finance as fundamentally cosmopolitan. Here then the tension between Lenin's two theoretical sources for the idea that under imperialism finance is dominant threatens to subvert the political conclusion he sought to draw from his analysis.

This tension is, in effect, resolved by Bukharin, who systematically builds on Hilferding's version of the dominance of finance. Brewer has noted 'the absence of any clear concept of imperialism in *Finance Capital* . . . The major elements of the idea were there, but they were never pulled together. The credit for that must go to Bukharin.'[76] Thus, for Bukharin, imperialism springs from

> the tendencies of finance-capitalist development. The organizational process, which embraces more and more branches of the 'national economy' through the creation of combined enterprises and through the organizational role of the banks, has led to the conversion of each developed 'national system' of capitalism into a 'state-capitalist trust'.

On the other hand, the process of development of the productive forces drives these 'national' systems into the most acute conflicts in their competitive struggle for the world market.[77]

On this account, imperialism has two fundamental features. The first is a consequence of the concentration and centralization of capital. The competitive accumulation of capital leads both to the growth in the size of the individual units of capital and to the incorporation, especially during economic crises, of smaller by larger capitals. Economic power accordingly becomes increasingly concentrated. Sectors become monopolized, dominated by a handful of large firms or perhaps by only one huge corporation. Furthermore, industrial capital tends to merge with the big banks to form finance capital. The final stage of this process of 'organization' is the growing integration of private capital with the nation-state, in other words, the emergence of state capitalism:

> Here 'economics' is organizationally fused with 'politics'; the economic power of the bourgeoisie unites itself with its political power; the state ceases to be a simple promoter of the process of exploitation and becomes a direct, capitalist collective exploiter, openly opposed to the proletariat . . . State capitalist relations of production are, logically and historically, a continuation of finance capitalist relations and constitute the completion of the latter.[78]

Secondly, however, this national organization of capitalism takes place in the context of the growing internationalization of the productive forces. The world economy, which Bukharin defines as '*a system of production relations and, correspondingly, of exchange relation on a world scale*', forms the arena in which the 'state capitalist trusts' compete. Competition between capitals is no longer simply the struggle between private firms for markets: increasingly, it assumes the form of military and territorial rivalries among state capitals on a global scale: 'The struggle between state capitalist trusts is decided in the first place by the relation between their military forces, for the military power of the struggling "national groups" of capitalists.'[79] Inter-imperialist wars of the kind that erupted in August 1914 are thus a necessary consequence of a world economy dominated by competing capitals.

The problematic aspects of Bukharin's version of the theory of imperialism are best considered in the context of the discussion of economic crises in the next section. The significance of his

51

contribution, particularly in *Imperialism and World Economy* (1917), is threefold. First, there is quite simply the greater rigour, consistency and economic sophistication that he brings to the subject in comparison to Lenin. Thus he elegantly detaches the outward drive of capitalism in the imperialist epoch from the kind of under-consumptionist explanations common to Luxemburg, Hobson and Lenin, locating it instead in Marx's conception of the circuit of capital as it is transformed from money, through the purchase of labour-power and means of production on the market, into its employment in the productive process that leads to the creation of new value (including surplus-value), which is then realized by a return to the market, where the commodities embodying this value are sold: 'the roots of capitalist expansion lie in the condition of buying as well as in the process of production itself, and finally in the conditions of selling. Three problems are generally related to that: the problem of the raw material markets and labour-power; the problem of new spheres for capitalist investment; lastly the problem of the market.'[80]

Secondly, though Bukharin builds on Hilferding, he takes the latter's argument a step further by arguing that the process of 'organization' culminates in the fusion of capital and the nation-state: this allows him to integrate into the analysis the retreat from laissez-faire very visible in late nineteenth-century economic policy-making – for example, in the spread of protectionism – and radically extended in the state-directed war economies of the First World War (see §4.2). Finally, as Brewer notes, 'where Hilferding saw one process at work, the concentration and centralization of capital, Bukharin saw two: the "internationalization" and "nationalization" of capital'.[81] He is remarkable both in his analytical and imaginative grasp of the growth and power of what he calls 'the contemporary imperialist robber state, the iron organization, which with its tenacious, raking claws embraces the living body of society', and also in his insistence on the commanding reality of the world economy; thus it is with the latter that he starts his book, arguing that 'the problem of studying imperialism, its economic characteristics, and its future, reduces itself to the problem of analysing the tendencies in the development of world economy and the probable changes in its inner structure'.[82] Bukharin thereby anticipated both the Leviathans that would in the 1930s and 1940s swallow tens of millions of lives (his own included) and, in his intellectual response to what is sometimes called the 'first globalization' at the end of the nineteenth century, established a bridgehead that can help connect the classical Marxist theory of imperialism with the world economy of our own day.

1.4   Organized capitalism and economic crises

The synthesis effected by Lenin and Bukharin represented a very serious attempt to develop a Marxist understanding of the form taken by capitalism at the beginning of the twentieth century. I consider how well it stands up to the historical record in chapter 4. But, even in its own terms, the synthesis posed two important questions. The first concerns the relationship between the account it offered of the current stage of capitalist development and the more abstract tendencies posited by Marx in *Capital*. The second centres on the question of whether the interstate antagonisms that both Lenin and Bukharin held to be inherent in imperialism could be transcended in a more advanced stage where capitalism succeeded in integrating itself across borders. We shall consider the latter question, which continues to haunt contemporary discussions of imperialism, in §1.5 below, and discuss the first now.

Marx describes his aim in *Capital* as 'to reveal the economic law of motion of modern society'. His focus, in other words, is on the dynamics of capitalist development. The competitive accumulation of capital leads to the growing concentration and centralization of capital, which, as we have seen, Hilferding and Bukharin regard as responsible for the emergence of finance capital. It also gives rise, thanks to rising productivity and the consequent emergence of an industrial reserve army of the unemployed, to the rather vaguely expressed 'general law of capitalist accumulation', according to which 'an accumulation of misery [is] a necessary condition, corresponding to the accumulation of wealth'. But these very general trends coexist with an increasingly elaborated account across the three volumes of *Capital* of capitalism's inherent tendency towards a short-term cycle of boom and slump. The possibility of economic crises is intrinsic to capitalism as a system of generalized commodity production. In such an economy, production and consumption are mediated by the exchange of commodities for money: it is, consequently, always possible that the money received in selling one commodity is hoarded, instead of being used to purchase another, leading to a shortfall in effective demand. But what makes this possibility a recurrent reality is the nature of the accumulation process, the competitive struggle among rival capitals driving them to expand production beyond the limit at which commodities can be profitably sold. In *Capital*, Volume I, Part 7, Marx sketches an initial account of the 'peculiar cyclical path of modern industry', which he relates to fluctuations in wage-rates – low at the beginning of the cycle but tending to rise as activity increases until, at the height of the boom, they cut into profit-rates – but themselves regulated by changes in the level of unemployment, which rises sufficiently in periods of recession to force down wages and thereby to help improve profitability and get the economy moving again.[83]

But it is in *Capital*, Volume III, Part 3, that Marx constructs the cornerstone of his explanation of economic crises, the theory of the tendency of the rate of profit to fall. The return on capital, he argues, is dependent on two variables. The first is the rate of surplus-value, which measures the degree of exploitation of the worker. The second is the organic composition of capital, the name that Marx rather unhelpfully gives to the ratio between capital invested in the purchase of means of production (constant capital) and capital invested in the employment of labour-power (variable capital). The reason why Marx attaches such significance to this distinction (as opposed to the more conventional one between fixed and circulating capital) is that, according to his theory of value, it is only variable capital, because it is embodied in labour-power, whose employment creates new value, including the surplus-value that is the source of profits, through the 'living labour' performed by the workers. His theory of the tendency of the rate of profit to fall depends on the process of competition that induces individual capitals to invest in improving their methods of production as a way of increasing labour productivity and thence reducing costs. Other things being equal, Marx believes, these investments will be labour-saving, and hence will increase the organic composition of capital. But, since labour is the source of surplus-value, the result will be a fall in the rate of profit. This is only a tendency, Marx emphasizes, because 'the same factors that produce the tendency for the rate of profit to fall also moderate the realization of this tendency'. For example, higher productivity may, by reducing the value of consumption goods, permit a rise in the rate of surplus-value, or, by cheapening the means of production, counter the rise in the organic composition of capital. Probably the most important counteracting tendency isn't formally listed as one by Marx, but is provided by economic crises themselves. During these, firms go bankrupt and their plant and equipment are sold off cheaply. The resulting depreciation of capital, together with the pressure that higher unemployment puts on workers to accept lower wages and worse conditions, tends to force the rate of profit back up. Consequently, Marx does not argue that capitalism is inherently liable to economic breakdown. On the contrary, '[c]rises are never more than momentary, violent solutions for the existing contradictions, violent eruptions that re-establish the disturbed balance for the time being'.[84]

As I noted in §1.1 above, the classical theorists of imperialism are best seen as continuing Marx's 'method of rising from the abstract to the concrete' by introducing new determinations capable of identifying the key features of capitalist development in their day. But this implies that these new determinations would be constrained by the more abstract ones developed by Marx. More specifically, how could his theory of crises be integrated into the accounts of imperialism developed in the early twentieth century? This was not merely a problem of intellectual coherence, since the authors of these accounts (with the exception of Luxemburg and Lenin, who were dead by then) were confronted after 1929 with the greatest crisis in the history of capitalism, the Great Depression, which was brought to an end only after the outbreak of the Second World War a decade later. The problem is compounded by one of the great puzzles of Marxist intellectual history. What Howard and King write of Marxist political economy in the 1920s can be applied to the entire first third of the twentieth century: 'One common strand unites these otherwise disparate schools. This is the almost total neglect of volume III of Marx's *Capital*, and in particular of the tendency identified there of the rate of profit to decline.'[85] What makes this neglect particularly puzzling is that the leading Marxist theorists were familiar with Volume III – Hilferding displays this in *Finance Capital*, and Lenin cites Marx's theory of rent extensively in his writings on the agrarian question in Russia, but they don't seem to have regarded the theory of the tendency of the profit to fall as relevant in their discussions of capitalist crises.[86]

Hilferding does cite the theory in his discussion of crises in *Finance Capital* but he places a much larger emphasis on the tendency of capitalism, because of its unplanned and anarchic nature, to generate disproportionalities between different branches of production and in particular between Departments I and II (respectively means of production and means of consumption) that could only be corrected by an economic downturn; this explanation of crises proved to be highly influential – a version was, for example, adopted by Bukharin.[87] But both Hilferding and Bukharin also argued that the current phase of development was dominated by the tendency of capitalism to become increasingly organized. Bukharin, as we have seen, views this process as culminating in the state increasingly assuming control over the accumulation process itself: '*state power absorbs virtually every branch of production. Not only does it preserve the general conditions of the exploitative process but, in addition, the state increasingly becomes a direct exploiter, organizing and directing production as a collective, joint capitalist.*[88] In 1915, the year that Bukharin drafted the text just cited, Hilferding wrote:

> In place of the victory of socialism there appears possible a society organized, indeed, but hierarchically and not democratically organized, at the apex of which stand the combined forces of the capitalist monopolies and the state, under whom the working class are engaged in a hierarchy of agents of production. Instead of the triumph of socialism over capitalist society we would have an organized capitalism, better adapted than hitherto to meeting the immediate material needs of the masses.[89]

But, if economic crises are caused by disproportionalities between different sectors and between production and consumption, could not an organized capitalism overcome these? In the mid-1920s Hilferding drew the conclusion that it could, and indeed that organized capitalism would rid the world of both economic slumps and imperialist wars.[90] Bukharin moved in the same direction, though he didn't go as far, reflecting their divergence in political commitments – Hilferding served as Social-Democratic Minister of Finance in Weimar Germany, while Bukharin was a leader of the Communist International. In various texts of the 1920s, Bukharin presents the difference between Victorian capitalism, still dominated by private market competition, and the state capitalism that he now believed to be becoming dominant as the difference between economic anarchy and 'organization'. Under the organized capitalism now emerging, production within each national economy was being subjected to conscious regulation and control: 'Capitalist "national economy" has moved from an *irrational system* to a *rational organization*, from a subject-less economy to an economically active subject.'[91]

In his critique of Luxemburg, Bukharin went as far as to argue that, in a state capitalist economy, 'no crisis can arise, since the mutual demand of all branches of production, and likewise consumer demand, that of the capitalists as well as of the workers, is given from the start. Instead of an "anarchy of production" – a plan that is rational from the standpoint of *Capital*.'[92] This argument was a consequence of Bukharin's commitment to a disproportionality theory of crisis:

> The disproportion between purchasing power and the growth of the productive forces and the disproportion between the various branches of production merely serve as an expression of the *absence of plan* in

56

capitalist economy. Under state capitalism . . . crises would be impossible, although the 'share' of workers may steadily decline. This diminishing share would be taken into account in the plan. In *anarchic* capitalist society, we have the elements of buying and selling, of money and the market. That is why the contradiction between the growth of the productive forces and purchasing power leads to crises.[93]

Quite consistent with his belief that 'organized capitalism' was becoming dominant in the West, Bukharin, not long before the Wall Street crash of 1929 and the subsequent disintegration of the banking system, poo-pooed the remarkably accurate prediction by the British Liberal economist Sir George Paish that '*the collapse of the international credit system becomes dangerously imminent*', saying: 'I rather doubt the accuracy of this author when he predicts catastrophe all along the line.'[94] This judgement did not reflect any reconciliation on Bukharin's part with capitalism, since he saw it as still based on class exploitation. More to the point, it was still subject to anarchic competition, but now on a world scale: 'The system of the world economy is just as blindly irrational and "subject-less" as the earlier system of *national* economy.'[95] But the economic contradictions of capitalism had, with the 'organization' of national economies, become displaced on to the geopolitical conflicts among the imperialist powers. Thus, on the eve of the Great Depression, Bukharin could identify the main contradictions of imperialism as politico-military: 'From the point of view of the economic analysis of present-day world economy, from the point of view of the specific relationships within imperialist states, from the point of view of the general crisis of capitalism – from all these points of view, war is the *central problem of the present day*.'[96]

Now Bukharin was right, of course, to insist against Hilferding that the world capitalist system remained liable to inter-imperialist war, as developments in the 1930s were to prove beyond any doubt. But his claim that the system was escaping the danger of economic crises was, equally plainly, wrong. One way of locating the source of Bukharin's error would be to remind ourselves that he had defined imperialism as constituted by two simultaneous but mutually contradictory tendencies, towards the internationalization and the statification of capital. But his discussions of crises take into account only one of these tendencies – towards state capitalism – and treat it as an accomplished result. But, from Bukharin's own theoretical perspective, treating both these tendencies as constitutive implies that each would limit the other. Consequently, the transformation of individual national economies into 'economically active subjects' fully in control of their fate could never be realized. Here again, the actual experience of the 1930s proved decisive, in this case confirming the impossibility of full economic autarky. The major powers did react to the slump by seeking to carve out autarkic economic empires in which each had sole access to markets and sources of raw materials. But it was their inability to achieve this objective peacefully that helped to drive Germany and Japan in the direction of territorial expansion and war (see §4.2). The power that came closest to attaining autarky along the lines envisaged by Bukharin in his theory of state capitalism was the Soviet Union, but even here the forced industrialization during the two first Five-Year Plans (1928–37) depended on imported plant and equipment. As Norman Stone notes, 'the background to the Stalinist collectivization of agriculture was a determination to export sufficient grain to pay for industrial machinery at a time when grain prices fell, by 1932, to a quarter of their level in 1925, itself two-thirds of the level of 1913'.[97] The share of agricultural output that had to be exported to pay for imported capital goods rose 0.14 per cent in 1928 to 7.33 per cent in 1931, at the price of the wholesale seizure of land and crops and the death by starvation of millions of peasants.[98]

A related problem with the larger Lenin-Bukharin synthesis is its association of imperialism with 'monopoly capitalism', since, strictly speaking, monopoly implies the absence of competition, but competition is an essential mechanism in both disproportionality theories of crisis and Marx's own theory of the tendency of the rate of profit to fall. Bill Warren observes:

> The rise of oligopolistic market structures – or monopolistic firms, as they are popularly called – has not reduced competition but on the contrary has intensified it. The development of oligopoly and various forms of association and combination (in individual economies) has been associated with the disappearance of monopoly on a world scale and its replacement by competition – the disappearance, that is, of the British world monopoly of manufactures with the rise of various competitors towards the end of the nineteenth century.[99]

A theory of monopolistic (or, more accurately, oligopolistic) competition forms part of the basis of the most serious single attempt to address the relationship between imperialism and crises, by Evgeny Preobrazhensky, in a book published in 1931, just as the world economy sank decisively into the Great Depression. Preobrazhensky, a leading figure in the Left Opposition led within the Bolshevik Party by Trotsky, focuses on the implications for the functioning of capitalist crises of the transition from 'classical capitalism' to 'monopolism' (a synonym for 'the economic structure of imperialism'), which he locates in the 1890s. Economic competition continues under monopolism, but primarily at the global level: 'I shall speak only of monopolism within the context of the entire world economy, presupposing not only the existence of capitalism's uneven development, but also competition and struggle between the trusts and national economies, using the methods of monopolistic capitalism.'[100]

Preobrazhensky, like Bukharin, sees economic crises arising from disproportionalities between branches of production and between production and consumption. But the most original aspect of his theory is the development of a suggestion by Marx that the rhythm of the business cycle is regulated by the turnover of fixed capital, and in particular by the tendency for the replacement of fixed capital to be, not gradual and continuous, but concentrated in relatively short bursts of time. It is this demand for the renewal of fixed capital that tends to pull the economy out of depression in the era of classical capitalism. This recovery is facilitated by an economic structure based on free competition and flexible prices: *'The lowering of prices and rapid technological progress, mercilessly smothering all the backward enterprises, is the mechanism that facilitates a new expansion based on orders for new fixed capital.'* But:

> the presence of enormous associations, outgrowing market methods of distributing new productive forces and even the frontiers of separate national economies, creates conditions in which regulation of production by the law of value is accompanied by a progressive reduction of the positive consequences of such regulation and by an intensification of the negative consequences.[101]

The monopolistic structure of the economy under imperialism acts as 'a constant source of thrombosis in the development of society's productive forces', since the trusts are able to prevent the falls in prices that stimulate competition and productive reorganization under classical capitalism, and to maintain large reserves of fixed capital that delay the bursts of replacement that would otherwise power economic recoveries.[102] The result would be protracted depressions, of which Preobrazhensky sees the world slump developing at the end of the 1920s as an instance, putting both war and revolution on the political agenda. His highly suggestive analysis was vilified by Stalinist hacks amid the febrile atmosphere of Russia under the First Five-Year Plan; in some ways its conclusions anticipated the

Table 1.1 Global GDP growth rates 1820–2003 (annual average compound growth rates)

	1820–70	1870–1913	1913–50	1950–73	1973–2003
Western Europe	1.68	2.11	1.19	4.79	2.19
USA	4.20	3.94	2.84	3.93	2.94
Japan	0.41	2.44	2.21	9.29	2.62
Asia (excl. Japan)	0.04	0.98	0.82	5.13	5.71
World	0.94	2.12	1.82	4.90	3.17

Source: A. Maddison, *Contours of the World Economy, 1–2030 AD* (Oxford, 2007), p. 380, table A5

'stagnationist' theories produced after the Second World War by Marxist economists such as Paul Baran, Paul Sweezy and Joseph Steindl, according to whom monopoly capital was responsible for a slowdown in the average rate of economic growth, though these versions tended to reassert Hobson's and Luxemburg's argument that advanced capitalism suffers from a chronic shortage of effective demand.[103] Both they and Preobrazhensky are vulnerable to Brewer's objection that '[t]he "long boom" of the 1950s and 1960s suggests strongly that monopoly capitalism is not incompatible with growth'.[104] As we can see in table 1.1, something very bad happened to the world economy between 1913 and 1950, but the very robust growth rates in the subsequent two decades indicate that the structures analysed by Preobrazhensky are not sufficient to explain the earlier slowdown.

The other major Marxist crisis theory of the 1920s did not rely on any claims about the specific structure of monopoly capitalism. Henryk Grossman used Otto Bauer's version of Marx's reproduction schemes in order to show that capitalism has an immanent tendency to breakdown because the investment required by a rising organic composition of capital in an expanding economy would eventually consume all the surplus-value, leaving nothing for the personal consumption of the capitalists. Grossman does not, however, believe that this tendency will be immediately realized, though the factors offsetting them will become less effective over time:

> Obviously, as Lenin correctly remarks, there are no absolutely hopeless situations. In the description I have proposed the breakdown does

60

not necessarily have to work itself out directly. Its absolute realization may be interrupted by counteracting tendencies. In that case the absolute breakdown will be converted into a temporary crisis, after which the accumulation process picks up again on a new basis.[105]

Grossman seems to have intended his attempt algebraically to prove that, on Bauer's assumptions, breakdown would follow in thirty-six years as an internal critique of the latter's argument, which had been strongly attacked by Luxemburg. The interest of his own analysis lies less in this proof than in the much more systematic account of the counter-tendencies to breakdown than that offered by Marx in *Capital*, Volume III. Grossman uses Bauer's assumptions to identify the main variables on which the counter-tendencies must act, by slowing down the rate of accumulation, devaluing constant capital and reducing the value of the labour-power. One interesting feature of his treatment of the counter-tendencies is the way he integrates imperialism and war into them. He writes: 'Imperialism is a striving to restore the valorization of capital at any cost, to weaken or eliminate the breakdown tendency . . . Because the valorization of capital fails in countries at a given, higher stage of accumulation, the tribute that flows in from abroad assumes ever increasing importance. Parasitism becomes a method of prolonging the life of capitalism.' If this argument serves as a way of giving more rigorous economic foundations to Lenin's theory of imperialism, Grossman's discussion of militarism develops an argument that anticipates later theories of the 'permanent arms economy' as an explanation of the postwar boom (see §4.3.2). Military expenditure is a form of unproductive consumption, inasmuch as the goods and services it purchases are not used directly or indirectly to produce new commodities. Hence, by diverting surplus-value from investment in the production of means of production or means of consumption and thereby reducing the rate of accumulation, it postpones the breakdown of capitalism:

> from the standpoint of the total capital, militarism is a sphere of unproductive consumption. Instead of being saved, values are pulverized. Far from being a sphere of accumulation, militarism slows down accumulation. By means of indirect taxation a major share of the income of the working class which might have gone into the hands of the capitalists as surplus-value is seized by the state and spent mainly for unproductive purposes.[106]

61

1.5 Spectres of ultra-imperialism

If this argument of Grossman's was to have a great future, so too was the second internal problem to confront the Lenin-Bukharin synthesis. This was the following: granted, as Hilferding and Bukharin argued, that capitalism was becoming increasingly organized, why should this process stop short at national frontiers? Why shouldn't the concentration and centralization of capital proceed to a further stage in which what we would now call a globalized capitalism succeeded in overcoming interstate antagonisms? As we have seen, Hobson had in his own way already sketched out this possibility. But, within the Marxist tradition, it was of course Karl Kautsky who predicted such an outcome in a famous article written on the very eve of the outbreak of the Great War:

> What Marx said about capitalism can also be applied to imperialism: monopoly creates competition and competition, monopoly. The frantic competition among the huge firms, giant banks, and multimillionaires compelled the great financial groups, who were absorbing the small ones, to devise the cartel. Similarly the World War between the great imperialist powers may result in a federation of the strongest, who renounce their arms race.
>
> From the purely economic standpoint it is therefore not impossible for capitalism to live through yet another phase, the transferral of this process of forming cartels into foreign policy; a phase of *ultra-imperialism*.[107]

The implication was that, *pace* revolutionaries such as Luxemburg, Lenin, Bukharin, Preobrazhensky and Grossman, inter-imperialist war did not arise from the nature of capitalism:

> There is no *economic* necessity for continuing the arms race after the World War even from the standpoint of the capitalist class, with the possible exception of certain armaments interests. On the contrary, the capitalist economy is seriously threatened precisely by these disputes. Every far-sighted capitalist today must call on his fellows: capitalists of all countries unite![108]

On this diagnosis, the epoch of wars and revolutions in which, according to the Third International, capitalism was culminating would prove merely a passing phase, leading to an era of global peace. Kautsky's prediction that inter-imperialist antagonisms could be peacefully reconciled within the framework of a global capitalist cartel proved to be of little help during what Arno Mayer has called 'the General Crisis and Thirty Years War of the twentieth century' between 1914 and 1945.[109] But the increasing integration of advanced capitalism under the hegemony of the United States since the end of the Second World War has frequently attracted theorists to versions of Kautsky's idea. Thus, summarizing an important debate in *New Left Review* at the end of the 1960s, Bob Rowthorn identified three main positions:

> *US super-imperialism* in which all other capitalist states are dominated by the United States and have comparatively little freedom to choose their policies and control their economies in ways opposed by the American state. America acts as the organizer of world capitalism, preserving its unity in the face of socialism. This domination may not, of course, operate smoothly – for antagonisms will not be eliminated but merely contained.

> *Ultra-imperialism* in which a dominant coalition of relatively autonomous imperialist states performs the organizing role necessary to preserve the unity of the system. For this to work the antagonisms between the members of the coalition must not be so severe that they overcome the interest they have in maintaining the coalition.

> *Imperial Rivalry* in which the relatively autonomous states no longer perform the necessary organizing role, or perform it so badly that serious conflicts break out between them and the unity of the system is threatened. For this to happen the antagonisms between states must be severe.[110]

At the time, few took up Kautsky's position. Theorists of American super-imperialism, particularly associated with the journal *Monthly Review*, slugged it out with Marxist economists such as Ernest Mandel who argued that, with US hegemony in decline, a new era of inter-imperialist rivalries beckoned.[111] Versions of both these positions are still very much represented in contemporary debates, but they have been joined by influential articulations of the same thought expressed by Hobson and Kautsky: now it is the economic globalization of the past few decades that is cited to support the idea that a new transnational capitalism is in the process of shaking itself loose from interstate antagonisms. The most celebrated statement of this idea is Hardt and Negri's theory of Empire, 'a *decentred* and *deterritorialized* apparatus of power that progressively incorporates the entire global realm within its open, expanding frontiers', but others such as William Robinson have argued along somewhat parallel lines.[112] I hope in the course of this book to provide a theoretical and empirical basis to assess rival Marxist conceptualizations of imperialism, both past and present. For the moment, however, I want to look at how Lenin and Bukharin responded to Kautsky's evocation of the possibility of ultra-imperialism.

It should be clear that both had strong political reasons for dismissing the idea, since if Kautsky was right then the entire revolutionary strategy that Lenin derived from his theory of imperialism would collapse. But on what basis did they do so? In a recent article that seeks, among other things, to demonstrate, against me, '[t]he poverty of Marxist imperialism theory', Hannes Lacher and Benno Teschke argue, quoting Lenin's Foreword to Bukharin's *Imperialism and World Economy*:

> For Lenin and Bukharin did not just concede that ultra-imperialism is conceivable (as Callinicos suggests). Lenin, in fact, argues: 'There is no doubt that the development is going *in the direction* of a single world trust that will swallow up all enterprises and all states without exception' . . . If this sounds more like Hardt and Negri's *Empire* than Lenin's *Imperialism*, Lenin saw no real chance of this inherent capitalist developmental logic ever being realized; for 'before a single world trust will be reached, . . . imperialism will inevitably explode, capitalism will turn into its opposite'.[113]

Citing a similar passage from Bukharin, Lacher and Teschke continue:

> Again, therefore, it is not the inexorable logic of uneven and combined development, which, according to Bukharin and Lenin, can be expected to maintain both the territorial sovereignty of capitalist statehood, and the dynamic of geopolitical competition. It was only the world revolution that in their perspectives prevents permanent ultra-imperialist concertation and global state formation. But the world revolution never came. Instead, World War II gave rise to something akin to the unipolar capitalist state system (within the bipolar Cold-War structure) envisaged by Bukharin.[114]

Lacher and Teschke cite Lenin and Bukharin accurately, but they fail to point out that the former's discussion of ultra-imperialism, in the Foreword to *Imperialism and World Economy*, amounts to two paragraphs and, much more seriously, they ignore his much more extended treatment of the subject in *Imperialism*. Here, *pace* Lacher and Teschke, Lenin develops what Arrighi calls 'his most original contribution in comparison with Hobson, namely, the thesis that "uneven development" would rekindle the conflict among capitalist countries for a fresh redivision of the world'.[115] His argument proceeds in two stages. First, he documents the extreme disparities of levels of economic development in the world of his day, in order to refute one implication of the idea of ultra-imperialism, 'i.e., that the rule of finance capital *lessens* the unevenness and contradictions inherent in the world economy, whereas in reality it *increases* them'. Then, a little later on in the book, Lenin considers the possibility of the kind of ultra-imperialist alliance that Hobson had discussed in the case of China:

> We ask, is it 'conceivable' that, assuming that the capitalist system remains intact – and this is the assumption that Kautsky does make – that such alliances would be more than temporary, that they would eliminate friction, conflicts, and struggle in every possible form.
>
> The question has only to be presented clearly for any other than a negative answer to be impossible. This is because the only conceivable basis under capitalism for the division of spheres of influence, interests, colonies, etc., is a calculation of the *strength* of those participating, their general economic, financial, military strength, etc. And the strength of these participants in the division does not change to an equal degree, for the *even* development of different undertakings, trusts, branches of industry, or countries is impossible under capitalism. Half a century ago Germany was a miserable insignificant country, if her capitalist strength is compared with that of the Britain of that time; Japan compared with Russia in the same way. Is it 'conceivable' that in ten or twenty years' time the relative strength of the imperialist powers will have remained *un*changed? It is out of the question.[116]

Here, in the first place, Lenin considers the possibility of a stable ultra-imperialism (as opposed to a temporary alliance of convenience among rival capitalist states) on the assumption that capitalism will continue to exist; in other words, he does not rely on the imminence of socialist revolution to discount it. Secondly, what makes ultra-imperialism 'out of the question' is not simply the immense disparities in the global economy, but the way in which the dynamic process of capitalist development continually alters the distribution of these disparities and thereby shifts the balance of power among states. This helps to explain, incidentally, Lenin's emphasis on the pressures towards the *re*division of the world under imperialism: there is no once-and-for-all sharing out of the spoils, since rising powers will seek some of what established but declining powers had seized earlier on. Howard and King are therefore correct to note: 'Coupled with the completed division of the world between the "great powers", uneven development was for Lenin the economic basis of military rivalry. It was not the result of competition being eradicated from national economies and wholly transferred to the interrelations of states, as it was for Bukharin.'[117]

Both the mechanisms responsible for uneven development and its political (and geopolitical) implications are matters for analysis and debate. Nevertheless, the concept is an important one, particularly since the contemporary world economy continues to be characterized by what Lenin called 'unevenness and contradictions'. His grasp of the extent and significance of these disparities is a major reason for regarding his *Imperialism* as more than an outdated pamphlet and continuing to engage with his arguments, even if we may choose to criticize or even reject many of his assumptions and conclusions. The richness of the larger body of Marxist writing on imperialism to which Lenin's *Imperialism* was merely one contribution – a richness that I have tried to convey in this chapter – justifies taking the same stance towards all the different theorists that helped to produce it. My aim in the rest of this book will be to pursue questions in many cases similar to those that they posed, starting where they did, from Marx's *Capital*, and seeking to use both it and the work of the classical theorists of imperialism as a resource that is neither to be dogmatically reaffirmed nor, on the basis of some misguided iconoclasm, to be as dogmatically dismissed.

— 2 —

CAPITALISM AND THE STATE SYSTEM

2.1 Rethinking the theory of imperialism

What distinguishes the Marxist approach to imperialism? Bob Sutcliffe answers this question very well:

> The distinctive feature of the Marxist or historical method of analysing imperialism consists in a special kind of dual vision which tries to integrate coherently two separate aspects of the world. One consists of the hierarchies, conflicts, and alliances – political, military, and economic – between countries; the other concerns the working of the productive system and the hierarchy of classes that it generates. The first is about dominance and exploitation of some countries by others, the second is about the stability of the productive system and the domination and exploitation of some classes over others.[1]

'Conventional thinking' – for example, mainstream International Relations theory or neoclassical economics – 'tends to look at only one level at a time . . . ,' Sutcliffe continues. 'Those who practise political economy, and Marxists in particular, try to break out of these disciplinary boundaries to say something about both of the superimposed layers, to recognize the elements of autonomy in each one as well as the links, complementary and contradictory, between the two.'[2] Marxist theorists of imperialism thus seek to think the articulation of the economic and the (geo)political – one should add, in the context of a larger understanding of the trajectory of capitalist development. We have seen in the preceding chapter how, in the high era of classical Marxism during the first decades of the twentieth century, a brilliant *galère* of theorists pursued this project. But the question with which I am concerned in this book is this: what form should this same project take nearly a hundred years later, in a world economy in many respects very different from the one analysed by Luxemburg or Bukharin?

Plainly the answer one gives to this question depends heavily on one's assessment of the facts. But, as Althusser insisted, no reading of the empirical evidence is theoretically innocent. What I want to consider in this chapter concerns the theoretical foundations on which contemporary Marxist approaches to imperialism should be based. One way into this subject is to look at some of the major weaknesses of the classical theories of imperialism. Of course, this can't be fully separated from considering the historical record. But identifying some of the key analytical problems to emerge from the classical theories may help to set an agenda for contemporary conceptualizations of imperialism. Three difficulties in particular emerge from the survey in chapter 1.

The first concerns the fit, or lack of fit, between the different interpretations of imperialism and Marx's more abstract theory of the capitalist mode of production. As should be plain from chapter 1, the classical theorists all knew *Capital* well and used this knowledge in their analyses and debates. But the main strategy they developed to continue Marx's project – setting the imperialism of their day in the context of a new phase of capitalist development – tended to short-circuit discussion of the relationship between the abstract tendencies that he identified and the concrete trends at work in the contemporary capitalist economy. This weakness was compounded, as I show in §1.4, by the general neglect of Marx's theory of the tendency of the rate of profit to fall, and the resort instead to disproportionality theories of crisis that proved inadequate when confronted with the Great Depression of the 1930s. The exceptions to this general pattern – Luxemburg and Grossman – relied on attempts to demonstrate capitalism's inherent tendency to economic breakdown that were, in the first case, wholly untenable, and, in the second, ambiguous about the relative weight to be given to the tendency and its counter-tendencies. One constraint, then, on any adequate Marxist theory of imperialism must be that it successfully articulates the account it gives of the particularities of economics and geopolitics with a more general theory of the relations, mechanisms and tendencies of the capitalist economic system.

The second problem with the classical theories of imperialism is one of empirical fit, rather than of intellectual coherence with the larger Marxist research programme. How well do they stand up when confronted, not just with the historical record, but with economic and geopolitical developments since the 1920s and 1930s? This question can only be properly answered when I look at the historical evolution of capitalism and imperialism up to the present in Part II. But there is one problem in particular that it is important to highlight here because of both its importance and its theoretical implications. As we saw in §1.3, the most rigorous version of the classical Marxist theory of imperialism, developed by Bukharin, relied on Hilferding's theory of finance capital as the fusion of banking and industrial capital under the dominance of the former. But, as Hilferding himself noted, this form of integration was far more advanced in Germany and the United States than in Britain. The explanation of this variation is very well stated by Michael Kidron in his classic critique of Lenin's *Imperialism*:

> German capitalism was a late developer. It found . . . that to break into the modern (in this case, British-controlled) market with backward (German) means it had to conserve every drop of saving and skill, even the very smallest, bring them together and invest them in plant bigger and better than that of their entrenched rivals. It had to make 'combined development', in Trotsky's phrase, work in its favour. Since the banks were structured around this task and since the future of German capitalism hinged on its effective performance, it is not surprising that they became the key, controlling institutions within it.[3]

Hilferding offers a very similar explanation, but adds the following rider: 'Although this difference was due to the backward and belated development of Germany, the close connection between industrial and bank capital nevertheless became, in both Germany and America, an important factor in their advance towards a higher form of capitalist organization.'[4] On this interpretation, the emergence of finance capital in late industrializing economies such as Germany and the US is a case of what Trotsky called the 'privilege of historic backwardness': the uneven and combined development of global capitalism may permit – and indeed require – a relatively backward state to overleap the more gradual evolutionary process undergone by the dominant states, and to adopt more advanced technologies and forms of organization than those prevailing in the latter.[5] But even if we grant this argument, there remains the difficulty that Hilferding's theory only partially fitted the major economies of his day – particularly it applied least to Britain, which remained the greatest imperialist power through the interwar era – and that, as we shall see in §4.3, it lost even this partial fit after the Second World War.

This does not, in my view, invalidate the attempt to develop a stadial theory of capitalism – that is, to differentiate specific phases of capitalist development; indeed, I attempt in chapters 4 and 5 to distinguish phases in the history of imperialism itself. But the case of finance capital carries two theoretical morals. The first is the fairly banal one that analysis must always seek to distinguish the authentically general from the particular. The second and more interesting one is that one should not seek to associate either imperialism itself or a particular phase in its evolution with one specific paradigmatic model of capitalist development. Different models may coexist within the same phase. Thus Giovanni Arrighi has pointed out that, even in the classical era of imperialism (1870–1945), the main challengers to British hegemony pursued very different strategies – Germany seeking through military expansion to carve out its own closed economic empire, the US instead seeking to open the world up to American investment and trade: 'Lenin did not concern himself with the fact that the newly-emerging powers were bearers of diverse models of expansionism, and that consequently shifts in the relationship of forces between nation-states – correlated to phenomena of uneven development – would not necessarily strengthen the model of imperialism which he analysed.'[6] The diversity of simultaneously existing 'models of expansionism' is an exceptionally important point for understanding the trajectory of capitalist imperialism, as I try to show in chapters 4 and 5.

The first two problems concern how classical theorists of imperialism conceptualized one of the two levels distinguished by Sutcliffe – the economic. The third addresses the other level – the political and geopolitical dimension of states and their interrelations. Particularly in the Lenin-Bukharin synthesis, the first level explains the second: the structural transformations undergone by capitalism in its monopoly stage – the emergence of finance capital and its tendency to fuse with the nation-state – provide the key to the territorial and military rivalries of the Great Powers. But this poses the question of how precisely these two levels are related and also provokes the accusation that has constantly haunted all Marxist discussion of the state – that of economic reductionism, in which the state is treated as a mere vehicle for predefined class interests. As is well known, there is no coherent theory of the state in the writings of Marx, Engels, and Lenin. Rather these texts contain elements of different theories, of which the two most important are what is usually called instrumentalism – i.e., the idea that the state is simply a tool that is used by the economically dominant class to advance its interests – and a much more interesting and politically radical structural theory, which conceptualizes the state as a set of specific institutions defined by the attempt to concentrate and monopolize the means of violence that of their very nature work in the interests of the exploiters and consequently must be destroyed by the working class if it is to emancipate itself. Plainly the first conception, if deployed within a theory of imperialism, would result in a reductionist treatment of the (geo) political – a possibility most fully realized in the theory of state monopoly capitalism developed by the Communist Parties after the Second World War, where the state is understood as the tool of the big monopolies.[7] Bukharin, who influenced Lenin's own adoption of the structural theory, goes beyond instrumentalism, in part because the state figures under both *explanans* and *explanandum* – as state capitalism and as the interstate rivalries that this explains. He certainly doesn't conceive the state instrumentally; on the contrary, in the era of imperialism *'the state absorbs into itself the whole multitude of bourgeois organizations'* and *'becomes the sole universal organization of the ruling class'*.[8] The problem here isn't economic reductionism – on the contrary, it is through this absorption of civil society by the state that national economies become 'active subjects' – but rather its opposite: Bukharin greatly overstates the conscious 'organization' of capitalist economies even when the tendency towards state capitalism was the strongest, between 1914 and 1945 (see §1.4).

How, then, to think the articulation of the economic and the (geo) political? One response is explicitly to make this the focus of the concept of capitalist imperialism. This is essentially the solution on which both David Harvey and I have converged. Let's start with Harvey's version: 'Imperialism of the capitalist sort arises out of a dialectical relation between territorial and capitalistic logics of power. The two logics are distinctive and in no way reducible to each other, but they are tightly interwoven.' The significance of calling the relationship a dialectical one is that it rules out any attempt to reduce one of its terms to the other:

> The relation between these two logics should be seen, therefore, as problematic and often contradictory (that is, dialectical) rather than as functional or one-sided. The dialectical relationship sets the stage for an analysis of capitalist imperialism in terms of the intersection of these two distinct but intertwined logics of power. The difficulty for concrete analyses of actual situations is to keep the two sides of this dialectic simultaneously in motion and not to lapse into either a solely political or a predominantly economic mode of argumentation.[9]

71

Harvey takes the distinction between capitalist and territorial logics of power from Arrighi, according to whom they must be conceived as

> opposite *modes of rule* or logics of power. Territorialist rulers identify power with the extent and populousness of their domains, and conceive of wealth/capital as a means or a by-product of the pursuit of territorial expansion. Capitalist rulers, in contrast, identify power with the extent of their command over scarce resources and consider territorial acquisitions as a means and a by-product of the accumulation of capital.[10]

Arrighi has pointed out that Harvey's use of this distinction differs from his own: 'In his, the territorialist logic refers to state policies, while the capitalist logic refers to the politics of production, exchange, and accumulation. In mine, in contrast, both logics refer primarily to state policies.'[11] Indeed, in the passage last cited from Harvey we see very clearly how he understands the capitalist and territorial logics not, as Arrighi does, as 'modes of rule', but in terms of the distinction between the economic and the (geo)political. Harvey has also spoken of 'imperialism as the outcome of tension between two sources of power. One is a territorial source of power lying in state organizations. The other is the capitalist logic of power, which is the control of money and assets, and the flow and circulation of capital.'[12] In order to resolve this potential ambiguity, it seems to me better to understand capitalist imperialism as the intersection of economic and geopolitical competition; this difference with Harvey is not, however, one of content but merely one of formulation.[13]

I have already said something about the merits of this refinement of the Marxist theory of imperialism in the Introduction to this book. Let me, in the light of the preceding discussion, emphasize two particular advantages that it has. The first is that it detaches the theory from any specific claims about the organizational structure that capitalist economies must necessarily take in the epoch of imperialism – something that, as we have seen, got Lenin and Bukharin into trouble with their use of Hilferding's theory of finance capital (not to speak of Lenin's attempt to integrate Hobson as well). The other is that conceiving imperialism as the intersection of two logics of power or forms of competition avoids economic reductionism, as Harvey's stress on the relationship between the two being 'problematic and often contradictory' highlights. But these strengths are also potential sources of weakness as well. In the first place, if not on the

Lenin-Bukharin synthesis, then on what account of capitalist development is the reconceptualization of imperialism to rest? For unless it is integrated in some such account, then the supposed refinement of the theory of imperialism offered by Harvey and me remains merely formal, offering nothing in the way of an enhancement of our substantive understanding of Sutcliffe's two levels. Secondly, if the (geo) political level is to be given the 'element of autonomy' that is certainly required if there is to be the kind of dialectical tension that Harvey treats as constitutive of imperialism, then there needs to be some kind of theorization of this level that both gives weight to its specificity and integrates it into the larger account of capitalist development that, as we have just noted, is also required. These are tough challenges, but I believe they can both be met. Harvey addresses the first in *The New Imperialism*, using his theory of capitalist crisis as over-accumulation as a lens through which to read world history, from the Revolutions of 1848 to the invasion of Iraq. I offer my own, partially overlapping, answer to the same question in chapters 3 to 5. But the rest of this chapter is devoted to considering the second challenge.

2.2 Conceptualizing the state system

The Marxist theory of the state is a minefield in which many unresolved problems and unfinished debates lurk. But it cannot be completely avoided in what I need to address here. The best way in is provided by an important intervention in one of these debates. Criticizing the approach taken by John Holloway and Sol Picciotto in the so-called 'state-derivation' debate, mainly among German and British Marxists in the 1960s and 1970s, Colin Barker writes:

> Their treatment of the state remains at an inappropriate level of abstraction, in particular in that it treats the state as if it existed only in the singular. Capitalism, however, is a world system of states, and the form that the capitalist state takes is the nation-state form. Any discussion, therefore, of the capitalist state form must take account of the state *both* as an apparatus of class domination and as an apparatus of competition among segments of the bourgeoisie.[14]

Barker doesn't simply make a fundamental point about Marxist state theory – that it can't talk about 'the' state, but about a plurality of states that jointly constitute a system. He highlights a key issue for the theory of imperialism, one that I tried to highlight in this last section by, no doubt rather clumsily, referring to one of the two dimensions or levels articulated by that theory as the '(geo)political'. The Lenin-Bukharin version of the theory was, implicitly at least, a theory of the international since it concerns the interrelationship between the capitalist world economy under the dominance of finance capital and the geopolitical rivalries among the Great Powers. Harvey's and my restatements make this property of the theory explicit by talking about two logics of power, capitalistic and territorial, or two forms of competition, economic and geopolitical. In my version, I understand geopolitics, very broadly, to refer to all conflicts among states over security, territory, resources and influence. The place it occupies within the theory of imperialism thus directs our attention towards the state system, the privileged theoretical object of mainstream International Relations, which, particularly in the more analytically sophisticated versions of structural realism stemming from the work of Kenneth Waltz, is conceived as having properties irreducible to those of its constituent units, the individual states.[15]

Thematizing the state system as a specific problem for Marxist theory launches a game where the stakes are particularly high. Back in the 1970s and 1980s, Weberian historical sociologists such as Anthony Giddens, Michael Mann, W.G. Runciman and Theda Skocpol developed a powerful critique of Marxism based especially on what they alleged to be its inability analytically to integrate interstate competition; the moral they drew was that social theory needed to base itself on an explanatory pluralism that treated class relations as merely one among an irreducible multiplicity of sources of social power.[16] This was a formidable challenge to the theoretical scope of historical materialism. The terrain has become even more tangled in recent years as a result of debates about the impact of globalization on geopolitics. The most influential Marxist intervention in these debates was made by Hardt and Negri, for whom, as a transnational network power, Empire represents the end of geopolitics, replacing national with imperial sovereignty and binding together states, transnational corporations and international institutions into a baroque constitutional structure that transcends and internalizes interstate conflict:

> It is in fact through the extension of *internal* constitutional processes that we enter into a constituent process of Empire. International right always has to be a negotiated contractual process among *external* parties . . . Today right involves an internal and constitutive institutional process. The networks of agreements and associations, the

74

channels of mediation and conflict resolution, and the coordination of the various dynamics of states are all institutionalized within Empire.[17]

But the most interesting exploration of the analytical problem posed for historical materialism by the state system has taken place within the school of 'Political Marxism'. This intellectual current takes its inspiration from the historical work of Robert Brenner, which I discuss in the following chapter, but its founding text is an intervention by Ellen Meiksins Wood in the state debates of the 1970s and 1980s. Here she makes two key moves. First, she criticizes the conventional Marxist treatment of the distinction within a mode of production between the economic base and the political, juridical and ideological superstructure, which tends to treat them as two distinct spheres or regions of the social:

> 'Political Marxism', then, does not present the relation between base and superstructure as an opposition, a 'regional' separation between a basic 'objective' economic structure, on the one hand, and social, juridical, and political forms, on the other, but rather as a continuous structure of social relations and forms with varying degrees of distance from the immediate processes of production and appropriation, beginning with those relations and forms that constitute the system of production itself.[18]

Accordingly, '[r]elations of production take the form of particular juridical and political relations – modes of domination and coercion, forms of property and social organization – which are not mere secondary reflexes but constituents of the productive relations as well.' Secondly, however, Wood argues that the politico-juridical form taken by capitalist relations of production is that of the separation of the economic and political, or, 'more precisely, a differentiation of political functions themselves and their separate allocation to the private economic sphere and the public sphere of the state'. This is a consequence of the specific nature of capitalist exploitation. In pre-capitalist social formations, the economic and political are fused, since what Marx called 'direct extra-economic force' is required to extract surplus-labour from dependent peasants or chattel slaves. But, where capitalist production relations prevail:

> the appropriation of surplus labour takes place in the 'economic' sphere by 'economic' means. In other words, surplus appropriation is achieved in ways that are determined by the complete separation of the producer from the conditions of labour and by the appropriator's

75

absolute private property in the means of production. Direct 'extra-economic' pressure or overt coercion are, in principle, unnecessary to compel the expropriated labourer to give up this surplus-labour.[19]

In its basic ideas, the approach to the state developed by Wood was by no means unique to her. It was, for example, anticipated in Joachim Hirsch's fundamental contribution to the German state-derivation debate.[20] In the Anglophone discussion, Holloway and Picciotto treat the state as a fetishized form of the capital-relation, an idea that continues to inform the work of the school of 'Open Marxism', which, like Wood and her co-thinkers, is increasingly active in the academic discipline of International Relations (IR).[21] But Wood's version is distinguished both by the clarity and rigour with which the argument is developed and by its association with a very important interpretation of the origins of capitalism, in Brenner's work (see §3.1). It is, however, just as vulnerable as Holloway's and Picciotto's to Barker's criticism – namely Wood also, in formulating her theory of the state, conceives the latter in the singular. In recent years, this problem has given rise to a debate within Political Marxism between Wood and two younger scholars, Hannes Lacher and Benno Teschke. Teschke, in an important book, *The Myth of 1648*, offers a historical deconstruction of a founding myth of International Relations theory, namely, that the modern state system originated in the Treaty of Westphalia that ended the Thirty Years War in 1648. He contends that the geopolitical system that took shape was pre-modern, and associated particularly with absolutism, a social formation that was neither feudal nor proto-capitalist but that involved the distinctive form of 'proprietary kingship', fusing the economic and the political. Hence,

> there is no constitutive or genetic link between capitalism and a geo-political pluriverse ... The formation of a territorially fragmented states-system preceded the onset of capitalism. This system was socio-economically and (geo) politically pre-modern, since its constitutive units were predominantly dynastic states and, to a lesser extent, oli-garchic merchant republics. This pre-modern international order was precisely IR's Westphalian system.[22]

Lacher presses the conclusion implied by this analysis, namely that the connection between capitalism and the state system is purely contingent. He criticizes Marxist theories of international relations because '[t]hey take the territorial boundedness of the capitalist state as given and proceed to ground the interstate system in essentially the same conceptual operations in which the Marxist state debate sought to derive the capitalist state. In this way, the theoretical problem why capitalist political space is territorially fragmented disappears from view.' This is precisely the criticism that Barker had made of the 1970s state-derivation debate. But, unlike Barker (whom he cites), Lacher argues that 'the interstate-ness of capitalist political space cannot be derived from the capital relation. Instead it should be regarded as a "historical legacy" from pre-capitalist historical development.' The European state system originated, not during the transition from feudalism to capitalism (the latter's advent, Lacher asserts, did not take place on the Continent until the early nineteenth century), but as a result of the replacement of feudalism, based on 'parcellized personal domination', by absolutism, where 'generalized personal dominion' 'was articulated precisely as a claim to sovereignty over the inhabitants of a particular territory by rulers who regarded their state as patrimony'. Capitalism, when it finally came, developed its own conception of sovereignty 'based on general impersonal possession', but it did so in a geopolitical context constituted by this pre-existing system of states. Consequently, though '[t]he interstate system is capitalist, because it has become capitalist in the process of the totalization of capitalism', 'it has simultaneously structured and configured the way in which capital operates'. Moreover, capitalism could dispense with the state system, and replace it with a different form of political sovereignty – for example, the 'transnational state' that William Robinson claims is emerging.[23]

Wood shares the same theoretical and historical framework as Lacher and Teschke, but she strongly resists this conclusion. Though she accepts capitalism developed (outside England) very late, and in a geopolitical context dominated by a pre-capitalist system of territorial sovereignties, she argues that state sovereignty itself could not take its full shape 'until capitalist property displaced both parcellized sovereignty and the fragmented economy entailed by politically constituted property' that was required to secure the coercive extraction of surplus labour from peasants, on which absolutism continued to depend. Moreover, 'the universalization of capitalism has also meant, or at least been accompanied by, the universalization of the nation-state'. Even in the era of globalization, classes remain nationally constituted, and 'global economic imperatives require local mediations' via nation-states. The resulting tensions between capitalism's global economic dynamic and its political fragmentation into a system of nation-states are inherent in the capital relation itself:

77

The critical point is that there is an irreducible contradiction between two opposing tendencies, both of which are rooted in the nature of capitalism.

While capitalism did not create the nation-state, nor did it invent state sovereignty or territoriality, its systemic logic has reproduced the territorial state no less than the universal globalizing force of the economy. It is, in other words, in the very nature of capitalism to intensify the contradiction between its expansionist imperatives and the territorial divisions of its original political (and economic) form.[24]

This formulation, interestingly, echoes Bukharin's conception of imperialism as constituted by tendencies to both the internationalization and the statification of capital. Wood's substantive conclusion, that 'the political form of global capitalism is not a global state but a global system of multiple territorial states', is in my view correct.[25] But can she ground this conclusion theoretically in terms capable of resisting Lacher's critique of traditional Marxist discussion of international relations – a critique that is particularly telling because it starts from the very terrain that Wood herself first mapped out? The core of her argument strikes an uncharacteristically uncertain note. The kind of transnational state whose advent is announced by Robinson is

at best a highly abstract *theoretical* possibility and one that is constantly undermined by capitalism's own logic of process. The kind of legal and political order required to enable capital accumulation, and to preserve social stability in conditions of market dependence, is for all *practical* purposes inconceivable without clear territorial demarcations and sharply defined jurisdictions.[26]

Elsewhere, Wood elaborates the point:

The new imperialism, by contrast to older forms of empire, depends more than ever on a system of multiple and more or less sovereign national states. The very fact that 'globalization' has extended capital's purely economic powers far beyond the range of any single nation state means that global capital requires *many* nation states to perform the administrative and coercive functions that sustain the system of property and provide the kind of day-to-day regularity, predictability, and legal order that capitalism needs more than any other social form. No conceivable form of 'global governance' could provide the kind of daily order or the conditions of accumulation that capital requires.[27]

Wood herself has acknowledged one point of weakness in this argument: 'I should, perhaps, concede that the impossibility of a global state to match global capital is not something that can be grasped entirely on the theoretical plane. To a large extent, this proposition is a lower-level practical observation about the impossibility of sustaining on a large geographical scale the close regulation and predictability capital needs.'[28] But this then highlights another weakness, well diagnosed by a sympathetic critic, Vivek Chibber, namely 'a tendency to presume that what exists does so because capitalism, or imperialism, requires it – a kind of soft functionalism'. As such, it suffers from the general problem of functionalism, namely that to identify a need doesn't either guarantee that it will be met, or, if it is actually met, specify the form this takes. Chibber makes the point well:

> It is difficult to see how the requisite *scale* of state construction can be deduced from the functional requirements of capital accumulation. That would appear to be a matter depending on other, more contingent factors. In remarking that the reason there cannot be a global state is that the demands of global capital are beyond the reach of any territorial state, Wood perhaps hints at this. But if so, this is not a fact about the deep functional requirements of capitalism, but a more contingent fact about administrative capacities and political reach. What would prevent these capacities from changing as technological capacity advances?[29]

Wood's strategy for integrating the state system into the Marxist theory of the capitalist mode of production thus fails to deliver the goods. The problem is partly that she has too undifferentiated a conception of capital. As we saw in §1.1, capitalist relations of production involve, not merely what Brenner calls the 'vertical' antagonism between capital and labour, but also the 'horizontal' competitive rivalries among individual capitals.[30] Marx himself argues that '[c]apital exists and can only exist as many capitals': it is, in other words, through the competitive pressures imposed on each other by rival capitals that the distinctive economic tendencies of capitalism – above all, accumulation and crises – develop and are sustained.[31] It follows that, from a Marxist perspective, 'global capital' cannot exist, but only a plurality of competing economic actors. Such a pluralization of capital might be thought of as supportive of a 'geopolitical pluriverse'. But, though suggestive as a point of orientation, it hardly amounts to an argument to insist on competition among capitals as (together with the exploitation of wage-labour)

79

constitutive of capitalist relations of production. I have tried to come up with something better by aiming at the same conclusion as Wood through a very different theoretical strategy.[32]

The thought informing this strategy is that Marx's method in *Capital* can be extended to incorporate the state system in the theory of the capitalist mode of production. This method consists in the progressive but non-deductive introduction of increasingly more complex determinations (see §1.1). Marx himself initially thought of *Capital* as merely the first volume of a larger work, of which Book 4 would be devoted to the state, though he probably changed his mind about this.[33] Nevertheless, his original intention indicates that, in principle, he considered it both appropriate and necessary to cover the state when analysing the capitalist mode of production. One way of attaching the state to Marx's existing theory would be to extend the division of surplus-value into the different forms of revenue that helps to organize *Capital*, Volume III: for, as Barker has noted, from the perspective of value theory, taxation represents a specific portion of surplus-value that is appropriated by the state.[34] But, more importantly (and also following Barker), rather than thinking in terms of 'the' state, we should conceive the state *system* as a set of complex determinations of the capitalist mode of production.

It is no argument against this proposal that, as both the Weberian historical sociologists and Political Marxists such as Lacher and Teschke point out, the state system antedates capitalism. An important theme of *Capital*, Volume III, concerns the capitalist economic forms that long pre-date the dominance of the capitalist mode of production. These forms, which Marx calls merchant's and usurer's capital, can coexist with pre-capitalist production relations, but, once capitalism conquers the process of production, they are restructured and integrated into a capitalist economic system that rests on the exploitation of wage-labour. Why shouldn't the state system be conceived analogously, as a social form that develops prior to the dominance of capitalism but that is incorporated into and adapted to the capitalist mode? Wood goes part of the way towards making such a suggestion, arguing that 'the territoriality and sovereignty of the state, while not created by capitalism, were, so to speak, perfected by it. It is only the separation of the political and the economic that permitted an unambiguously sovereign state, without challenge from, or overlapping jurisdictions with, other forms of "politically constituted property".'[35] But she prevents herself from further developing this argument by a persistent tendency to conceive geopolitical competition as essentially pre-capitalist. Thus she contrasts the development of industrial capitalism in France and Germany with that in Britain:

> The driving force here [i.e. in France and Germany] was not [as in Britain] domestic social property relations, impelling the capitalist imperatives of competition, capital accumulation and increasing labour productivity, but rather the same geopolitical and military rivalries, and their commercial consequences, that had prevailed in the non-capitalist economies and states of Europe.[36]

Or again: 'States [such as France and Germany] still following a precapitalist logic could become effective agents of capitalist development.'[37] This is the opposite of Hilferding's argument, cited in §2.1 above, that overcoming backwardness compelled Germany to develop particularly advanced capitalist forms. Wood's treatment of geopolitical competition as pre-capitalist is only intelligible against the background of an interpretation of capitalist development that privileges a misreading of English history as the norm against which all other cases must be judged. Why this is wrong will only begin to become clear when we take a closer look at the historical development of capitalism in the next chapter. For the moment I simply want to register a protest against what on the face of it is the arbitrary and dogmatic assumption that geopolitical competition cannot reflect a purely capitalist logic. The only argument I can think of that might justify such an assumption is that a dynamic driven by geopolitical competition could not give rise to the intensive development of the productive forces characteristic of capitalism. But this is demonstrably false, as chapters 3 and 4 will show in detail. Indeed, Wood herself concedes the point when she says that France and Germany were able to promote capitalist development despite 'still following a precapitalist logic' of geopolitical competition – a dangerous claim for her to make, since it potentially weakens the connection between capitalist property relations and the modern pattern of economic growth that is central to her and Brenner's interpretation of the history of capitalism (see §3.1).

To appreciate the strategy I am proposing to incorporate the state system in the theory of the capitalist mode of production, it is important to bear in mind one key feature of Marx's method in *Capital*, namely that new determinations are introduced *non-deductively*. A deductive argument is content-preserving: the conclusion of such an argument, when validly inferred, makes explicit content implicit in the premisses. By contrast, the introduction of each more complex determination in *Capital* adds new content to the analysis. Consequently, each determination cannot be reduced to those that precede it: Marx's exploration of the functioning of finance markets in *Capital*, Volume III, for example, is not somehow implicit in his analysis of the commodity and money at the start of *Capital*, Volume I, though it depends on that analysis. Introducing the state system as a set of determinations in this way is thus, by definition, non-reductive. It is a way, therefore, of integrating the state system in the Marxist theory of the capitalist mode that isn't simply consistent with, but demands attention to and analysis of the specific properties and tendencies of the state system.

In the paper where I originally outlined this strategy I sought to underline the argument by offering a provocation: 'One implication of this point is that there is, necessarily, a realist moment in any Marxist analysis of international relations and conjunctures: in other words, any such analysis must take into account the strategies, calculations, and interactions of rival political elites in the state system.'[38] This has evoked a cogent and well-argued protest by Gonso Pozo-Martin. His main thought seems to be that the narrowness and rigidity particularly of the original version of structural realism developed by Waltz, which restricts the scope of international theory to the properties of a state system conceived as inherently anarchic, disables it from offering a remotely adequate account of geopolitics: 'it can be argued that realist theory leaves policymakers and analysts orphaned of any indications as to the specific content of geopolitics . . . realists are gagged by the tight cloth separating theory from everything else'. This is certainly a valuable corrective to what Pozo-Martin justly describes as my fairly 'vague claims' about realism.[39] My aim here is not to discuss realism, but to develop Marxism's understanding of imperialism (though to do the latter I will have to say a little more about realism in the next section). Two points are worth making here. First, it remains the case, as I argued in my original article, that 'there will be issues on which Marxists and realists will find themselves on the same side – for example, in contesting exaggerated expectations of interstate harmony after the end of the Cold War and criticizing idealist conceptions of the international offered by constructivists', though such convergence neither implies nor requires that Marxists sign up to realist axioms: rival research programmes may (and indeed usually will) partially overlap in some of the consequences entailed by the theories they generate without losing their individual identity.[40] Secondly, developing an adequate Marxist theory of the international requires, among other things, a critical engagement with the main theoretical ideologies of the international – not just realism, but also liberal internationalism and constructivism, which, in the general spirit of Marxist critique, would involve not just rejection and refutation but also the incorporation of valid elements of these ideologies. But, again, developing such a theory is not my main aim here.[41]

The main point of relevance is that, on the strategy being defended here, the state system is treated as *a dimension of the capitalist mode of production.* Here we see one advantage of conceptualizing imperialism as the intersection of two forms of competition. Harvey's formula of two logics, capitalistic and territorial, is vulnerable to attack from Weberians and Political Marxists because it implies that the territorial logic (geopolitical competition in my version) is external to capitalism. I don't think this is Harvey's intention and it certainly isn't mine. Economic competition among 'many capitals' is constitutive of the capitalist mode of production. My claim is that any development of Marx's theory on the assumption that the capitalist mode is dominant must introduce, at the appropriate stage in the analysis, a distinct form of competition with its own patterns and goals, as a property of the state system. From this perspective, in a certain way it is misleading to pose the issue in terms of *two* logics or forms of competition, however necessary this may be when conceptualizing imperialism, since the state system and the interstate conflicts inherent in it are simply one among a multiplicity of determinations that, when correctly conceptualized and ordered, a theory of the capitalist mode must incorporate. But also – and this is important when addressing Pozo-Martin's criticisms – we should recall another feature of Marx's method as described in §1.1, namely that each determination is explained by its placing within this larger theory. Thus any analysis of the state system as such a determination would take into account the entire preceding account of the capitalist mode. Far from reproducing the reified conception of the international to be found in realism, which abstracts states from the social relations and economic structures in which they are embedded, such an analysis would explore the features of a specifically *capitalist* state system, shaped by class antagonisms, competitive struggles, capital accumulation, crisis-tendencies, and social and political movements. Hence Pozo-Martin's call 'to theorize a *capitalist* geopolitical logic' is not simply consistent with, but required by, this approach.[42]

But understanding the state system as a determination of the capitalist mode of production would remain completely formal without some account of the mechanisms that bind states and capitals together.

A great strength of approaches such as Political Marxism and Open Marxism, which have emerged from the state-derivation debate, is that they treat the state as a reified or fetishized form of capitalist relations of production. Holloway, for example, writes: 'To criticize the state means in the first place to attack the apparent autonomy of the state, to understand the state not as a thing in itself, but as a social form, a form of social relations.' Hence '[t]he existence of the state implies a constant process of separating off certain aspects of social life and defining them as "political" and hence as separate from the economic.'[43] There is a valuable insight here that is of direct contemporary relevance in understanding, for example, the attempts characteristic of neoliberalism to depoliticize economic policy-making by, for example, transferring control over interest rates to 'independent' central banks and franchising out the provision of public services to private firms that allow politicians, bureaucrats and business executives to hide from democratic accountability behind the mantle of commercial secrecy.

Nevertheless, simply to remain at the level of this kind of form-analysis limits attempts to understand the state system. Peter Burnham seeks to adapt Open Marxism to the international: 'By viewing states as political nodes in the global flow of capital, it is possible to avoid both the Smithian bias introduced [into world systems theory] by focusing uncritically on the market and the mistakes of orthodox IPE (international political economy) which treat state and market as independent variables.' In line with this perspective, Burnham argues that 'state managers are above all circuit managers' who 'seek to remove barriers to the accumulation of capital, which flows through their territories'.[44] The trouble is that there have been different strategies for capital accumulation, both historically and in the contemporary world economy. Thus the managers of the Chinese state continue to promote a very high rate of accumulation while maintaining tight capital controls, a policy abandoned by the United States and Britain in the 1970s. Form-analysis doesn't seem to provide the tools needed to explain these differences. More broadly, even if we were to accept the abstract proposition that 'state managers are . . . circuit managers', we would still need to understand why, in general, they are motivated to act in this way.

Addressing this problem requires us to go beyond seeing the state as a reified form of capitalist social relations. If we do not 'treat state and market as independent variables', then, at the very least, we must assume that capitalists and state managers constitute distinct groups of actors with different interests – respectively, in expanding their capital and in maintaining the power of their state against both the population subject to it and other states. Taking this step is essential if we are properly to integrate the state system within the capitalist mode of production by identifying the micro-mechanisms through which state managers are motivated to act in the interests of capital.[45] This strategy was first developed by Fred Block in the 1970s, though essentially the same approach was also sketched out by Claus Offe, Ralph Miliband, and Chris Harman, among others. Block posits

> a division of labour between those who accumulate capital and those who manage the state apparatus. Those who accumulate capital are conscious of their interests as capitalists but, in general, they are not conscious of what is necessary to reproduce the social order as a whole. Those who manage the state apparatus, however, are forced to concern themselves to a greater degree with the reproduction of the social order, because their continued power rests on the maintenance of political and economic order.[46]

Furthermore, Block notes that

> those who manage the state apparatus – regardless of their own political ideology – are dependent on the maintenance of some reasonable level of economic activity. This is true for two reasons. First, the capacity of the state to finance itself through taxation or borrowing depends on the state of the economy. Second, public support for a regime will decline sharply if the regime presides over a drop in economic activity.[47]

But:

> In a capitalist economy the level of economic activity is largely determined by the private investment decisions of capitalists. This means that capitalists, in their corrective role as investors, have a veto over state policies in that their failure to invest at adequate levels can create major political problems for the state managers. It also means that state managers have a direct interest in using their power to facilitate investment, since their continued power depends on a healthy economy. There will be a tendency for state agencies to orient their various programmes toward the goal of facilitating and encouraging investment. In doing so, the state managers address the problem of investment from a broader perspective than that of the individual capitalist. This increases the likelihood that such policies will be in the general interest of capital.[48]

This elegant argument predicts a tendency for the state to act in the interests of capital without any need to posit a conspiracy by big business to shape public policy to its needs, or even to suppose particularly close connections between capitalists and state managers. All that is required is that individual capitals make investment decisions calculated to maximize their own profitability; the net, unintended effect of these atomistic, self-seeking actions will be to push state policy in a direction that tends to promote capital accumulation. To the extent that conspiracies – or, to use the language of political science, policy networks – exist (for example, in the intense lobbying efforts through which corporations seek to shape contemporary public policy), they serve merely to reinforce this tendency. But an important qualification needs to be added to this argument. Block acknowledges that this process may involve considerable conflicts between capitalists and state managers, particularly to the extent that the latter seek to maintain order by accommodating working-class pressures for social reforms. Moreover, he notes that 'there are certain periods – during wartime, major depressions, and postwar reconstruction – in which the decline of business confidence as a veto on government policies doesn't work. These are the periods in which dramatic increases in the state's role have occurred.' This underlines the importance of conceiving state managers as independent actors with their own interests that may lead them, in conjunctures where this seems both necessary and possible, to intervene to reshape the accumulation process in ways that the capitalists would not have freely chosen: a case in point is National Socialism in Germany (see §4.2).[49] Harman's formulation of a *'structural interdependence'* between the state and capitals is helpful in articulating the recognition that the relationship between capitalists and state managers is a two-way street.[50]

The point is an important one because Harvey's conception of imperialism as the intersection of capitalist and territorial logics has been attacked by Brenner, in part on the grounds that 'it is difficult to specify an actual social force in the state that possesses interests in conflict with those of capital in terms of foreign policy'. He supports this claim partly by rhetorical questions intended to expose the absurdity of such a conflict in the case of the postwar United States. Thus: 'Does it really make sense to understand any of the teams of state managers who fashioned US imperial policy between World War II and 2000 . . . as representing a state interest as opposed to the interests of capital? To ask these questions seems to answer them.' Actually the answers are considerably less obvious than

86

Brenner suggests. As we shall see in §4.3, US policy in Western Europe after 1945 involved on several occasions restraining American economic interests in order to achieve the foreign policy objective of rebuilding and integrating European capitalism. Moreover, Brenner himself, briefly in the article cited and at greater length elsewhere, has argued that the militarist unilateralism adopted by the administration of George W. Bush after the 9/11 attacks is not in the interests of American capital, an argument that, if valid, would suggest quite a big conflict between capitalists and state managers.[51]

Brenner also appeals to what he calls 'the standard Marxist conception', by which he means the kind of analysis of the relationship between state and capital developed by Block: 'The general result is the operation of a homeostatic mechanism, which confines government policy to that which is compatible with, or falls within the limits set by, the requirements of capital accumulation.'[52] But this interpretation of 'the standard Marxist conception' does not rule out state managers taking independent initiatives, since the final outcome, however favourable to the interests of capital, may result from a protracted succession of interactions in which the equilibrium position is discovered through a process of trial and error. Moreover, if this outcome is conceived as somehow fixed in advance – in the way in which a central heating system is programmed to maintain a pre-set temperature – then Brenner's argument is badly mistaken. For the higgling among capitalists and state managers may serve to redefine the equilibrium position at a very different point, in terms of institutions and policy mix, from where they started. This is one way of conceiving major changes in economic policy regime – say, the shift from laissez-faire to Keynesianism in the 1930s and 1940s, or the adoption of neoliberalism in the 1970s and 1980s (very far from being simply a return to the starting point before the 'Keynesian revolution') – as a partially blind, partially ideologically directed, discovery process that, in seeking to restore favourable conditions for capital accumulation, may significantly redefine the character of the accumulation process. A further complication is that the concept of the interests of capital is itself a somewhat misleading abstraction; as Marx noted, '[c]apital exists and can only exist as many capitals'.[53] The convergence posited by Block actually occurs between the interests of the managers of a given state and those of specific constellations of individual capitals particularly concerned with and having leverage over the state in question (a set that is unlikely to be coextensive with that of the capitals based in the state in question). The result is the formation of specific, institutionalized, and (as we shall see) geographically demarcated nexuses between *particular* states and *particular* capitals.

Brenner does concede that there is 'potential for a significant gap to open up between a state's foreign policy and the needs of capital', but says this is best addressed 'not by reference to a dubious conflict between the interests of capital and that of states, but, more simply and straightforwardly, by reference to the problematic character of the form of state that historically emerged to carry out the political function required for the reproduction of capital: the system of multiple states'.[54] In my view, this 'problematic' state-form is no mere contingent historical inheritance, as Brenner, like Lacher and Teschke, believes, but a necessary concomitant of the capitalist mode of production. As we have seen (§1.5), Lenin argued it was the uneven development inherent in capitalism at its imperialist stage that would prevent the overcoming of national antagonisms in ultra-imperialism. Trotsky developed the notion of uneven and combined development, initially to explain the peculiarities of Russian historical development, but later to extend Lenin's concept of uneven development. Like Bukharin, he insists that 'world economy, which dominates its separate parts, is taken as the point of departure':

> the entire history of mankind is governed by the law of uneven development. Capitalism finds various sections of mankind at different stages of development, each with its profound internal contradictions. The extreme diversity in the levels attained, and the extraordinary unevenness in the rate of development of the different sections of mankind during the various epochs, serve as the *starting point* of capitalism. Capitalism gains mastery only gradually over the inherited unevenness, breaking and altering it, employing therein its own means and methods. In contrast to the economic systems that preceded it, capitalism inherently and constantly aims at economic expansion, at the penetration of new territories, the surmounting of economic differences, the conversion of self-sufficient provincial and national economies into a system of financial interrelationships. Thereby it brings about their *rapprochement* and equalizes the economic and cultural levels of the most progressive and the most backward countries . . . By drawing the countries economically closer to one another and levelling out their stages of development, capitalism, however, operates by methods of *its own*, that is to say, by anarchistic methods which constantly undermine its own work, set one country against another, and one branch of industry against another, developing some parts of world economy while hampering and throwing back the development of others. Only the correlation of these two fundamental tendencies

– both of which arise from the nature of capitalism – explains to us the living texture of the historical process.[55]

It is possible to give a more precise economic statement of Trotsky's claim that uneven and combined development are 'fundamental tendencies ... which arise from the nature of capitalism'. Marx posits the search for differential profits – or what are sometimes called technological rents – as a prime motive for technical innovation under capitalism. A capital that introduces a labour-saving technique will be able to reduce its costs of production below the average level of the sector and thereby to gain a super-profit, either by leaving the price of its output unchanged or by lowering the price to gain additional market share. In his discussion of the tendency of the rate of profit to fall, Marx argues that other capitals in the sector typically will copy the innovation in order to defend their market share; the net effect will be to reduce average costs of production and eliminate the innovator's advantage and super-profit, in the process raising the organic composition of capital and lowering the general rate of profit.[56] But the innovating capital may use the additional profit it has already made to make further productivity-enhancing investments that once again put it ahead of the game, so it gains more technological rents that both compensate it for any fall in the average rate of profit and provide it with the resources to continue the same pattern. The result may be a self-reinforcing process that gives rise to privileged concentrations of high-productivity capital. The technological innovation induced by competition among capitals is thus a force at once of equalization and of differentiation.[57]

This argument has important spatial implications, as the work of Marxists influenced by Harvey's 'geo-historical materialism' has shown. Michael Storper and Richard Walker have analysed the development as part of the process of capitalist industrialization of geographically concentrated Territorial Production Complexes; Sam Ashman argues capitalist development is inherently 'clumpy' spatially, as high-productivity complexes attract suppliers, retail and service industries, and skilled labour.[58] If correct, these arguments cast light on the contemporary processes of economic globalization, suggesting that they are unlikely (contrary to the claims of both neo-liberal boosters and Hardt and Negri) to even up the huge economic inequalities that currently prevail. Writing from a non-Marxist perspective, Robert Wade has developed a similar analysis:

To understand the 'fact' of non-convergence – or uneven development, or failure of catch-up – we have to understand a general property of modern economic growth. Some kinds of economic activities and production methods have more positive effects on growth and productivity than others. They are activities rich in increasing returns (to scale, to agglomeration), in contrast to activities with decreasing returns . . . Countries and regions with higher proportions of increasing return activities enjoy higher levels of real incomes, in a virtuous circle; countries and regions with higher proportions of diminishing return activities have lower incomes, in a vicious circle . . . Thanks in part to the communications advances associated with globalisation, manufacturing value-chains have become spatially disarticulated, and value-added has 'migrated' to the two ends of the value chain – to R&D, design, distribution and advertising. Activities within the value chain that are more subject to diminishing returns have been shifting to low wage zones while those more subject to increasing returns tend to stay at home.[59]

I return to the implications of these arguments for the contemporary global political economy in chapter 5. For the moment I want to focus on the significance of uneven and combined development as constitutive tendencies of the capitalist mode of production for an understanding of the state system. Harman has argued that capitalist state-formation is historically driven by the emergence of geographically concentrated clusters of productive, commercial and money capital that

act together to try to shape the social and political conditions in that territory to suit their own purposes . . . This does not mean that the structures of the state are an immediate product of the needs of capital. Many of the elements of the pre-capitalist state are restructured to fit in with the needs of the capitals that arise within them, rather than simply being smashed and replaced. But they are actively remoulded so as to function in a very different way than previously, a way that corresponds to the logic of capitalist exploitation.[60]

Harvey has argued along rather parallel lines that 'a certain informal, porous but nevertheless identifiable territorial logic of power – "regionality" – necessarily and unavoidably arises out of the molecular processes of capital accumulation in space and time', leading to both the capture of the state 'by some dominant regional interest or coalition of interests within it' and the state itself using 'its powers to orchestrate regional differentiation and dynamics'.[61] But one very important implication of these arguments is that the tendency of capitalist development to generate spatially concentrated economic complexes creates very powerful centrifugal forces that would strongly work to sustain the political demarcation of the world into territorial states. Capitalists in such a complex would have an interest in preserving the existing state to which they had privileged access; equally, state managers would be reluctant to surrender the control they currently exercised over the resources of this complex. It is important to emphasize that this centrifugal dynamic represents only a *tendency*: in other words, it is possible to specify conditions in which it could be overcome, allowing at least local and partial transcendence of existing territorial sovereignties. The European Union is a case in point, but it is important to appreciate the particularity of the historical conditions that permitted its formation – especially, as we shall see in §4.3, the existence of an economic region (the Ruhr) to which the two leading states (France and West Germany) had an interest in regulating access, and a geopolitical configuration – the Cold War partition of the continent and the presence of a hegemonic power (the US) with an interest in giving West European states incentives partially to pool sovereignty among themselves. These conditions are evidently not generalizable to other regions and therefore it is quite wrong, as even some Marxists have tended, to portray EU-type 'rescaling' of sovereignty (upwards to the Community, downwards to sub-state regions) as the teleological fate of the contemporary state system.[62]

If this argument is correct, then Lacher and Teschke are mistaken when they assert:

> There simply is no straight line from capitalism to any specific geo-territorial matrix or set of international relations. Counterfactually, it is perfectly possible to imagine that had capitalism emerged within an imperial formation – let us say, the Roman Empire – it would not have required its political break-up into multiple territorial units. Capitalism did not develop out of itself the system of territorial states that fragments capitalist world society; inversely, capitalism is structured by an international system because it was born in the context of a pre-existing system of territorial states.[63]

It is not disputed that capitalism 'was born in the context of a pre-existing system of territorial states'. The issue is whether the persistence of such a system is pure historical contingency. I affirm that it is not: as it happens, capitalist production relations *did* first become dominant in part of a transnational empire, namely the Northern Netherlands, which rebelled against Habsburg Spain and formed the

United Provinces in the late sixteenth century, in the process reinforcing the tendency for Europe to develop politically as a system of multiple states (see §3.3). To assert this is not to say that the processes of uneven and combined development are the *sole* force sustaining the system of territorial states. Thus the formation of collective, mainly national, identities is another such force that is particularly important in explaining both the precise territorial demarcations between states and mass political investments in them. But the fact remains that capitalism's inherent tendencies to uneven and combined development are the source of a powerful centrifugal drive that helps to keep states multiple.

Lacher and Teschke make a more useful historical point when they draw attention to the variations in the kinds of modern territorial sovereignty:

> even the most cursory glance over the history of capitalist international orders – from the establishment of the liberal trade system of the Pax Britannica and the 'New Imperialism' of Salisbury or Chamberlain, with its oscillation between 'formal' and 'informal empire' via the territorially expansive and economically autarchic *Mitteleuropa* and *Lebensraum* conceptions of German *Geopolitik* and the Japanese project of a 'Greater East-Asian Co-Prosperity Sphere', to the US-sponsored (but multilateral) post-war liberal world order within the Cold War context and contemporary European integration – shows how the historical record exhibits an immense co-variation in the nexus between capitalist states and projects of territorialization.[64]

It is certainly true that the generalization of the nation-state as the dominant political form is a very recent development, only taken close to relative 'completion' by the disintegration of the multinational empire that was the Soviet Union. But the fact that, as Frederick Cooper has emphasized, it is only in the past few decades that territorial empires have ceased to be a living political form does not alter the fact that capitalism has historically coexisted with a system of multiple states, albeit states of different kinds.[65] In other words, the limits to the 'co-variation' of capitalism and 'projects of territorialization' have been exactly those predicted by my argument from uneven and combined development. In any case, what conclusions do Lacher and Teschke draw from the existence of a variety of forms of political territoriality? They recommend 'a constant attentiveness to the rich diversity of socio-political constructions of IR' and criticize Harvey and me for attributing 'one *generic* rationality' respectively to capitalists and to state managers: 'The question is never what state managers or capitalists *ought* to do or *ought* to have done, but what they actually did.' Marxist IR analysts should therefore proceed by 'first reconstructing the real historical socioeconomic and (geo) political conflicts in order to then arrive at the multiple "logics" of capitalist geopolitical competition and cooperation'.[66] Attention to historical variety is indeed necessary, but, despite their disclaimers, Lacher's and Teschke's apparent adoption of inductivism amounts to giving up theory in favour of empirical description. Part of the significance of Marx's method in *Capital* is that it seeks to break down this kind of theoretical/empirical polarity through the production of progressively more definite concepts that integrate an increasingly complex factual content into the theory. It is this method that I try to follow in chapters 3 to 5 – not abandoning theory in the face of history but developing the theory by means of the concepts necessary to capture the changing interrelations of economic and geopolitical competition.[67]

2.3   Interests and ideologies

So far my argument has proceeded entirely in structural terms, exploring the relationship between capitalist production relations and the state system without any consideration of the mental and linguistic representations used by the individual and collective actors caught up in these structures. Though, in my view, an entirely legitimate way of proceeding, this cuts across the tenets of the currently most fashionable school in IR theory, that of constructivism, whose 'central thesis' is summarized by Alexander Wendt as the claim that 'the meaning of power and the content of interests is largely a function of ideas'. Wendt develops quite a sophisticated defence of constructivism that characterizes and rejects realism in IR as based on the claim that 'the effects of power are constituted by brute material forces', whether the latter are found in human nature or in technology. This then leads to the argument that 'the effects of [interstate] anarchy and material structures depend on what states *want*', the starting point for Wendt's now celebrated differentiation between three kinds of international anarchy, each of which depends on how states conceive each other – as Hobbesian (the Other as enemy), Lockean (the Other as rival), or Kantian (the Other as friend). Thus we can see that Wendt's actual theory of the international does not exclude 'brute material forces', but rather holds that their 'effects interact with interests and culture to dispose social interaction and systems in certain directions and not others'.[68]

Wendt's detailed account of these effects raises a fine analytical point. He says that '[t]he distribution of actors' material capabilities affects the possibility and likelihood of certain outcomes'. But what is the ontological status of this distribution? Does it derive from the nature of the items distributed, in which case the material includes more than brute bodies or tools? Or, if the nature of the distribution (essentially a relationship connecting actors and capabilities) is distinct from that of these items, in what does it consist? In his discussion of Marxism, Wendt seems to opt for a version of the latter:

> The problem is that Marxism defines the mode of production not only in terms of forces but also in terms of *relations* of production. Forces of production ('tools') are plausible candidates for being brute material forces. But relations of production are thoroughly ideational phenomena, namely institutions or rules – which are ultimately shared ideas – that constitute property and exchange relationships, who works for whom, class powers and interests, and so on. The fact that relations of production are ideational means that capitalism is mostly a *cultural* form, not material, and as such Marxism's 'material base' is actually shot through and through with ideas.[69]

Wendt is right that Marxism gives explanatory primacy to the forces and relations of production, and that the latter cannot be understood as 'brute material forces' in the sense that he gives to this expression. But his conclusion that 'relations of production are ideational' depends on a question-begging and narrow counter-position of the ideal and the material. Even if we were to grant the highly doubtful premiss that institutions and rules are 'ultimately shared ideas', the relations of production are not reducible to institutions or rules. If we take the two constitutive dimensions of capitalist relations of production, the capital–labour relation in the first place certainly *requires* institutions and rules for it to function – for example, the legal forms and processes through which a stable labour-contract can be maintained, but, as the historical record amply demonstrates, wage-labour can be institutionalized in *various* forms, differentiated, for example, according to the degree to which 'extra-economic coercion' is involved.[70] The distinction between relations, on the one hand, and institutions and rules, on the other, is even clearer in the case of the capital–capital relation: competing capitals can exert pressure on another, even if trading relations between the states where they are based are only very weakly institutionalized, through the impact they have on each other in other markets. Philosophically, Wendt, rightly in my view (though a bit confusingly, since he rejects realism in IR theory), espouses scientific realism, according to which explanatory theories refer to a world that exists independently of individual minds and of language and is often not directly observable, but he wrongly restricts the scope of this realism by denying social relations an irreducible ontological status. To follow him in this would make it impossible to conceptualize what I call the relationality of capital.[71]

Marxism thus represents a considerably more sophisticated form of materialism than that attacked by constructivists in IR. One index of its sophistication is that it provides a framework that is perfectly habitable by explorations of the role played by ideologies and domestic interests and forces in shaping transnational relationships. These are, by contrast, something of an embarrassment for structural realism, which, in the Waltzian version, eschews unit-level analysis of processes internal to states, in favour of systemic explanations couched in terms of the instrumentally rational behaviour of states conceived as unitary actors making the best of their share in the distribution of material capabilities among the units of the system. But the discrepancies between predictions based on such austere assumptions and the empirical record have forced theorists in the realist tradition to crack open the black box of the state and engage in unit-level analysis. The most celebrated example of this is provided by John Mearsheimer's and Stephen Walt's introduction of the domestic US Israel lobby, in order to explain what they regard as the irrational invasion of Iraq by the administration of the younger Bush. But this is a relatively ad hoc adjustment by analysts who, apart from assuming that states aim to maximize their power relative to that of others instead of, as Waltz argues, seeking survival, remain committed to his minimalist conception of the international.[72]

Other 'offensive realists' have, however, gone considerably further in integrating unit-level analysis in the explanation of how states behave relative to one another. Fareed Zakaria, for example, defends 'state-centred realism', which predicts that *nations try to expand their political interests abroad when central decision-makers perceive a relative increase in state power*'. Such perceptions are in turn likely to reflect both the state's material capabilities, relative to those of others, and its strength. State strength is a complex variable, depending on the scope of the state's activities, on its autonomy of 'societal interests' and on its 'possession of sufficient capacity and cohesion to carry out its wishes', which in turn is a function of 'the state's ability

95

to extract wealth' and 'the degree of centralization of decision-making within the state'. Thus the time lag between the acquisition by the US of the material capabilities to act as a Great Power in the 1860s, and the adoption of an assertive foreign policy that actually began to cash in this increase in relative power in the 1890s, is to be explained by the absence of sufficient state strength in the *post-bellum* era.[73] An even more radical integration of state–society relations into realism is provided by Christopher Layne, who in a powerful historical critique of American grand strategy since 1940 argues that 'it has driven the United States to attempt to establish its hegemony in the world's three most important regions outside North America itself: Western Europe, East Asia, and the Persian Gulf'. This pursuit of 'interregional hegemony' has to be explained not just by 'systemic' factors – i.e., by the relative power of the US to that of other states – but also by 'domestic variables', notably the influence of the liberal internationalist ideology of the Open Door, based on 'two pillars: the economic Open Door (maintaining an open international economic system) and the political Open Door (spreading democracy and liberalism abroad)'. This 'grand strategy has served the interests of the dominant elites that have formed the core of the US foreign policy establishment since at least the late 1930s', a 'multinational liberal coalition' at whose core 'were large capital-intensive corporations that looked to overseas markets and outward-looking investment banks'.[74]

Layne's analysis has much to commend it as an interpretation of US grand strategy from FDR to Obama, as we shall see in chapters 4 and 5. Moreover, as Layne acknowledges, in many respects it corresponds to the radical critique of American foreign policy pioneered by William Appleman Williams. The difference is that, first, Layne's critique is located politically on the libertarian right, in the opposition to imperial adventures mounted by, for example, the Hayekian think-tank the Cato Institute. Secondly, theoretically Layne's analysis remains embedded in the conceptual universe of structural realism, in particular in its assumption that, other things being equal, states act instrumentally rationally. Thus he commends to the US the strategy that Mearsheimer argues it has historically pursued – that of an offshore balancer that does not seek to dominate other regions, but only intervenes in the rare cases where a power, or coalition of powers, emerges that represents a serious threat to its regional interests in the Western Hemisphere. In a certain sense, Layne's difference with Mearsheimer is one of historical interpretation rather than underlying theory – that is, over whether since the outbreak of the

Second World War the US has generally behaved as an interregional hegemon (as Layne contends) or as an offshore balancer (as Mearsheimer affirms). In both cases, 'domestic variables' appear primarily to explain deviations from what they agree to be the instrumentally rational strategy of offshore balancing – in Layne's case, the 'multinational liberal coalition' behind the Open Door, and in Mearsheimer's the Israel lobby allegedly responsible for Washington's Middle East blunders. But, perhaps because the deviation diagnosed by Layne is much more deeply embedded historically, he seeks to provide a general theory capable of accommodating such deviations by thematizing the role of 'domestic variables', and hence distinguishes his 'extra-regional hegemony theory' from Mearsheimer's 'first-wave offensive realism'.[75]

If these different interpretations of American foreign policy provide evidence of the intellectual fertility of the efforts by gifted analysts to escape from the straitjacket of structural realism, Marxist approaches to the international have no need to don similar confining garments. Thus the ancient debate among historians of modern Germany over *Der Primat der Innenpolitik* and *Der Primat der Aussenpolitik* – the primacy respectively of domestic and foreign policy – should be regarded by Marxists as a false dilemma: *both* domestic class relations and interstate relations enter into the determination of foreign policy. As Pozo-Martin notes, the idea common to Harvey and myself that imperialism consists in the intersection of economic and geopolitical completion has been 'taxed . . . with indeterminacy'.[76] I would prefer to say that treating state policy as multiply determined is a theoretical strength provided that the relative explanatory openness that this entails is used to develop robust, historically-informed analysis. I should add that these determinations should not be confined simply to domestic class and interstate relations; thus, as Kees Van Der Pijl has consistently sought to demonstrate, *transnational* class relations constitute another important determination.[77]

But I want to conclude this chapter with a brief discussion of the role played by ideological representations of these and other relations. The functions of ideologies include: the legitimation and delegitimation of relations of domination; contributing to the constitution of individual and collective identities; and the displacement of social antagonisms.[78] All these functions are plainly relevant to the formulation of states' external policies, but they pose the question of how ideologies in this area relate to the determination of state interests. This issue is implicit in the realist interpretations of American foreign policy that I have been discussing. Realists tend to conceive interests

97

as the maximization of some variable – survival in the case of Walt-zian defensive realism, relative power in the case of the offensive realism common to Mearsheimer, Zakaria and Layne. To the extent that ideologies play any explanatory role it is to help to account for states' failure to pursue their interests, as in the case of the ideology of the Open Door in Layne's critique of US grand strategy. Wendt's constructivist approach is more helpful here. He makes two relevant points. First, one condition of a state constituting itself as a corporate agent is that 'powerful and enduring notions of *collective* identity among individuals' are sufficiently shared. Secondly, to the extent that states succeed in becoming corporate actors, they possess objective interests, that is, 'needs or functional imperatives which must be fulfilled if an identity is to be reproduced'. Wendt identifies four such 'national interests' – physical survival, autonomy, economic well-being and collective self-esteem:

> These four interests are needs that must be met if state-society com-plexes are to be secure and as such they set objective limits on what states can do to their foreign policies . . . While in this respect national interests are a selection mechanism, their real significance lies in the fact that they dispose states to try to understand them, to interpret their implications for how subjective security interests should be defined.[79]

I have reservations about Wendt's conceptualization of states as corporate agents; it seems to me better to think in terms of state managers whose specific rules of reproduction endow them with certain interests – in particular, maintaining and, if possible, expand-ing the internal and external power of the state. This doesn't alter the fact that state managers' capacity to constitute themselves as a collective actor – typically jointly with, at the very least, substantial fractions of the capitalist class – depends on the prevalence of beliefs about their shared identity. But what is really valuable here is Wendt's identification of certain *objective* interests that states (or state manag-ers) have, though more complex ones than those posited by realists. Any exploration of the strategies pursued by individual states would need to involve some assessment of what securing these interests would mean, given the domestic and transnational context within which a state finds itself: apart from anything else, such an assessment is necessary in order to specify the alternatives confronting state managers at critical junctures – think, for example, of the choice set of British state managers before each of the world wars, or of the US foreign policy establishment at the end of the Cold War.

But Wendt also stresses the importance of objective interests in that state managers seek to *interpret* them. Here the important point is that, even if what is in a given state's interests is ultimately a matter of fact, the correct answer to the question is likely to be essentially contested. This is partly because of difficulties inherent in the decision-making process – for example, the fallibility of knowledge and the problem of how to weigh multiple goals. But, more importantly from our point of view, it is also because of the presence of social antagonisms – for example, those arising from the differing interests of specific branches of the state apparatus and of individual capitals or fractions of capital, not to speak of the more fundamental conflict between capital and wage-labour. From a Marxist perspective, then, identifying the 'national interest' is likely to be an inherently ideological operation since, in postulating the existence of a unitary set of interests, it represses or displaces class antagonism. At the same time, ideologies also perform the more specific function of offering representations of the state's interests that can advance the case put by a particular interest-group and/or provide a framework for resolving conflicts among or between state managers and capitalists. This is, incidentally, a case where intellectuals play a part: one aspect of the significance of the differing realist interpretations of American foreign policy is that they amount, not simply to academic conceptualizations, but to ideological interventions in policy debates about where US 'national interests' currently lie. Understanding the ascertainment of state interests as essentially contested is important because it should block simplistic counter-positions of 'rational' and 'irrational' policies pursued by governments. Establishing the 'national interest' of a capitalist state is always likely to be a conflictual process in which social antagonisms and ideological representations play an ineliminable part.

All of this is consonant with a broadly Gramscian approach to ideology that focuses on its role in constituting collective class actors and representing their interests as universal. This approach has become increasingly influential in Marxist and *marxisant* approaches to the international, where the focus has been on how ideological representations and international institutions and networks can facilitate the transnational hegemony of a specific capitalist class. Recently, the fairly loose version of this 'neo-Gramscian' conception developed by Robert Cox, where structural determinations effectively disappear, has been tightened up in the more rigorously Marxist work of Adam Morton and Andreas Bieler, among others.[80] In principle this work is perfectly consistent with the theory of capitalism and the state system set out in the present chapter, but to my mind the problem of hegemony in the international system is most helpfully explored historically. And it is to exploring how the theoretical framework elaborated here illuminates the history of capitalism and imperialism that I now turn.

Part II

HISTORY

— 3 —

CAPITALISM AND *LA LONGUE DURÉE*

3.1   What is capitalism?

Two leading International Relations theorists, Barry Buzan and Richard Little, pause midway through a book that, admirably, seeks to open up IR to world history to confront 'a causal puzzle':

> the striking parallel occurrence during the nineteenth century of three things:
>
> • economic liberalization;
> • the industrial transformation of physical interaction capacity; and
> • the internal evolution of the leading modern states into their mass national and then democratic forms.
>
> It beggars belief to think that these concurrent developments are mere coincidences. Yet thinking of them as connected implies the existence of a very considerable transformation in the international system whose causal pathways are not at all clear.[1]

To anyone familiar with Eric Hobsbawm's great trilogy on the long nineteenth century, there is a simple resolution of this puzzle: the common denominator connecting the phenomena listed by Buzan and Little is the formation of an integrated, genuinely global economy dominated by the capitalist mode of production.[2] This perspective is relevant to any approach to the history of capitalist imperialism, since, as Hobsbawm puts it, '[a] world economy whose pace was set by its developed or developing capitalist core was extremely likely to turn into a world in which the "advanced" dominated the "backward"; in short into a world of empire'.[3] But the connection goes in the other direction as well: to what extent and in what ways did the establishment of European domination of the rest of the world between the sixteenth and nineteenth centuries contribute to the eventual triumph of capitalism? These are enormous questions and I address them only insofar as it is necessary to do so in order to establish some understanding of the historical formation of capitalist imperialism. But confronting them then begs two even larger questions – what is capitalism, and how and when did it become globally dominant? The two are connected, as Ellen Wood, a leading contemporary contributor to Marxist debates on these questions, puts it, 'we can hardly begin to talk about the origin of capitalism if we offer no account of its specificity, what differentiates it from non-capitalism, how we know when we have moved from one to the other, from a non-capitalist systemic logic to a new, capitalist set of "rules for reproduction"'.[4]

There have, in fact, been two major waves of Marxist controversy about the origins of capitalism that have posed the question of its specificity. The first, immediately after the Second World War, was provoked by Maurice Dobb's *Studies in the Development of Capitalism* (1946). Dobb argues that the merchant oligarchies that dominated the cities of early modern Europe and the guild systems over which they presided constituted an obstacle to the development of capitalist production relations based on the exploitation of wage-labour. The decisive change came with 'the birth of a capitalist class from the ranks of production itself', as 'the yeoman farmer of moderate means or handicraft small master' began 'to place greater reliance on the results of hired labour than on the work of himself and his family, and in his calculations to relate the gains of his enterprise to his capital rather than to his own exertions'.[5] Dobb's interpretation was forcefully challenged by Paul Sweezy, who insisted that the main causes of the decline of European feudalism were the rise of the towns and the spread of the market, precipitating a flood of rebuttals.[6] Though probably a minority position during this original debate on the transition from feudalism to capitalism, Sweezy's argument received powerful reinforcement with the emergence in the 1960s and 1970s of a closely connected constellation of theories known, according to their authors and emphases, as dependency theory and as world systems theory. Anthony Brewer has admirably summarized a common presupposition of these theories:

> In this approach, oversimplified, capital accumulation is seen, not as a precondition for genuine qualitative advance in the level and methods

of production, but rather as a redivision of a fixed magnitude, a transfer of resources from the exploited periphery to the centre. Development in some areas and the 'development of underdevelopment' in others are opposite sides of the same coin.[7]

The 'development of underdevelopment' is a phrase coined by Andre Gunder Frank to sum up the chronic backwardness, over several centuries, of Latin America; as Brewer puts it, 'Frank identified capitalism as a system of (world-wide) exchanges characterized by monopoly and exploitation. He also (implicitly) argued that any part of the world which is affected in any fundamental way by "capitalism" (exchange) is "capitalist".'[8] This is an analysis that offers a way of historically situating capitalist imperialism as the systematic exploitation of the South by the North. It also admits theoretical and historical extension, which was provided by Immanuel Wallerstein. His starting point was 'that the correct unit of analysis was the world-system, and that sovereign states were to be seen as one kind of organizational structure among others, within this single social system'. This methodological stance offered a new perspective on the origins of capitalism:

> In the late fifteenth and early sixteenth century, there came into existence what we may call a European world economy. It was not an empire yet was as spacious as a grand empire and shared some features with it. But it was different, and new. It was a kind of social system the world has not really known before and which is the distinctive feature of the modern world system. It is an economic, but not a political entity, unlike empires, cities, and nation-states. In fact, it precisely encompasses within its bounds (it is hard to talk of boundaries) empires, city-states and the emerging 'nation-states'. It is a 'world' system, not because it encompasses the entire world, but because it is larger than any juridically defined political unit. And it is a 'world *economy*' because the basic linkages between the parts of the system is economic, although this was reinforced to some extent by cultural links and eventually . . . by political arrangements and even confederal structures.[9]

This conception of the world system allows Wallerstein to give a more precise formulation to the kind of view of capitalism expressed by Sweezy and Frank, where it is identified in effect with the integration of societies into a transnational network of market exchanges. Thus Wallerstein denies that the capital-relation necessarily involves the exploitation of formally free wage-labour. Different forms of 'coerced cash-crop labour' in the 'periphery' of the early modern world system – indigenous people assigned under the *encomienda* system to Spanish settlers in Habsburg America or peasants tied to the land in Central and Eastern Europe under the 'second serfdom' – were subsumed under the capital-relation insofar as they 'produced for a capitalist world-economy', since '[t]he economic limits of his [the eastern lord's] exploitive pressure were determined by the demand-supply curve of a market':

> The point is that the 'relations of production' that define a system are the 'relations of production' of the whole system, and the system at this point in time [the sixteenth and seventeenth centuries] is the European world economy. Free labour is indeed a defining feature of capitalism, but not free labour throughout the productive enterprises. Free labour is the form used in core countries, whereas coerced labour is used for less skilled work in peripheral countries. The combination thereof is the essence of capitalism; when labour is everywhere free, we shall have socialism.[10]

Wallerstein's theory of the capitalist world system was developed under the influence of, and in dialogue with, Fernand Braudel's grand history of early modern capitalism. Like Wallerstein, Braudel conceives a world economy as a centred and hierarchical structure where the key differentiation is geographical – '*at least* three different areas can be distinguished: a narrow *core*, a fairly developed middle zone [called by Wallerstein the 'semi-periphery'] and a vast *periphery*'. But Braudel more clearly perhaps than other world systems theorists brings out the essential features of their conception of capitalism. He rigorously distinguishes capitalism from a market economy,

> with its many horizontal communications between the different markets: here a degree of automatic coordination usually links supply, demand and prices. Then alongside, or rather above this layer, comes the zone of the anti-market, where the great predators roam and the law of the jungle operates. This – today and in the past, before and after the industrial revolution – is the real home of capitalism.[11]

On Braudel's view, then, capitalism seeks to maximize profits typically through the establishment of monopoly. Thus historically its privileged terrain was not production, but circulation, for example, in search of the super-profits to be gained from *Fernhandel*, long-distance trade usually in luxury goods, between the fifteenth and eighteenth centuries: 'Until the industrial revolution of

106

the nineteenth century, when capital moved into industrial production, now newly promoted to the rank of large profit-maker, it was
in the sphere of circulation, trade and marketing, that capitalism
was most at home, even if it sometimes made more than fleeting
incursions on to other territory.' Thus, what provides the system
with its dynamic is less the transformation of the productive forces
induced by the competitive accumulation of capital that Marx
emphasizes than geographical changes in the locus of power at the
centre of the global trade network: 'In the face of pressures, both
internal and external, there may be shifts of the centre of gravity:
cities with international destinies – *world-cities* – are in perpetual
rivalry and may take one another's place:' hence 'the classical
sequence of dominant cities of Western Europe – Venice, Antwerp,
Genoa, Amsterdam, London'.[12]

Giovanni Arrighi and his collaborators have more recently developed the most theoretically and empirically compelling attempt to
substantiate the idea, common to Braudel and Wallerstein, that the
history of the capitalist world system can be understood cyclically,
as the rise and fall of successive hegemonies. Arrighi argues that the
history of this system is best understood as a succession of overlapping 'systemic cycles of accumulation', each characterized by 'the
leadership of communities and blocs of governmental and business
agencies' that promote specific 'strategies and structures' constituting
a distinct 'regime of accumulation on a world scale'. There have been
four such cycles to date, each associated with the hegemony of a
particular state – Genoa (1340s to c.1630), the Netherlands (c.1560
to 1780s), Britain (c.1740 to the 1930s), the United States (1870s to
?). Each systemic cycle has a universal form that Arrighi characterizes
by using Marx's general formula of capital, M-C-M' (the investment
of money in the production of commodities that are then, thanks to
the extraction of surplus-value in production, sold for a larger sum
of money than that initially invested):

> The central aspect of this pattern is the alternation of epochs of mate-
> rial expansion (MC phases of capital accumulation) with phases of
> financial rebirth and expansion (CM' phases). In phases of material
> expansion money capital 'sets in motion' an increased mass of com-
> modities (including commoditized labour power and gifts of nature);
> and in phases of financial expansion an increasing mass of money
> capital 'sets itself free' from its commodity form, and accumulation
> proceeds through financial deals (as in Marx's abridged formula MM').
> Together, the two epochs or phases constitute a full *systemic cycle of
> accumulation*.[13]

Within this framework, periods of financial speculation are 'a recurrent phenomenon' marking 'the transition from one regime of accumulation on a world scale to another', the decline of one hegemonic power and its regime and the ascent of their successors. Financial replace material (or trade) expansions because the rate of profit on the production and sale of commodities inevitably falls, encouraging the investment of surplus money capital in speculation in financial markets. Each financial expansion begins and ends with a crisis of the dominant regime of accumulation, the first a 'signal crisis' announcing the beginning of a new cycle, the second the 'terminal crisis' marking the end of the old cycle. The US regime of accumulation experienced its signal crisis around 1970, and, Arrighi now argues, the fatally misjudged invasion of Iraq in 2003 marked the beginning of its terminal crisis.[14]

World systems theory has undoubtedly made a most valuable contribution to our understanding of the history of capitalism particularly in the work of Braudel and Arrighi. The concept of the capitalist world system itself, in conceiving transnational economic relationships as constituting an integrated entity, represents an important analytical advance (though one anticipated within the classical Marxist tradition by Bukharin and Trotsky). Nevertheless, in detaching the concept of capitalism from the precise account of the relations of production developed by Marx in *Capital*, world systems theory loses sight of what was one of the key aims of that account, namely to specify the distinctive economic dynamic that, he believed, distinguished it from other modes of production and shaped its pattern of development. This fundamental point is made with great force by Robert Brenner in the most important single intervention in the second wave of the debate about capitalism, first in an article taxing Frank, Sweezy and Wallerstein for a 'Neo-Smithian Marxism' that equates the development of capitalism with that of the world market and the division of labour, and then in a more generalized version of the argument. In the latter text, he argues that 'modern economic growth', that is, 'the presence in the economy of a *systematic* and *continuous* tendency or drive to transform production in the direction of greater efficiency', presupposes that economic actors, whether (in Marxist terms) exploiters or direct producers, are dependent on the market for their reproduction. The premise of this argument is that the prevailing 'property relations', 'the relationships . . . which determine the regular and systematic access of the individual economic actors . . . to the means of production and the economic product', also 'determine the economic course of action which is rational for

108

the direct producers and the exploiters' if they are 'to continue to maintain themselves as they were – i.e. in the class position they already held', in other words, 'the rules for the reproduction of the direct producers and the exploiters'.[15]

Under pre-capitalist property relations, both the direct producers and the exploiters have direct access to the means of subsistence. Consequently, they are under no systematic pressure to increase their income by introducing new methods of production that would raise productivity. Surplus-labour is extracted through extra-economic coercion; hence the exploiters 'will direct their resources to strengthening their means of coercion' to squeeze more out of the direct producers or dispossess other exploiters of their land and labour. Given these rules of reproduction, 'the long-term developmental trend will be toward stagnation, if not crisis'. This pattern changes only with the advent of capitalist property relations, 'where all the direct producers are separated from their means of subsistence, *above all the land*, and where no exploiters are able to maintain themselves through surplus-extraction by extra-economic coercion'. The market-dependence of both capitalists and workers introduces the rules of reproduction necessary to support 'modern economic growth':

> It is only where the organizers of production and the direct producers (sometimes the same person) have been separated from direct access to the means of subsistence, that they *must* buy on the market the tools and means of subsistence they need to reproduce themselves. It is only where the producers must buy on the market their means of reproduction, that they must be able to sell *competitively* on the market, i.e. at the socially necessary rate. It is only in the presence of the necessity of competitive production – and the correlative absence of the possibility of cutting costs, or otherwise raising income, by forcefully squeezing the direct producers – that we can expect the systematic and continual pressure to increase efficiency of production which is the *sine qua non* of modern economic growth.[16]

Capitalists have to compete to reproduce themselves and hence have an interest in reducing their costs of production (and therefore the price of their products) through productivity-enhancing investments. But, even more important, it is only where the immediate producers themselves have no direct access to the means of subsistence – as is, above all, true of wage-labourers who do not control the means of production – that they can be induced to cooperate in increasing productivity through a combination of market-based sanctions (unemployment or even starvation) and rewards (for example, higher wages for improved productivity).[17] Hence the distinctive dynamic of 'modern economic growth' can only be sustained once, not merely the world economy, but capitalist property relations – and in particular the relationship between capital and wage-labour – have been fully constituted. A crucial implication of this argument is that producing for the market does not necessarily constitute market-dependence. Thus Brenner attacks Wallerstein's contention that coerced cash-crop production in early modern Central and Eastern Europe represented the subsumption of labour under capital. Even though the Polish nobility reorganized their estates to supply grain to West European markets (particularly the Netherlands), the economic dynamic governing lord and peasant was different from that of capitalism:

> Since the serf-lords had direct (non-market) access to their own means of subsistence (serf-peasant output from their demesnes), they did not have to buy on the market necessities for reproduction; their ability to survive, to reproduce, was independent of their ability to 'hold their place on the market'. Indeed, from the point of view of the Polish economy, the goods imported from the West (almost exclusively by the Polish lords) were in the fullest sense luxuries. The Polish producers might not be able to hold their own in the world market, and consequently might be less able to buy luxury imports, but this would not 'put them out of business'. As a result, no entrepreneurs, either from inside or outside the system, no matter how great the superiority of the productive methods they could potentially put into play, could replace the serf lords through competition. Far from being capitalist, Poland remained impervious to capitalist development. Its serf class structure ensured that existing means of production – land, labour power and means of production – remained locked away from potential capital accumulation. Precisely because free wage labour had failed to emerge, neither labour power nor means of production had emerged as commodities; as a result, these use values simply could not constitute a field for capitalist investment and development, because they were not, could not be, combined as exchange values under the sway of capital for production at the socially necessary rate. They were already merged by means of a class structure which fused the direct producers with the means of production and subsistence.[18]

Brenner's intervention provides a powerful reformulation of the case for focusing on the constitution of capitalist production relations rather than simply on the development of trade in tracing the emergence of capitalism. This is particularly important when considering the history of capitalist imperialism since, as we shall see in the next section, empires and markets have tended always to coexist. Nevertheless, in the hands of Wood and other Political Marxists, Brenner's writings have been used to present a very one-sided conception of capitalist development. This is in large part a consequence of the debate among early modern economic historians when Brenner's specific conception of capitalist development first emerged. This debate was inaugurated by his contention that the decisive breakthrough to capitalism in Europe came with the formation, as a result of the specific outcome taken in England of continent-wide clashes between lord and peasant, of capitalist property relations, based on the trinity of commercial landowner, capitalist tenant farmer and wage-labourer, in the English countryside. It was the resulting increase in agricultural productivity that allowed England to weather the general economic crisis of the seventeenth century and, by the end of that century, to support 40 per cent of the population in industrial pursuits.[19] In the ensuing controversy, the French Marxist historian Guy Bois coined the expression 'Political Marxism', attributing to Brenner 'a voluntarist vision of history in which the class struggle is divorced from all other contingencies and, in the first instance, from such laws of development as may be peculiar to a specific mode of production'.[20] The accusation was manifestly unfair, but Bois's label was embraced as a badge of pride by Wood, who advances an essentially normative conception of capitalist development, according to which cases of economic change that are not founded on the emergence of English-style agrarian capitalism cannot be counted as capitalist. Thus she denies that the United Provinces in the sixteenth and seventeenth centuries represented a case of capitalist development, despite the Republic's high level of urbanization and heavy involvement in international trade because, in the first instance, '[t]he growth of cities . . . did not depend on agricultural productivity', and then because, although 'the Dutch pioneered many improvements in labour-productivity, it is not at all clear that they were driven by the kinds of competitive pressure associated with capitalism'.[21]

As we shall see in §3.3 below, this represents a profoundly mistaken interpretation of Dutch socioeconomic development (and, incidentally, one not shared by Brenner). Underlying it is one side of what seems to me a false polarity concerning mercantile capitalism. In *Capital*, Volume III, Marx calls merchant's capital 'the oldest historical mode in which capital has an independent existence': 'In all earlier modes of production, . . . , commercial capital . . . appears as the function of capital *par excellence*, and the more so, the more production is directly the production of the producer's means of subsistence.'

This state of affairs reflects the fact that '[t]he circulation of money and commodities can mediate spheres of production with the most diverse organization, which in their internal structure are still oriented to the production of use-values'. The compatibility between mercantile capitalism and pre-capitalist modes of production, where, to put it Brenner's terms, the direct producers and exploiters are still not market-dependent, leads Marx to distinguish between two paths to capitalism:

> The transition from the feudal mode of production takes place in two different ways. The producer may become a merchant and capitalist, in contrast to the agricultural natural economy and the guild-bound handicraft of mediaeval industry. This is the really revolutionary way. Alternatively, however, the merchant may take direct control of production himself. But however frequently this occurs as a historical transition . . . it cannot bring about the overthrow of the old mode of production by itself, but rather preserves and retains it as its own precondition.[22]

This last passage was much quoted in the original postwar debate on the transition from feudalism to capitalism, because it seemed to support Dobb's contention that the adoption by small producers of capitalist rules of reproduction was the real lever of socioeconomic transformation. What in effect Political Marxists do is to take as a matter of faith Marx's final sentence, which rules out the possibility of mercantile capitalism providing a framework for the subsumption of labour under capital. This is the mirror image of the position taken by Braudel and Wallerstein, for whom trade is capitalism's 'home ground' and incorporation of direct producers in transnational commercial networks is a necessary and sufficient condition of their subsumption under capital. Boring though it may seem, this is a case where the truth lies in the middle. In other words, there seems no reason in principle to foreclose the possibility that specific forms of merchant capitalism provide conditions under which capitalist rules of reproduction develop. Indeed, Marx remained open to this possibility. A page after drawing the famous distinction between 'two ways', he apparently changes his mind, writing: 'The transition can thus take *three* forms', the first of which is that 'the merchant becomes an industrialist directly'.[23] This is a valuable reminder that the second and third volumes of *Capital* are posthumously edited and published manuscripts in which Marx struggled with what proved to be the unfinished process of developing concepts capable of grasping the complex realities of capitalist development.

112

Among these complexities is the emergence during the early modern era of what might best be called 'transitional forms', economic hybrids combining pre-capitalist and capitalist production relations that in important ways helped to facilitate the development of full-blooded capitalism. One of the most significant cases of such forms is provided by what Robin Blackburn calls the 'systemic slavery' of the Atlantic economy between the sixteenth and nineteenth centuries – the large-scale exploitation of the labour of chattel slaves producing either mass consumption goods (sugar, tobacco, coffee) or industrial inputs (cotton) primarily for the growing markets of Europe. The slaves were not directly subject to capitalist rules of reproduction since they represented part of the fixed capital of the master, who therefore had an incentive to ensure that they had access to the means of subsistence, typically through the allocation of plots that they cultivated themselves. But since the plantations were integrated into global networks of trade and credit, and obtained slaves, tools and fertilizers via the market, the masters themselves cannot be regarded as having direct access to the means of subsistence; their rules of reproduction required them to calculate profit-and-loss on capital that might have been lent them by merchants (or amassed by the masters themselves functioning as merchants) and to seek to reduce the costs of production. As Blackburn puts it:

> The slave plantations were dependent and hybrid socio-economic enterprises, not animated by a pure capitalist logic but closer to it than European serfdom or slavery would have been, or were. Plantation slavery was an artificial extension of mercantile and manufacturing capital in the age of capitalist transition, extending their reach at a time when fully capitalist social relations were still struggling into existence.[24]

Brenner himself in his monumental study of the role played by merchants in the English Revolution of 1640–60 draws an important distinction between two kinds of mercantile capital in early seventeenth-century England. The dominant faction in the City of London, increasingly represented by the East India Company and merchants importing from the Levant, depended for their control over particular lines of trade on Crown charters granting them monopolies. Free trade in colonial products from the Americas, such as tobacco, bore no attraction to the company merchants. Moreover, crucial to the state regulation of trade on which they depended was the reservation of monopolies to 'mere merchants', specializing exclusively as intermediaries between producers and consumers. Thus the chartered companies sought 'to prevent entry into overseas commerce by the City's shopkeepers, small producers, and ship captains', all of whom 'were well positioned to undersell the "mere merchants" (overseas trading wholesalers) . . . by going directly to the final consumer, either with English exports or foreign imports'. But the profitability of the chief colonial enterprises – tobacco and (from the 1640s onwards) sugar production – depended on long-term investments requiring, at the minimum, informal partnerships between merchants and planters, and, at the maximum, the direct ownership of plantations by merchants. Colonial merchants thus could not be 'mere merchants', but had to superintend the production of the commodities in which they traded, in a manner incompatible with the traditions of the chartered companies. Exploiting the Americas could therefore only be the work of City outsiders, whom Brenner dubs the 'new merchants': 'Originally men of the "middling sort", they were mostly born outside London and were, in many cases, the younger sons of minor gentry or prosperous yeomen. A few came from borough commercial families.' Brenner traces their careers, from their beginnings, some as colonial planters who used their profit to set up as merchants, others as London captains, retailers or artisans who entered colonial trade to cut out the middle man, through to the formation of a distinctive group marked, not only by definite patterns of economic behaviour, but by identifiable political and religious alignments that led some of them to play leading roles in supporting Oliver Cromwell and the Independents during the Revolution, and to direct the financial and foreign policies of the Commonwealth.[25]

In a sense Brenner is presenting here the metropolitan face of the hybrid economic forms whose development the other side of the Atlantic is traced by Blackburn. But in identifying a cleavage within the London merchant community, between a section which continued to depend on pre-capitalist 'politically constituted forms of property' in which the direct application of coercion was required to constitute economic relations (the state-regulated commodity circuits from which the company merchants derived their profits), and another whose members were beginning the process of subsuming labour under capital, Brenner encourages a more nuanced approach to our understanding of the role played by mercantile capital in the formation of a world dominated by the capitalist mode of production.[26] I now turn to consider aspects of this process relevant to our understanding of modern capitalist imperialism.

3.2 Markets and empires

One trend in recent historical research has sought to relativize the distinctiveness of Western modernity by highlighting the existence of robust market economies in the great civilizations of the pre-modern East, particularly China and India, and the active role played by non-European empires that often proved remarkably resistant to Western pressures – the Ottomans, Safavids, Mughals and Qing – in the constitution of the modern world.[27] This is a welcome corrective to Eurocentrism, as are the efforts of economic historians, most notably Kenneth Pomeranz, to demonstrate that Europe and North America began to outdistance China, India and Japan only after 1750, and then (according to Pomeranz) for highly contingent reasons, largely to do with how a combination of English coal and colonial raw materials allowed some Western regions to overcome the Malthusian resource barrier to which their economies, like those of their Eastern counterparts, were increasingly subject.[28] But the scale of Pomeranz's 'great divergence', as shown by table 3.1 (which dates its emergence earlier than he does), is now so vast, and apparently entrenched (despite all the boosterism about globalization), as to require sustained attention. The discussion in the preceding section offers one orientation for such attention – namely that it is Europe and North America's role as, till very recently, the favoured location of modern industrial and agrarian capitalism, with its dynamic of sustained economic growth driven by productivity-enhancing investments, that explains its ability to outpace the rest of the world over the past five centuries.

But this of course merely begs other questions, and in particular the ancient one that obsessed Max Weber – why did modern capitalism originate in Western Europe rather than in one of the great

Table 3.1 Levels of per capita GDP AD 1–2003 (1990 international dollars)

	1	1000	1500	1820	1870	1913	1950	1973	2003
West	569	426	753	1,202	2,050	3,988	6.297	13.379	23,710
Rest	453	451	538	580	609	880	1.126	2,379	4,217
World	467	450	567	667	873	1,526	2,113	4,091	6,516
West/Rest Spread	1.3 : 1	0.9 : 1	1.4 : 1	2.1 : 1	2.3 : 1	4.5 : 1	5.6 : 1	5.6 : 1	5.7 : 1

Source: A. Maddison, *Contours of the World Economy, 1–2030 AD* (Oxford, 2007), p. 70, table 2.1

civilizations of the East? Here too the efforts to decentre world history have shifted the focus of discussion. Recent research has highlighted the development in the first half of the second millennium AD of significant enclaves of merchant capitalism scattered across Eurasia, all of them associated with relatively developed industrial complexes. Janet Abu-Lughod, for example, has written a distinguished study of what she calls 'the Thirteenth Century World System' – the circuits of trade and investment that between AD 1250 and 1350 bound together merchants and producers of luxury and industrial goods in a vast zone stretching from France to China, in which Western Europe was a backward 'sub-system' peripheral to more advanced Asian civilizations. It was the intrusion of Portuguese predators at a moment of systemic disorganization in the late fifteenth and early sixteenth centuries, caused by demographic crisis and geopolitical instability (above all, the implosion of the Mongol Empire, which blocked the land route for trade across Central Asia), that permitted a shift in the centre of the world economy westwards.[29]

This is a much more congenial perspective on world history than triumphalist and teleological narratives of the 'rise of the West', or 'why the West won'. But, even if we grant that what Abu-Lughod calls the 'restructuring' of the world system depended at least in part on the opportunistic exploitation of a particular conjuncture by European rulers and merchants, important analytical problems remain. She writes:

> It must be recognized . . . that the 'takeover' of that system was certainly not according to the old rules. The old world system that was deeply penetrated by Portuguese intruders in the early sixteenth century offered little resistance. Why? In part, it could not, since it was already at a low (albeit possibly temporary) point of organization. Perhaps it had adapted so completely to the coexistence of multiple trading partners that it was unprepared for players interested in short-term plunder rather than long-term exchange. More than anything else, then, it was the new European approach to trade-plus-plunder that caused a basic transformation in the world system that had developed and persisted over some five centuries.[30]

Here again, then, the question of the specificity of European development – of what Abu-Lughod calls 'the European approach to trade-plus-plunder' – presents itself. Getting a better handle on it necessitates paying more careful attention to the different properties of pre-capitalist economic systems. Historical materialism has identified three main kinds of class society prior to capitalism – the slave, feudal and

116

tributary modes of production. Only in very exceptional conditions has chattel slavery provided the exploiting class with its main source of surplus-labour – in classical Athens, Rome under the late Republic and the early Principate, and the plantation economies of the early modern Atlantic world.[31] The feudal and tributary modes, by contrast, have prevailed over much longer spans of world history. Both involve the extraction of surplus-labour from a smallholding peasantry by means of extra-economic coercion. The key difference between them lies in how the exploiting class organizes itself. Chris Wickham in the most important single discussion of the tributary mode defines it as 'a state bureaucracy taxing a peasantry', as opposed to the feudal mode of production, which is based on 'rent-taking . . . backed up by coercion'. He argues that 'state tax-raising and coercive rent-taking by landlords cannot be conflated. They represent two different economic systems,' involving 'divergent interventions in the peasant economy'. Thus, under the tributary mode, 'it is not in the state's purview to control the production process'. It 'does not need to control the economic and social lives of its subjects; it just needs the funding that enables it to pursue its objectives'.[32]

The feudal mode, by contrast, requires that the exploiting class are much more intimately involved in the process of production:

> Landowners relate to peasants much more closely. Their interest is not just in the amount of surplus, though this is important enough; it is in the recognition of local power, local control . . . But this control is not just political, i.e. coercive; it extends to involvement in production itself. This involvement is structural, rather than necessarily conscious . . . everywhere, landlords control access to the land, even if in practice how much power this gives them is variable, and largely dependent on the strength or weakness of peasant resistance.[33]

In effect, what Wickham is offering here is a sketch of the differing rules of reproduction for exploiters in the two modes of production. Under the tributary mode, the exploiters' interest lies in perfecting and reproducing the tax system as a machine of surplus-extraction, and maintaining control over it and over the army needed to back up its claims on other classes – control that has to be defended against both state officials and private landowners, as well as against the peasants themselves. Under the feudal mode, by contrast, the process of exploitation is decentralized, the lords seek to maintain and extend the military and juridical power needed to regulate the peasants' lives and ensure a regular flow of rents, dues and other revenues, and a typically much more rudimentary state struggles to gain access to

income and the means of coercion. Where the tributary mode prevailed, as it did in the greater civilizations of the pre-capitalist East,
as well as in Western Late Antiquity, it usually had to struggle to
contain the tendency of its local agents to develop into feudal lords
with their own landed estates and armed retainers or (as in the case
of the western Roman Empire) to accommodate a landed aristocracy
with considerable independent economic and political power. Irfan
Habib's classic study of the Mughal Empire in the sixteenth and
seventeenth centuries portrays a particularly stark case of such a
tributary economic system, where approximately half the agricultural
product was extracted from peasant communities in the form of the
central government's land revenue; the right to this income from
specified territorial zones (*jāgīr*) was assigned on a temporary basis
to the *jāgīrdārs*, high-ranking state officials who typically were
expected in return to supply a military contingent to the imperial
army. Habib identifies a tension in this system:

> The imperial administration, which could contemplate the long-term
> interests of the empire and the ruling class, did, probably, strive to set
> a limit to the revenue demand . . . But there was an element of contra-
> diction between the interests of the imperial administration and the
> individual *jāgīrdār*. A *jāgīrdār*, whose assignment was liable to be
> transferred at any moment and who never held the same *jāgīr* for more
> than three or four years at most, could have no interest in following
> a far-sighted policy of agricultural development. On the other hand,
> his personal interests would sanction any act of oppression that con-
> ferred an immediate benefit upon him, even if it ruined the peasantry
> and so destroyed the revenue-paying capacity of that area for a long
> time.[34]

Here a state strategy designed to prevent officials from transforming
themselves into a landed aristocracy tended to undermine long-term
agricultural productivity. Mark Elvin describes a version of the same
kind of tension under the early Han Empire in China during the first
and second centuries BC that this time pitted landowners and peasants
against the state:

> The collection of revenue and the enlistment of soldiers [by the Chinese
> state, which relied on peasant conscripts,] were both imperilled by the
> growth of latifundia, huge properties owned by officials or merchants,
> worked by tenants or slaves, and able to resist most of the demands
> made on them by the local government authorities. A primary reason
> for their spread was the pressure of taxation on the independent
> peasants.[35]

118

The coexistence of tributary and feudal production relations, whatever the sociopolitical tensions it might produce, was facilitated by the fact that both economic forms involve surplus-extraction from the same exploited class of smallholding peasants. It also, depending on the circumstances, offered the peasantry alternative strategies of resistance: confronting two different kinds of exploiter, they might be able to play one off against the other – appealing to the central government against oppressive local magnates, or (as in the Chinese case just cited) allying with landowners in defence of local autonomy against the tributary state. Finally, the interweaving of what Wickham calls 'tax-based' and 'land-based' systems of surplus-extraction could create the conditions for a transition from one mode of production to the other. This is precisely how he understands the 'other transition' from Late Antiquity to the Middle Ages (though he no longer treats this as a change in mode of production, but rather in 'sub-types' of the same mode): he argues that 'the Roman fiscal system', 'arguably the most effective way of extracting surplus from a large population yet known', largely vanished in the West following the establishment of the barbarian successor kingdoms in the fifth century AD and fragmented in the East after the seventh-century crisis of the Roman Empire, induced by the Persian wars and the Arab invasions. The long-term result of this change in the West was the predominance of private landownership, though the Byzantine state and some Arab polities in the East were able to retain relatively effective tax systems.[36]

Tributary production relations could nevertheless provide the basis for imperial states to maintain long-term stability and offer a framework for extensive market relationships. Thus Wickham sees the 'Roman world system' that economically bound together the Mediterranean in a web of exchanges during Late Antiquity as unified by the fiscal system – more specifically, 'the tax spine', connecting the flows of revenues and key commodities (above all, grain, oil and wine) to the imperial capitals of Rome and Constantinople and to their armies; when this spine broke, in the fifth and sixth centuries in the West, and in the seventh century in the East, the Mediterranean world system fragmented, with many regions experiencing a decline in economic complexity. But this was a world economy where, as Wickham writes of the Byzantine Empire, the state acted as 'a structuring device for all exchange activity, including commerce'.[37] Habib has shown how the marketing of agricultural produce to raise the money for the land revenue, which was typically paid in cash, helped to support an extensive market economy in Mughal India; commodity circulation was facilitated by advanced financial techniques, including bills of exchange and forms of insurance, and supplied a substantial urban population that included skilled artisans manufacturing high-quality goods for the city-based ruling class.[38] The decline of the Mughal state in the early eighteenth century helped to marginalize the great port of Surat in Gujarat, a key centre of the pre-colonial trading system in Western Asia, and thereby to give an opening to the factories of the English East India Company.[39]

But the most important case of a tributary society that coexisted with developed market relationships is provided by China between the tenth and eighteenth centuries AD. Following the reunification of the empire – far and way the most long-lived large territorial state in world history – under the Song dynasty (AD 960–1276), Elvin writes,

> what happened was that an economic and technological revolution reduced the burden of the imperial administrative superstructure, increased the efficiency of the Chinese war machine, and created enough economic integration to be a real obstacle to renewed political fragmentation. At this point, therefore, Chinese historical evolution began to diverge significantly from that of Europe, to which in one way or another it had run nearly in parallel for over a millennium . . . Chinese society, like that of Europe at this time, developed in the direction of manorialism (*regime seigneurale*); but since the state retained control over defence functions, as it did not in Europe, there was no feudal superstructure (*regime feodale*), in the sense of a dominant specialist military class disposing of fiefs granted in return for military service and ruling these as more or less unquestioned lords.[40]

What subsequently emerged under the Song was a distinctive combination of a tributary state whose professional bureaucracy promoted scientific and technical innovation, landowners whose estates were typically worked by tenant serfs, and a highly commercialized economy in which grain and land were bought and sold as a matter of course. These institutional developments reinforced the process that had begun in the eighth century, where, thanks to the mastery of wetland rice cultivation, the centre of gravity of China's vast population shifted southwards. A cluster of new technologies (the sluice-gate, moria, treadle water-pump, woodblock printing, movable type, a water-driven hemp spinning machine) made China in this era the most advanced economic region in the world. The pace of innovation was not sustained under later dynasties (notably the Ming, 1368–1644, and Qing, 1644–1912), but the imperial state sought consistently to maintain and improve what were remarkably efficient inland communications by pre-modern standards. The disappearance of

120

serfdom and the manorial system in the eighteenth century promoted a further commercialization of economic relationships, reflected, for example, in the spread of rural and urban industries. In the cotton industry of the Yangtze Valley, for example, contractors acted as middlemen between merchants and artisans: 'an industry enormous in the aggregate was created not by expanding the size of the units of production but linking a growing multitude of small producers, with a minimum of direct functional integration between the various parts of the structure'.[41]

Arrighi has praised China under the Ming and Qing as a model 'non-capitalist market economy' and favourably compared 'the China-centred tribute trade system' in East Asia, characterized by 'near-absence of intra-systemic military competition and extra-systemic geographical expansion' for five hundred years (*c.*1400–1900), with the notoriously belligerent and expansionist European state system. He regards the Ming decision not to follow up on Admiral Zheng He's famous naval expeditions to the Indian Ocean in the early fifteenth century, and instead to run down the fleet and discourage the previously flourishing overseas trade conducted from the Chinese coast, despite China's superiority in maritime technology at the time, as 'entirely reasonable': 'For China's rulers, . . . control over these trade routes [connecting Europe and Asia] was far less important than peaceful relations with neighbouring states and the integration of their populous domains into an agriculturally based national economy.'[42] This picture leaves out of account the Chinese empire's biggest strategic problem, its long land frontier in Central Asia, rendering it vulnerable to the predations and invasions of mainly Turkic nomad peoples, and demanding policies that combined warfare, protection payments, diplomatic alliances and cultural assimilation. The trade- and ocean-oriented Song first lost northern China to sinicized Jürchen nomads and were finally overwhelmed by the Mongols; the Ming retreat from the sea was in part a defensive response to nomad pressure on the inner Asian land frontier.[43] In any case, China in this era remained less a non-capitalist economy than a *pre*-capitalist one, in which a state bureaucracy continued to extract surplus-labour from a peasantry whose direct access to the means of subsistence, in the shape of the land, actually increased thanks to the disintegration of the manorial system. Arrighi accepts Elvin's argument that the Chinese economy found itself caught by the eighteenth century in a 'high-level equilibrium trap' where it could support a large population at a low per capita income: 'Both in technological and investment terms, agricultural productivity per acre had nearly

121

reached the limits of what was possible without industrial scientific inputs, and the increase of the population had therefore steadily reduced the surplus product above what was needed for subsistence'. Consequently:

> With falling surplus in agriculture, and so falling per capita demand, with cheapening labour but increasingly expensive resources and capital, with farming and transport technologies so good that no simple improvements could be made, rational strategy for merchant and peasant alike tended in the direction not so much of labour-saving machines as of economizing on resources and fixed capital.[44]

For all its remarkable achievements, then, pre-capitalist China failed to generate the pattern of what Brenner calls 'modern economic growth', where output grows thanks to investment in technical innovations that raise the productivity of labour. Indeed, in a characteristically mammoth critique of Pomeranz written jointly with Christopher Isett, he has cited precisely the persistence of pre-capitalist property relations in China to explain this divergence. Brenner and Isett argue that in the seventeenth and eighteenth centuries, both the main classes of Chinese rural society continued to have direct, non-market access to the means of subsistence: the peasants had, as we have seen, gained control of their plots; the landlords, though they had largely withdrawn from the countryside to the cities, secured, thanks to the support of the Qing state, 'an essentially politically fixed level of rent'; 'In the Yangtze delta, the Chinese elite was thus able to extract roughly 30 to 40 per cent of agricultural output.' This pattern diverted surplus-product from agriculture; moreover, '[p]easants thus involved themselves in the market to secure the gains of trade, but did so only to the extent that doing so did not render them subject to the competitive constraint, and thus compelled to eschew highly desired objectives' – especially achieving social and symbolic insurance against old age and death by raising sons, a strategy that promoted population growth and the subdivision of plots. This conjunction encouraged efforts to raise (or maintain) household production and income by applying more labour per unit of output – in other words, by reducing agricultural productivity. Falling plot sizes and productivity encouraged the reallocation of primarily female rural labour to industry. Peasants were thus 'adding labour inputs in domestic manufacturing that they had previously applied – and would have wished to continue to apply – in agriculture, only because they were obliged to do so in order to keep up household consumption, even despite manufacturing's reduced rate of return, compared to their already existing labour inputs in agriculture'; thus the return on paddy rice cultivation in the Yangtze delta was two-and-a-half times that on spinning and weaving. China by the nineteenth century found itself caught in a vicious cycle of population growth, labour intensification and ecological crisis (for example, deforestation), while in England the market-dependence of all the main classes of economic actors – landowners, capitalists and workers – encouraged them, under the pressure of competition, to cooperate in specializing and in raising productivity, thereby allowing the economy to support a much larger population at a much higher standard of living than had prevailed before the agricultural and industrial revolutions.[45]

Properly to adjudicate the complex analytical and historical issues posed by Brenner's and Isett's critique of Pomeranz is beyond my competence. This critique, however, has the merit of offering an explanation of Elvin's high-level equilibrium trap rooted in the specific properties of the particular articulation of tributary and feudal rules of reproduction that shaped the strategies of economic actors in Qing China. It both offers a distinctively Marxist explanation of Pomeranz's Great Divergence and vindicates the insistence on the specificity of capitalism that is one of the main themes of this chapter. This is where – finally – we begin to rejoin the connected problem of what distinguishes modern imperialism. Here the account that Arrighi – more attentive to historical specificity than many other world systems theorists – gives of the 'Great Divergence' is helpful, because it takes into account differences in geopolitical as well as economic structures. As we have seen, he contrasts the East Asian state system, 'in which a growing introversion of the power struggle generated a combination of political and economic forces that had no tendency towards "endless" territorial expansion' with 'the extroverted European path' where geopolitical and economic competition drove states to seek to trump their rivals by expanding to other continents.[46] Addressing this contrast requires us, once again, to consider the differences between capitalist and pre-capitalist relations of production.

3.3 The sinews of capitalist power

Feudal relations of production, in the sense given it by Chris Wickham of the extraction of surplus-labour from smallholding peasants by means of extra-economic coercion that predominantly takes the form of 'coercive rent-taking', has only comparatively rarely been the

dominant pre-capitalist economic system. But, as he notes, 'the mediaeval and post-mediaeval West was one of the few societies where
feudalism has *dominated*'.[47] For some mediaeval scholars, for example
Guy Bois, the emergence of this historically distinctive phenomenon
can be dated around the year AD 1000; the 'Feudal Revolution' represented the definitive displacement of the imperial political structures that the Romano-German successor states and the Carolingian
Empire had sought unsuccessfully to preserve and of the juridical
form of slavery that had continued to shape social relations long after
the slave mode of production had been economically marginalized.
From the ruins of Late Antiquity there emerged new production relations, involving the fusion of economic and political power in decentralized lordships, extracting rent from a smallholding peasantry with
a significant degree of control over the process of production.[48]

Whether or not the transition from Antiquity to feudalism took the
punctual form of a relatively concentrated 'revolution' or was a more
protracted process seems less important for our purposes than the
significant change in geopolitical structures involved. While tributary
production relations can exist in a variety of contexts, their most historically significant role lay in providing the socioeconomic base for
the great pre-modern empires. Now one distinctive feature of an empire
as a political form is that it tends to be *centred*: power radiates outwards from the imperial court, while resources tend to flow inwards
from the provinces (or transversally to the frontier armies). Typically
also the boundaries of empires blur ambiguously rather than ending
in a clear-cut frontier, reflecting the tendency for what Michael Mann
calls the 'infrastructural power' of pre-modern states, that is, their
'capacity to actually penetrate society and to implement logistically
political decisions', to decline sharply beyond a limited distance from
the capital, compelling the imperial government to strike compromises
with local elites and even (as in the case of successive Chinese dynasties) to divert some of the flow of tribute to the nomadic polities on
its periphery.[49] This doesn't mean that empires can never meet or fight
– Rome waged long wars with the Arsacid (Parthian) and Sassanid
(Persian) dynasties that successively ruled Mesopotamia and Iran, the
Ottomans and the Safavids in a sense inherited this conflict in the early
modern era, and, of course, the European empires were forged in
mutual rivalries. But there is nothing inherent in empire as a political
form that requires such conflicts, and their existence undermines the
common claim of imperial rulers to bring peace to their 'world' – for
example, under Rome, the *oikoumenē* of the Mediterranean world
and its Western extensions.

The political structures characteristic of feudalism as it came to predominate in Europe after AD 1000 are by contrast inherently fragmented, less because of the overlapping jurisdictions that make mediaeval history so hard to follow, but rather as a consequence of the relations of production, constituted as they are by the coercive extraction of rent by the lord and his retainers from peasants by virtue of specific politically constituted property rights covering delimited territories. Is it purely random whether, where the feudal mode prevails, this political fragmentation grows or declines? Brenner answers this question in the negative:

> In view of the difficulty, in the presence of precapitalist property relations, of raising returns from investment in the means of production (via increases in productive efficiency), the lords found that if they wished to increase their income, they had little choice but to do so by *redistributing* wealth and income away from their peasants or from other members of the exploiting class. This meant that they had to deploy their resources toward building up their *means of coercion* – by investment in military men and equipment. Speaking broadly, they were obligated to invest in their politico-military apparatuses. To the extent that they had to do this effectively to compete with other lords who were doing the same thing, they would have had to maximize both their military investments and the efficiency of these investments. They would have had, in fact, to attempt, continually and systematically, to improve their methods of war. Indeed, we can say that the drive to *political accumulation*, to *state-building*, is the *precapitalist analogue* to the drive to *accumulate capital*.[50]

There was another option that this situation presented to the lords: instead of squeezing their own peasants harder or stealing someone else's, they could expand into the 'barbarous' or 'infidel' periphery of Western Christendom, exporting feudal relations and finding new direct producers to subsume under them (and exploit). The quantitative extension of the area under cultivation that was a crucial dimension of the progress achieved by the mediaeval economy between AD 1000 and 1300 was accompanied by the outward drive of military conquest and colonization by land-hungry knights and lords – Westwards (England and Ireland), North-eastwards (the Slav lands beyond the Elbe), South-westwards (Muslim Spain and the Two Sicilies) and South-eastwards (Greece, Syria and Palestine).[51] But Brenner's fundamental point stands – that the limits set to productive development by feudal social relations gave the lords a powerful incentive to pursue a military logic of territorial expansion and state-building.

When a lethal combination of technical stagnation and population growth induced a Malthusian crisis of subsistence in the fourteenth and fifteenth centuries, the result was an intensification of intra-ruling class warfare that, notably during the Hundred Years War (1337–1453), reached a catastrophic pitch of destruction, as Bois demonstrates in his great study of late mediaeval Normandy.[52] Both Bois and Brenner agree that out of this process of feudal 'political accumulation' came the development of centralized monarchies that began to experiment with the formation of professional bureaucracies and armies – absolutist states whose extractive capacities no longer depended on their rulers' ability to play the game of lordship and suzerainty with vassals who might have more resources than they did.

Brenner sees the formation of absolute monarchy in France as a response to the falling rate of seigneurial levy that Bois documents in the late mediaeval and early modern eras (1300–1600), which Brenner argues was a consequence of the success of French peasant communities, unlike their English and East-Elbian counterparts, in taking possession of much of the land:

> A more effective system of surplus-extraction against the peasantry required a more effective, tightly knit political association of the ruling class, a stronger 'state'. This was in fact constructed in the large part through the recreation of 'private property in the political sphere' for the benefit of the crown's servants – and this meant, paradoxically, the renewal of the crown's ultimate dependence upon a (reconstructed) ruling class (heavily, though only partially, based on office).[53]

One need not dispute this assessment to recognize that it needs supplementation by what Brenner himself in his discussion of capitalist crisis calls the 'horizontal' dimension of conflict within the ruling class (see §1.1). Indeed, his own account of political accumulation requires us to see the centralization and bureaucratization of juridical and military power in late mediaeval and early modern Europe as involving not merely the 'vertical' struggle between lord and peasant but the territorial rivalries among the lords themselves. Charles Tilly calls the latter 'a ruthless competition, in which most contenders lost. The Europe of 1500 included some five hundred more or less independent units, the Europe of 1900 about twenty five.'[54] Mann's study of early modern European state finances finds that, till the nineteenth century, war dominated state functions: 'A state that wished to survive had to increase its extractive capacity over defined territories to obtain conscripted or professional armies or navies. Those that did not were crushed on the battlefield and absorbed into others.'[55]

How this Darwinian process of irreducibly plural state-building and expansion intersected with the development of capitalism in Europe is a very large question. Feudal production relations, like those of the tributary mode, are consistent with extensive commodity exchanges. Wickham argues that the development of a market economy driven by aristocratic demand can be traced back to around AD 800.[56] Chris Harman has even written of the 'birth of market feudalism' during the later Middle Ages, despite the structural crisis that developed after 1300:

> Parts of the rural population, especially the lords, had become too dependent on the goods produced in the towns for society to revert on a system of production on virtually self-contained estates. As their demand for goods grew, so did their demand for cash, which they could only get by selling a growing proportion of rural output. Market networks continued to penetrate the countryside, linking each village and household to the traders of the towns.[57]

No doubt the political fragmentation inherent in feudal relations facilitated the crystallization of particularly concentrated nodes of mercantile capitalism in urban centres from central Italy to the Baltic.[58] Moreover, increased demand for industrial products encouraged the development of what some economic historians have called 'proto-industrialization' – the expansion of rural industries bypassing the restrictions imposed by city guilds and based on the putting-out system, in which merchants would supply raw materials and credit to artisan households in exchange for their final product.[59] But, for the reasons discussed extensively in the preceding sections of this chapter, these developments do not necessarily represent the subsumption of significant numbers of economic actors under capitalist relations of production; peasant households switching to rural industry might amount to an attempt to maintain their income through an intensification of labour that actually reduced productivity. Moreover, to the extent that merchant capitalism advanced significantly in the European late Middle Ages, it doesn't seem qualitatively superior to what existed further East, in China, India and the Islamic world. The emergence of the first capitalist states – really breaking the mould of world history – seems to have been the result of an interaction between intra-European developments, leading to the dominance of capitalist economic relations in the Northern Netherlands and England in particular, and the manner in which geopolitical conflict and mercantile ambitions pushed European states and private adventurers to seek wealth in the rest of the world.

The first major European intrusion involved a relatively marginal player, Portugal, initially motivated both by Crusading ambitions against the Muslim states of north Africa and by a desire for west African gold; its extraordinary successes in the early sixteenth century in wresting control of the seaborne trade of the Indian Ocean and laying the basis of a plantation economy in Brazil, rather than strengthening its hand in the European cockpit, made it a target of more powerful predators, notably the Dutch.[60] Nor did conquests in the Indies necessarily lead to the transformation of socioeconomic relations in Europe. The biggest initial winner, Habsburg Spain, inherited the tributary imperial structures of the Mexica and Incas its agents had overthrown; the substantial indigenous population that survived the massacres and epidemics inflicted on them by their conquerors were allocated to settlers as forced labour under the *encomienda* system. The vast silver deposits discovered almost simultaneously in the mid-1540s in the high Andes and northern Mexico reinforced the power of Habsburg absolutism; the annual treasure fleet to Seville gave Charles V, Philip II, and their successors the resources to pursue their European ambitions. The actual dynamic of English expansion in North America was much more decentralized, and (in part because the settlers sought to seize the Native Americans' land, not to exploit their labour) much more genocidal in its practice of war, but, in his superb comparative study of Spain and England in the Americas, J.H. Elliott conjures up a counterfactual history:

If Henry VII had been willing to sponsor Columbus's first voyage, and if an expeditionary force of West Countrymen had conquered Mexico for Henry VIII, it is possible to imagine an alternative, and by no means implausible, script: a massive increase in the wealth of the English crown as growing quantities of American silver flowed into the royal coffers; the development of a coherent imperial strategy to exploit the resources of the New World, the creation of an imperial bureaucracy to govern the settler societies and their subjugated populations, the declining influence in parliament in national life, and the establishment of an absolutist English monarchy financed by the silver of America.[61]

A genuinely capitalist version of extra-European expansion was in actuality pioneered by the United Provinces formed out of the Dutch Revolt against Habsburg Spain (1568–1609). Marxist historians have sometimes been quite dismissive of the Dutch Republic. Ellen Wood treats it as a case of 'non-capitalist commercial imperialism'.[62] This isn't so different from Eric Hobsbawm's much earlier description of the Republic as ' "feudal business" economy; a Florence, Antwerp or Augsburg on a semi-national scale'.[63] Such claims do not stand up to serious examination. For one thing, treating the United Provinces as just another city-state does not match up to the scale of its commercial empire. As Jonathan Israel puts it, '[e]xcept for Britain after around 1780, no one power in history ever achieved so great a preponderance over the processes of world trade as did the Dutch, for a century and a half, from the end of the sixteenth century down to the early eighteenth century.' By the middle of the seventeenth century the Dutch merchant elite were the main trading force in the Baltic, Mediterranean and Atlantic, and, through the agency of the Dutch East India Company (VOC), had succeeded in largely displacing the Portuguese in the Indian Ocean and the Indonesian archipelago. To quote Israel again: 'a fully fledged world entrepôt, not just linking, but dominating, the markets of all continents, was something totally outside human experience. The fact is that never before – or perhaps since – has the world witnessed such prodigious concentration of economic power at a single point.'[64]

Israel argues that Dutch dominance of world trade depended critically on control of the 'rich trades', primarily in commodities imported from the Americas and Asia such as silver, sugar, spices, silks and (from the late seventeenth century onwards) textiles. The growth of the early modern European economy generated demand for scarce goods from Asia – initially spices, later manufactures. These were precisely the kind of long-distance luxuries from trade in which significant profits could be secured. This gave the European trading companies in Asia – first the VOC but soon enough the English East India Company – an incentive to control the region's trade networks (and, in the case of spices, production as well), where necessary with the support of military power, as a means of regulating supply and prices. But European producers offered little that was in great demand in the sophisticated markets of the great Asian civilizations. Hence the importance of Spanish silver, a money commodity that could be exchanged for Indian and Chinese goods; hence also the significance for Dutch merchants of trade with their Republic's former sovereign and great rival, Habsburg Spain, and its American colonies. This in turn required the development of industries – for example, in fine cloths, whose producers migrated on a large scale from the Southern to the Northern Netherlands during the Dutch Revolt – as well as other activities, such as Dutch ships dominating the carrying trade in the Mediterranean and within Asia, that could help earn the necessary specie.[65]

What made this achievement possible was the development in the Northern Netherlands itself of a capitalist economy that developed a dynamic of rising productivity. As Jan de Vries and Ad van der Woude put it in their massive economic history of the Dutch Republic, '[T]he economic strength of the Northern Netherlands lay in its broadly based productivity, which lent profitability to a considerable range of activities in many cities and, especially, in the countryside and towns.' This was true in the first instance in agriculture: between the early sixteenth and late eighteenth century population doubled, but agricultural production tripled. It was also true of an advanced and diversified shipping industry: developed in the fifteenth century, the herring buss was 'a veritable factory ship'. Equally, a broader industrial base was established: by the early seventeenth century, wage-earners were 'a large minority', and the labour market showed 'no hint of Malthusianism': 'On the contrary, the wage evidence is consistent with an economy where heavy investment is expanding employment opportunities and increasing productivity' till the mid-seventeenth century.[66] Brenner makes a similar judgement:

> The Dutch economy as it emerged in the Early Modern Period thus appears to have been quite fully capitalist. It was unburdened by systems of ruling class surplus extraction by extra-economic compulsion . . . Moreover, its producers, notably its agricultural producers, were entirely dependent on the market and subject to competition in production to survive, so it had no choice but to maximize their price-cost ratio by specializing, moving from line to line in response to market signals, and seeking to bring in the latest techniques. High levels of investment obtained which resulted in rising capital/labour ratios, rapid productivity growth, and, ultimately, high income per person more generally.[67]

The final element in this pattern is, as Israel puts it, the 'specific form of the Dutch state' as a federation of urban mercantile elites: 'Despite all that has been said to disparage the Dutch Republic as cumbersome and slow-moving, the fact is that it was an exceptionally strong and efficient state compared with seventeenth-century France or Sweden, or for that matter pre-1688 England.' More specifically:

> Dutch world-trade primacy was built on an unprecedentedly broad foundation of shipping, fishing, and industrial resources, the bulk of which were based outside Amsterdam and which were dispersed right

across the country, albeit weighted towards the maritime zone. In this unique situation, so different from the past hegemonies of Venice, Antwerp, and Genoa, Amsterdam was merely the hub of a large clustering of thriving towns, all of which directly participated in the process of Dutch penetration of foreign markets. The federal machinery of the Dutch state, by linking the many towns, waterways, and outports which collectively constituted the Dutch entrepôt, provided a context of continuous political and economic collaboration.[68]

Formidable though the United Provinces was as an economic and political actor, its position was progressively undermined by the spread of mercantilist policies across Europe in the late seventeenth and early eighteenth centuries. This encouraged a reconfiguration of the Dutch economy around Amsterdam's highly developed capital markets and a more passive warehousing role in international trade. The most serious challengers were England and France, both of which developed trade sanctions and waged several wars against the Republic in the second half of the seventeenth century. Bourbon absolutism remained fundamentally a feudal sociopolitical form, though one that sought self-consciously to promote French industry in a way that the Spanish Habsburgs proved incapable of doing, and hence was consistent with a significant degree of capitalist development (during the eighteenth century France's overseas trade grew faster than Britain's, while equalling its industrial output[69]). Louis XIV's minister Colbert succeeded in the 1660s in luring enough Dutch fine-cloth workers to develop a local textile industry that, helped by French maritime power during the Nine Years War (1689–97), had driven the Dutch out of the crucial Ottoman market by the end of the century.[70] But England's developing capitalist agrarian and industrial economy proved to have the edge. The most important outcome of the English Revolution of the 1640s, as consolidated by the Glorious Revolution of 1688, was the installation of a new form of state that, though more centralized than the United Provinces, also facilitated further capitalist development.

Christopher Hill summarizes the changed nature of the English state as a result of 1640 and 1688:

Nobody, then, willed the English Revolution: it happened. But if we look at its outcome, when the idealists, the men of conscious will on either side had been defeated, what emerged was a state in which the administrative organs that most impeded capitalist development had been abolished: Star Chamber, High Commission, Court of Wards, and feudal tenures; in which the executive was subordinated to the men of property, deprived of control of the judiciary and yet strengthened in external relations by a powerful navy and the Navigation Act; in which local government was safely and cheaply in the hands of the natural ruler [i.e. the gentry], and discipline was imposed on the lower orders by a Church safely subordinated to Parliament.[71]

The significance of this new form of state – as Hill puts it, 'strong in external relations, weak at home' – is best brought home in his discussion of Braudel.[72] Hill argues that Braudel strives unsuccessfully to explain why it was first the United Provinces and then England, not France (despite the efforts of Louis XIV and Colbert), that dominated the world economy in the seventeenth and eighteenth centuries because 'he underestimates the role of politics in the consolidation of Amsterdam's hegemony and its replacement by London's'. More specifically: 'An absolute monarchy with a standing army and a permanent bureaucracy may intermittently favour trade and industry for its own military purposes; but it can control them. The looser, freer Dutch and English states allowed capitalist interest to dominate permanently.' The decisive factor in French failure and Dutch and English success was thus 'the differences between the two types of state', between an absolute monarchy and early capitalist states forged by revolution.[73]

The formidable character of the post-revolutionary English state is brought out by its capacity drastically to increase military expenditure in order, in the course of the eighteenth century, to secure its dominant position in the world economy. The real spending of the British state rose fifteenfold between 1700 and 1815, with civil expenses never rising above 23 per cent of total outlays.[74] It was this increase in military spending that allowed Britain to win its long series of wars with France between 1689 and 1815, in the process driving the French from North America and India and taking over from the Dutch in penetrating and cherry-picking the colonial empires of Spain and Portugal (as well as that of the VOC). The extractive capacity of the post-revolutionary state allowed it to become, as early as 1714, what Brendan Simms calls 'the most advanced national security apparatus of the time'; the tax burden in Britain during the eighteenth century was not only higher than that in France but rose steadily, reaching a high point of 35 per cent of physical output during the Napoleonic Wars.[75]

This reflected the commitment of the dominant landed aristocracy, based in a capitalist agriculture and with interests in industry, finance and the colonies, to find the resources needed to establish global hegemony. In his outstanding study of the eighteenth-century rise of the British 'fiscal-military state', John Brewer has shown that, though it was based on a uniform system of taxation to which landowners contributed through the land tax, there was a significant shift after 1713 from direct to indirect taxation, and in particular the excise levied on a range of basic commodities. The revenues generated by this tax (which was imported from Holland) reflected the huge expansion of Britain's commercial economy during the eighteenth century. The demands of administering this tax led to the development of the Excise Commission into a professional and disciplined bureaucracy, with a staff of around 5,000 by the 1780s, employing advanced mathematical techniques and exercising extensive powers of social surveillance.[76] The establishment of the Bank of England and of the National Debt in the 1690s allowed Britain to also raise money by borrowing, especially from Holland.[77]

The British state's ability to extract the resources for external expansion reflected its dynamic economic base, as well as its class character. By contrast, the continental absolute monarchies suffered endemic difficulties in financing their activities. Low productivity and high population growth limited the resources available. On the continent, the landed aristocracy, integrated into the absolute state, generally enjoyed considerable tax immunities; the fiscal burden therefore fell mainly on the peasantry. The lords represented the main obstacle to reforming the tax system. As Gabriel Ardant puts it, 'it was difficult to do without the backing of the nobility which provided part of the administration and the greatest part of the military cadres, and which strung throughout every region a string of landlords, all interested in maintaining order.'[78] The ultimately feudal character of the absolute state, its roots in a landowning class dependent on the coercive extraction of surplus-labour, set limits to reform. It was, of course, the Bourbon monarchy's efforts at restructuring – after the fiscal crisis caused, ironically enough, by France's successful intervention against Britain in the American Revolution – that precipitated the French Revolution.

What we see then in early modern Europe is a transformation in the nature of geopolitical competition. What began as a process of political accumulation – of territorial and dynastic rivalries among state-building magnates driven into expansion by the late mediaeval crisis of feudalism – is drastically changed by the emergence of a new kind of actor, the first capitalist states in Holland and England. The processes that generated these states were heavily shaped by internal social, political and ideological forces, though of course rebellion against Habsburg Spain provided the occasion for the formation of the United Provinces (and the Stuarts' failure to confront the traditional Spanish foe was one of the main Parliamentary grievances in the lead-up to the English Revolution). Nevertheless, the novel form of state created by the Dutch and English Revolutions facilitated external expansion, bringing its exemplars into collision. Barely had the Commonwealth been proclaimed after the execution of Charles I than it passed the Navigation Act 1651, directed against the trade primacy of its fellow Protestant republic, and provoked the First Anglo-Dutch War (1652–4).[79]

But, more crucially, the capitalist economic base of these states gave them a selective advantage in their geopolitical struggles with the great absolute monarchies. As Simms puts it, by the mid-eighteenth century 'Britain's dominance overseas was believed to be the key to defending the European balance of power'; 'Colonial expansion was not an end in itself, but designed to secure the resources necessary to pursue European interests, or to deny these resources to the enemy.'[80] Bourbon France finally cracked open and imploded under the pressure of the global struggle with Britain. The growing European lead in military technologies, generated by these conflicts, also facilitated the eventual conquest or penetration of the Asian tributary empires. Moreover, in different ways the process of external expansion promoted capitalist development at home. We have seen how the fiscal demands of war-making encouraged the bureaucratization and rationalization of the British state. William McNeill has highlighted the significance of the very high levels of military spending, during the wars with Revolutionary and Napoleonic France between 1793 and 1815, in directly and indirectly stimulating demand during a crucial phase of the Industrial Revolution, and the impact of army and navy contracts on the iron industry in particular:

> Thus both the absolute volume of production and the mix of products that came from British factories and forges, 1793–1815, was profoundly affected by government expenditures for war purposes. In particular, government demand created a precocious iron industry, with a capacity in excess of peacetime needs, as the postwar depression 1816–20 showed. But it also created the condition for future growth by giving British ironmasters extraordinary incentives for finding new uses for the cheaper product their new, large-scale furnaces were able to turn out. Military demands on the British economy thus went to shape the subsequent phases of the industrial revolution, allowing the improvement of steam engines, and making such critical innovations

as the iron railway and iron ships possible at a time and under conditions which simply would not have existed without the wartime impetus to iron production . . . massive governmental intervention in the marketplace had the effect, only half recognized or intended at the time, of hurrying on the industrial revolution in Great Britain and helping to define its path.[81]

There is, finally, the highly controversial question of the economic costs and benefits of the colonies into whose conquest so much blood and treasure was poured. I discuss the very important case of India in §4.2.3. The plantation economies of the Caribbean were seen at the time as the other great prize; despite being engaged in a desperate struggle for the mastery of Europe, both Pitt and Napoleon dispatched major military expeditions to seize the richest of the sugar islands, St Domingue, but disastrously failed to defeat the slave revolution that proclaimed the Republic of Haiti in 1804. Robin Blackburn's careful analysis suggests that, on a cautious estimate, the profits generated by the triangular trade connecting Africa, Britain and the Atlantic colonies in the era of systemic slavery amounted to between 20.9 and 35 per cent of Britain's gross capital formation, supporting Eric Williams's celebrated thesis that the triangular trade 'fertilized the entire productive system' of Britain.[82] Of course, a positive relationship between capitalist state-form and modern economic growth cannot be taken for granted. By the early eighteenth century the Dutch Republic had developed what de Vries and van der Woude call 'a state-rentier complex' in which a mammoth public debt held by urban oligarchs was serviced by a contracting tax base; this economic involution was a consequence of the United Provinces' progressive loss of markets to mercantilist rivals.[83]

But the case of Dutch decline underlines the general moral of this survey of early modern geopolitics: when successful, a state geared to the promotion of capitalist interests could both achieve external expansion *and* domestic economic development. Moreover, the economic pay-off that the primarily military activities of the state could generate – both in higher demand for manufacturing industries and in the seizure of lucrative colonies – suggests that the contrast that is usually drawn between late industrializing economies where the state intervenes actively to promote capitalist development, and the more laissez-faire English path of development, must be formulated with some care. Similar caution should be taken in approaching the separation of the economic and political under capitalism on which Political Marxists lay such stress (see §2.2). The post-1688 English state did in certain respects reflect and promote such a separation. It rested on a revolutionary settlement that had definitely broken with the 'politically constituted property' of the old regime. It began, as we have seen, to develop rational-bureaucratic apparatuses of the kind that Weber would have recognized – though this was a protracted process: the franchise was first reformed in 1832 and the purchase of army commissions was not abolished until the Gladstone government of 1868–74 (interestingly, the Royal Navy, the main instrument through which the British state projected power, was much more meritocratic[84]). Structurally, then, we can say that there was a strong tendency for the economic and the political to become separated in early modern Britain. But this did not mean that the state did not directly intervene in the economy (for example, in the efforts under the Navigation Acts to ensure that British producers and ships monopolized trade with the colonies, and in the extensive system of tariffs and subsidies introduced by Sir Robert Walpole in 1721, designed to favour domestic manufacturing industries), or that its activities lacked economic effects that might either promote or impede capitalist development. A symbiotic relationship thus emerged between state-building and geopolitical expansion, on the one hand, and capitalist economic development, on the other. One way of thinking about capitalist imperialism is that its emergence marks the point where this relationship is generalized.[85]

— 4 —

AGES OF IMPERIALISM

4.1 Periodizing imperialism

Discussing David Harvey's *The New Imperialism*, Robert Brenner poses a really good question:

> in seeking to interpret both classical imperialism (1884–1945) and American hegemony in the advanced capitalist world (1945–2000) in terms of Arendt's and his own proposed tendency for ever-greater expanded territorial expansion to follow the ever more expanded accumulation of capital, Harvey elides the fundamental question of the difference between the two periods. Why, with respect to the advanced capitalist world, did the imperialist expansion leading to inter-imperialist rivalry leading to war that prevailed before 1945 fail to obtain after that? Why, with respect to Europe, Japan, and indeed much of East Asia, did American hegemony for much of the postwar period fail to take an imperialist form, in Harvey's sense of the word – that is, the application of political power to consolidate, exacerbate, and make permanent already-existing economic advantage?[1]

The reason why the question is so important is that, as Brenner goes on to say, the answer 'will say much about the form we expect inter-capitalist competition will take in the current era'. In a real sense the rest of this book is an attempt to answer it. In this section I want to make a few preliminary analytical points. The first is that it is important that the terms of the question are posed properly. As Brenner notes, in setting out his conception of imperialism, Harvey draws on Hannah Arendt, and notably on the following affirmation: 'A never-ending accumulation of power must be based on a never-ending accumulation of property . . . The limitless process of capital accumulation needs the political structure of so "unlimited a Power" that it can protect growing property by constantly growing more powerful.'[2] This passage, like Arendt's entire treatment of imperialism in *The Origins of Totalitarianism*, is highly suggestive. Nevertheless, it comes from a discussion of Hobbes's *Leviathan*, and, as so often in Arendt's writings, relies on metaphor and extrapolation; consequently, her formulation does not lend itself to precise statements of mechanisms and tendencies. Together with Harvey's borrowing from Arrighi of the idea of distinct capitalist and territorial logics, it can be taken to imply, in my view quite contrary to Harvey's own intentions, that capitalist imperialism necessarily involves boundless geographical expansion, a proposition that is both historically false (the British Empire did expand as late as 1919, but was plainly suffering from growing difficulties in hanging on to what it had) and ill fits the particular dynamics of American imperialism. Hence I prefer to conceptualize capitalist imperialism as the intersection of economic and geopolitical competition, a formulation that leaves open the different and changing forms in which this intersection has historically manifested itself.

This leads us to a second point. As we saw in chapter 2, the classical theorists of imperialism typically saw it as constituting a new phase of capitalist development, most usually arising from the greater concentration and centralization of capital and the resulting dominance of finance capital. In this and the following chapter I take this approach a step further, distinguishing between three phases in the history of imperialism:

1   *Classical imperialism, 1870–1945*: this is the phase analysed by Hobson and Kautsky, Luxemburg and Hilferding, Lenin and Bukharin, the imperialism that gave rise to Arno Mayer's 'Thirty Years War' (§4.2).
2   *Superpower imperialism, 1945–1991*: the period when the world was partitioned geopolitically and ideologically between the two blocs headed respectively by the United States and the Soviet Union (§4.3); and
3   *Imperialism after the Cold War*: the period since 1991, marked by US primacy and a shifting global distribution of economic power (chapter 5).[3]

Periodizing imperialism in this way underlines that interrelationship of economic and geopolitical competition is both complex and changing. Ellen Wood seems to express a doubt about such periodizations when she criticizes François Chesnais for

> treat[ing] all stages of modern imperialism as equally capitalist, today as in Lenin's and Luxemburg's time. The effect is to make it difficult to explain where we are today and why. If the early twentieth century, as Lenin saw it, already represented late capitalism with fully developed capitalist imperatives and contradictions, then how are we to explain the specificities of capitalism and capitalist imperialism in the early twenty-first century? If, in the 'classic' age of imperialism, major colonial powers were engaged in inter-imperialist rivalries to divide and redivide the territories of a largely non-capitalist world, how should we compare it to the capitalist imperialism of today, when conflicts among capitalist powers take a different form?[4]

Wood's comment amounts to a less felicitous version of Brenner's Question. It is less felicitous because it implies that capitalism, an eminently historical product, itself lacks a history and that 'fully developed capitalist imperatives and contradictions' cannot manifest themselves in different, historically evolving, forms. But this seems inconsistent with Marx's method in *Capital* (see §1.1), where the very abstractness with which the relations, mechanisms and tendencies constitutive of the capitalist mode are conceptualized implies the possibility of their being actualized in a variety of different forms, depending on historical circumstances and the economy's position in the global constellation. It is certainly inconsistent with the actual diversity of capitalisms – in the sense of nationally institutionalized articulations of the state, the banking system and industrial firms – coexisting in the contemporary global economy, if we simply consider the entrenched differences between the US, Japan, Germany and Britain, for example.[5]

Of course, there is a danger in simply highlighting 'varieties of capitalism', namely that such talk may serve to mask the constitutive contradictions of capital. As Wood rightly says, '[i]f we obscure the very nature of the capitalist logic, we can talk about the stages of capitalism till the cows come home, but we will not give an adequate account of the changes involved'.[6] More specifically, Robert Brenner and Mark Glick make a good point when they argue the French Regulation School's 'project of conceptualizing the history of capitalism as a progression of institutionally determined, nationally situated modes of development' is undermined by the manner and degree to which, not only the broader framework of social-property relations, but also the nature of the world economy, shapes local process of capital accumulation . . . This is because the given international distribution of productive power will have a central role in determining what institutions are even viable within national economies at a given historical juncture, as well as what will be their effect on capital accumulation, since, unless they are shielded in some way, these institutions must directly respond to international competition.[7]

But what follows from this is not that it is wrong in principle to differentiate phases of capitalist development or specific institutionalized variants of capitalism, but that any attempt to do so must be set in the context of an analysis of the dynamic of capital accumulation at a global level. This analysis should start from Marx's relatively abstract theory of the capitalist mode of production, but it should involve a more concrete treatment of the form taken by that system's structures and tendencies at a given moment in its history. As we saw in §1.4, a major weakness of the classical theory of imperialism was that its different versions typically operated with inadequate understandings of the mechanisms that make capitalism prone to economic crisis. By contrast, it is a strength of *The New Imperialism* that Harvey seeks systematically to situate the history of imperialism within capitalism's tendency to over-accumulation. My own emphases are somewhat different, in part because I don't fully agree with Harvey's theory of crisis, but in this, as in many other respects, I regard his work as a model.[8] What follows, then, are *elements* of a sketch of an evolutionary history of imperialism. Rather than offering a detailed narrative, they focus on specific issues – in particular, the relationship between the formation of a liberal world economy and European territorial expansion, the specific nature of the different conflicting imperialisms of the first half of the twentieth century (§4.2), the dominance in the second half of the same century of a distinctive kind of non-territorial imperialism centred on the United States (§4.3.1), and the changes this helped to bring in both the forms of geopolitical competition (§4.3.2) and North–South relations (§4.3.3).

Erik Olin Wright argues that any evolutionary theory of society 'involves a typology of social forms which potentially has some kind of directionality to it'.[9] As Wright notes, an evolutionary theory thus understood need not be teleological – in other words, it doesn't have to explain the progression from one stage to another by their approximation towards some implicit goal of the entire process. Nor need it be deterministic: the move from one stage to another is not inevitable, either for teleological reasons or because of causal processes that drive history forward in a particular direction. What gives the history of capitalist imperialism a certain directionality is chiefly, as Bukharin argued in the most rigorous version of the classical Marxist theory of imperialism, the tendency, inherent in the accumulation process, for the concentration and centralization of capital, which leads both to a growth in the scale and relative weight of individual capitals and to an increased propensity for them to operate on a transnational basis. But, consistent with the theoretical approach I outlined in chapter 2, different aspects of the state system – geopolitical structures, the relationships between states and capitals, and military organization and technologies – need also to be treated as explanatory variables. Moreover, contingency plays an irreducible role. My periodization has, at its hinges, political events – the wars (the American Civil War, 1861–5, and the Austro–Prussian and Franco-Prussian wars, respectively 1866 and 1870–1) that mark the historical moment at which the United States and Germany emerged as Great Powers of the same (or even greater) range of capabilities as Britain, France and Russia, and the outcomes of the Second World War and the Cold War. But there was nothing inevitable about how any of these played out – wars notoriously turn on the uncertainties involved in strategic choices and the chances of battle, and historical research since the end of the Cold War has underlined just how close the world came to thermonuclear war during the Cuban missile crisis of October 1962.[10] Finally, though there are differences in the form taken by imperialism in its successive phases, this does not imply or require that a single model of capitalism prevailed, even among the leading powers, in the same phase. I argued in §§1.3 and 2.1 that Lenin and Bukharin were mistaken in generalizing, and applying to all the main capitalist states, the results of Hilferding's analysis of the emergence of finance capital, particularly of that in Germany at the end of the nineteenth century. Subject to the general constraints imposed by the global process of capital accumulation, there is no privileged form of imperialism in a given phase. The institutional configuration taken by a specific national capitalism and its associated territorial state is a consequence of, among other factors, economic structure, geographical location and character, and sociopolitical history, and cannot be deduced from the general properties of imperialism at a given phase. (It is probably worth adding that when I refer to countries, here as elsewhere in Part II, unless the context indicates otherwise, I am using shorthand for the managers of the state in question, or, at most, the constellation of state managers and the capitalists with whom they are in partnership.)

One final methodological point: in what follows, I proceed on the basis that, first Britain, and then the United States, can be understood as the hegemonic power in the international system in the epoch (in which we still live) of capitalist imperialism, and the historical discussion that follows takes their position and problems as its focus. I am aware of the strong historical objections to such an approach. For example, according to John Darwin, '[t]hose writers who have likened America's "hegemonic" status to that of Victorian Britain betray a staggering ignorance of the history of both'.[11] By contrast, Bernard Porter, a leading historian of the British Empire, thinks such comparisons are helpful.[12] I look more closely at the similarities and differences between British and American imperialism in §5.1. Here I simply want to say that it seems to me fairly clear that Britain between 1815 and 1914, and the US after 1945, performed a similar role in the international system both in organizing the world economy and in regulating conflicts between the Great Powers, even though the resources they had at their disposal and the kinds of states they related to were significantly different. In conceiving Britain and the US as hegemons, I am happy to follow the approach developed by Giovanni Arrighi, who understands 'world hegemony' as 'the power of a state to exercise functions of leadership and governance over a system of sovereign states'. In specifying the concept, Arrighi draws on Gramsci's famous distinction between domination and hegemony: 'Whereas dominance will be conceived of as resting primarily on coercion, hegemony will be understood as the *additional* power that accrues to a dominant group by virtue of its capacity to place all the issues around which conflict rages on a "universal" plane.'[13] Or, as Arrighi and Beverley Silver put it, where hegemony obtains, 'a dominant state leads the *system* of states in a desired direction and, in so doing, is widely perceived as pursuing a general interest.'[14] All this is very helpful, for example anchoring discussion of the role played by ideological representations in securing support for a hegemonic power by capitalists and state managers in other states (see §2.3).

But I do *not* find helpful the idea that the British and US hegemonies are the latest in a succession of world hegemonies, each associated with a 'systemic cycle of accumulation' in which the same features (in particular a tendency to financialization) recur. Arrighi and his collaborators seek to rebut the attribution to them of a cyclical philosophy of history (for example, by Hardt and Negri, who argue that in Arrighi 'the history of capitalism thus becomes the eternal return of the same') by explaining that each cycle involves an increase in the scale and complexity of the world economy – from Genoa to the United Provinces to Britain and finally (so far) to the US: 'Our model thus describes a pattern of recurrence (hegemony leading to expansion, expansion to chaos, and chaos to a new hegemony) that is also a pattern of evolution (each new hegemony reflecting a greater concentration of organizational abilities and a higher volume and density of the system than the preceding hegemony).'[15] But the real problem is less the cyclical element of the theory (which is partly compensated for by the attention to historical specificity that is one of the great strengths of Arrighi's version of world systems theory) than the plausibility of the idea that, for instance, the merchants and bankers of tiny Genoa, even when piggy-backing on the armoured mammoth of Habsburg Spain when military heavy-lifting was needed, constituted a 'world-hegemon' in the same sense as Victorian Britain or the contemporary US. Too much has to be packed into the *mutatis mutandis* clause for the claim to begin to be credible.

As for the United Provinces, Arrighi himself writes: 'Geopolitically, the system of states established at Westphalia under Dutch leadership was truly anarchic – characterized, that is, by the absence of central rule.'[16] But then in what sense was the Dutch Republic hegemonic? It is true that it helped to ensure that the Habsburg project of a dominant Catholic empire in Europe failed, through waging the Eighty Years War with Spain (1568–1648), but it was Bourbon France whose intervention in the Thirty Years War (1618–48) was pivotal in ensuring the Habsburgs' defeat. Holland's geographical vulnerability to attack by both land and sea enjoined, as Charles Wilson puts it, 'policies that were marked by extreme caution of alliances or embroilments'.[17] The one historical moment when one can see the United Provinces playing a decisive role in orchestrating the balance of power came at the end of the seventeenth century, when Stadtholder William III, strengthened by his installation as King of England thanks to the Glorious Revolution of 1688, constructed a coalition that eventually contained the power of Louis XIV of France, the latest aspirant to universal monarchy. But this project, which required heavy expenditure on the military and on subsidizing allies, vastly expanded the public debt, and thereby played a critical role in subordinating the Dutch Republic to an oligarchy of patrician and aristocratic bondholders; this weakened financial position prevented the United Provinces from maintaining sufficient military forces to pursue an independent foreign policy, and therefore imposed

143

neutrality in European conflicts (with the exception of the Republic's disastrous intervention against Britain in the American War of Independence).[18] All in all, then, Genoa and Holland are not plausible candidates for the exercise of world hegemony, and I shall restrict the extension of this concept to the era when industrial capitalism can genuinely be regarded as globally dominant.

4.2 Classical imperialism (1870–1945)

4.2.1 A liberal world economy

The starting point, then, to understanding capitalist imperialism is that it emerges at the historical moment when, not only does a new constellation of Great Powers appear following the American Civil War and the foundation of the German Reich, but a genuinely global capitalist world economy takes shape. Eric Hobsbawm has painted a superb portrait of the 1850s and 1860s as the decades when 'observers [first] saw the world not merely as a single interlocking complex, but as one where each part was sensitive to what happened elsewhere, and through which money, goods and men moved smoothly and with increasing rapidity, according to the irresistible stimuli of supply and demand, gain and loss and with the help of modern technology'. Hobsbawm highlights the significance in this transformation of the 'extraordinary acceleration in the speed of communication', closely connected to huge reductions in transport costs, which were all made possible by the new technologies emerging from the maw of industrial capitalism – above all, the railway, the steamship and the telegraph.[19] But this process of physical integration was associated with the knitting together of a global web of economic relations, facilitating the flows of commodities, money and capital. Berrick Saul writes:

> the pattern of world trade for most of the nineteenth century consisted of a number of self-contained networks of multilateral trade, with only unimportant links between them. There was no reason, therefore, why, apart from psychological influences, a change in economic activity should communicate itself directly from one multilateral network to another, except through the effects of such changes on the trade of Britain, standing at the centre of these numerous trade patterns.[20]

Britain's position as the common factor in these different networks, and the scale of its overseas investments, allowed it to

144

play a stabilizing role during economic crises in the 1870s and 1880s, as British investors tended, for example, to react to a slump in the US by putting money into the colonies. But, already in the 1890s, and certainly by 1914, Saul argues, 'a large part of multilateral trade was based . . . upon a complex net of activity embracing whole continents or sub-continents, derived from a new world-wide division of functions'. The emergence of this 'single complex interlocking pattern' of trade and investment was reflected in the US and continental Europe becoming major export markets for British colonies such as Australia, New Zealand and India. Consequently, '[t]he possibility of fluctuations being transmitted directly from one part of the world economy to another, instead of through Britain as before, was now growing more and more real'.[21] This global articulation of trade and investment was institutionally reinforced by the rapid spread after 1870 of a liberal economic policy regime based on the gold standard, which put governments under pressure to react to outflows of gold by cutting spending and raising taxes.[22] Peripheral states that failed to pursue 'sound' policies satisfactory to their mainly Western European bondholders found themselves liable to foreign intervention and sometimes military takeover, as in the case of Egypt in 1882.

Of course, industrial capitalism in the form that Marx analysed in *Capital* – the real subsumption of wage-labour under capital in conditions of technology-driven mass production – remained geographically confined to relatively small (though rapidly expanding) enclaves in North-western Europe and the North-east and mid-west of the US. Most of the world's population remained small producers, mainly peasants. But the *structural logic* of this socioeconomic system was increasingly governing the world as a division of labour crystallized, binding together agricultural suppliers of food and raw materials and the industrialized regions. Mike Davis has shown in a masterly study, *Late Victorian Holocausts*, how integration into the liberal world economy tended, above all in India and China, to undermine food security (for example, encouraging the erosion of the famine prevention strategies pursued under the Mughal and Qing tributary empires), to lead to deteriorating terms of trade for peasant producers, especially in the context of the Great Depression of 1873–96, and to restrict state managers' options when confronted with subsistence crises. These changes reacted malignly with unfavourable climatic conditions, generated by the El Niño/Southern Oscillation, to precipitate appalling famines that took between 12 and 30 million lives in India, 19.5 and 30 million lives in China, and 2 million lives in Brazil, in the last quarter of the nineteenth century.[23]

4.2.2   An economically and politically multipolar world

As we saw in §3.3, from the fifteenth century onwards European history was dominated by a ferocious and continuous process of military and territorial competition among the Great Powers. One way of summing up the nature of imperialism is to say that it marked the point at which this process fused – in the dialectical and hence potentially contradictory form highlighted by Harvey – with the expansion of industrial capitalism (table 4.1). Hobsbawm remarks of late nineteenth-century capitalism that 'the world economy was now notably more pluralist than before. Britain ceased to be the only fully industrialized and indeed the only industrial economy.'[24] An important factor in this change was what William McNeill calls the 'industrialization of war' in the mid-nineteenth century – the increases in mobility made possible by the railway and the steamship, and the mass production of weapons such as the breech-loading rifle and the machine gun. States' military power now depended directly on their level of industrialization. The great quasi-absolutist monarchies of Central and Eastern Europe – Prussia (after 1871 Germany), Austria-Hungary, Russia – were now compelled to promote the expansion of industrial capitalism in order to provide the material basis of modern armed strength. At the same time, the spread of industrial capitalism exacerbated the rivalries among the Great Powers, particularly as Britain found its industrial and naval supremacy challenged by Germany. The result was a race in naval armaments driven by rapid technological innovation, and Britain's eventual incorporation into one of the two great military blocs into which Europe was divided by 1914. Economic and geopolitical competition mutually reinforced each other in a world dominated by a handful of mainly European states.[25]

The development of this conflict between Britain and Germany decisively shaped the first half of the twentieth century. Britain's hegemonic role in the nineteenth-century world economy depended partly on its position as the first centre of industrial capitalism – though by the latter decades of the century this was under challenge from new centres, above all the United States and Germany, which adopted protectionist policies that allowed them to industrialize while keeping British competition at arm's length.[26] But British hegemony was closely associated with the role of the City of London in managing the liberal world economy – in part a reflection of Britain's increasing dependence on earnings from financial services, insurance and shipping to fund the growing balance of payments deficit on

Table 4.1 Relative shares of world manufacturing output, 1750–1980 (percentages)*

	1750	1800	1830	1860	1880	1900	1913	1928	1938	1953	1963	1973	1980
Britain	1.9	4.3	9.5	19.9	22.9	18.5	13.6	9.9	10.7	8.4	6.4	4.9	4.0
Habsburg Empire/ Austria-Hungary	2.9	3.2	3.2	4.2	4.4	4.7	4.4	–	–	–	–	–	–
France	4.0	4.2	5.2	7.9	7.8	6.8	6.1	6.0	4.4	3.2	3.8	3.5	3.3
Germany	2.9	3.5	3.5	4.9	8.5	13.2	14.8	11.6	12.7	5.9	6.4	5.9	5.3
Italy	2.4	2.5	2.3	2.5	2.5	2.5	2.4	2.7	2.8	2.3	2.9	2.9	2.9
Russia/USSR	5.0	5.6	5.6	7.0	7.6	8.8	8.2	5.3	9.0	10.7	14.2	14.4	14.8
United States	0.1	0.8	2.4	7.2	14.7	23.6	32.0	39.3	31.4	44.7	35.1	33.0	31.5
Japan	3.8	3.5	2.8	2.6	2.4	2.4	2.7	3.3	5.2	2.9	5.1	8.8	9.1
Developed countries	27.0	32.3	39.5	63.4	79.1	89.0	92.5	92.8	92.8	93.5	91.5	90.1	88.0
China	32.8	33.3	29.8	19.7	12.5	6.2	3.6	3.4	3.1	2.3	3.5	3.9	5.0
India	24.5	19.7	17.6	8.6	2.8	1.7	1.4	1.9	2.4	1.7	1.8	2.1	2.3

*Triennial annual averages 1750–1900, 1928–38; annual averages 1913, 1953–80

Sources: P. Bairoch, 'International Industrialization Levels from 1750 to 1980', *Journal of European Economic History*, 11 (1982): 296, 304, tables 10 and 13

trade in goods.[27] The City's global role dovetailed in with what Giovanni Arrighi, Kenneth Barr and Shuji Hisaeda describe as the 'extroverted, decentralized, and differentiated business structure' that continued to prevail in British industry, while US capitalism was pioneering the vertically integrated, bureaucratically, multi-branch corporation: 'in the last quarter of the nineteenth century, the British system of business enterprise was more than ever an ensemble of highly specialized medium-sized firms held together by a complex web of commercial transactions – a web that was centred on Britain but spanned the entire world'.[28] The distinctive structure of British capitalism dovetailed with issues of military strategy. Thus the negotiations over naval disarmament that bedevilled Anglo-American relations during the 1920s involved different strategic priorities: the US wanted a relatively small number of big cruisers that could match Japan's, while Britain insisted on maintaining a fleet of 70 smaller cruisers, reflecting, according to Stephen Roskill, 'the British Empire's need for a large number of cruisers, on account of the length of the trade routes to be protected'.[29]

Against this background, one can understand why Andrew Gamble highlights 'two momentous choices' taken by British state managers in the early decades of the twentieth century. 'One was the continued adherence to free trade and to the institutions of the liberal world order long after conditions which had originally recommended it had disappeared. The second was the decision to fight Germany rather than the United States.'[30] The decentralized transnational structure of British capitalism may help to account for the first decision; it is worth pausing over the second. After all, by the beginning of the twentieth century, the US had overtaken Britain industrially, and was building a powerful navy. Writing at the time, Brooks Adams used trends in industrial growth and the evidence of English 'decadence' provided by the South African War (1899–1902) to announce 'America's economic supremacy', and to affirm that 'there is no reason why the United States should not become a greater seat of wealth and power than ever was England, Rome, or Constantinople'.[31] Various theories have been constructed to rule out the possibility of a third Anglo-American war (after 1776 and 1812): liberal internationalist theorists of the 'democratic peace' argue that wars among liberal states are highly improbable; on the left, Kees Van Der Pijl has developed the theory that Britain and the US have successively led the 'Lockean heartland', 'a self-regulating transnational social space' dominated by Anglophone liberal capitalism, that has seen off a series of economically statist 'contender states' – France, Germany and the Soviet Union.[32]

148

Such theories involve a kind of reverse teleology that projects backwards the partnership, firmly under US leadership, that was established between Washington and London in 1939–41. Fareed Zakaria makes the point very well:

> Since the middle of the twentieth century, historians have commonly asserted that through most of the previous century, the United States enjoyed a kind of tacit alliance with Great Britain and was, in particular, protected from the vagaries of the world by the virtually omnipotent Royal Navy. This interpretation of nineteenth-century history would certainly have stunned American statesmen of the late nineteenth century, who without exception regarded Britain as the greatest threat to the United States and its interests and the Royal Navy, in particular, as the greatest single threat to the physical safety of the country. This could hardly be considered peculiar, since the United States had fought two wars with Britain in the last century and a half – the last of which it lost resoundingly as the Royal Navy sailed up the east coast, shelling Washington and setting fire to the White House.[33]

Equally, as Kenneth Bourne puts it, 'for a very long time, British statesmen, like their counterparts on the other side of the Atlantic, tended to see a special danger and a special hostility in Anglo-American relations'. There were two war crises, provoked by frontier disputes between the US and Britain's colonies in Canada, in the 1840s, and another during the early part of the American Civil War in 1861–2. Far from feeling a sense of shared 'values' with the US, the Whig and Tory aristocrats who ran the British state tended for much of the nineteenth century to see the American democracy as a subversive and expansionist threat.[34] Herfried Münkler, eager to justify a benevolent imperial role for the contemporary European Union, ridicules the idea of a British attack on the US during the Civil War, declaring that the British 'would have been opposing their own imperial mission' of ridding the world of slavery.[35] This pronouncement is symptomatic of Münkler's rather uncertain grasp of the historical record; he seems, for example, unaware of the dependence of the British textile industry on raw cotton produced by slave labour in the American South, not to speak of the market Britain provided for the products of the other major slave economies, Cuban sugar and Brazilian coffee. Robin Blackburn writes: 'Capitalism as an economic system . . . thoroughly permeated and integrated the expanding slave systems of the Americas in the 1850s. British capital found advantageous outlets in each of the expanding slaves states . . . ,

149

helping to build railways, equip plantations, and finance trade.'[36] The antebellum South was in many ways an enclave of the British economy, with an interest therefore in free trade; its political representatives in Congress blocked Northern lobbying for higher industrial tariffs. Michel Aglietta has gone as far as to describe the Civil War as 'the final act of the struggle against colonial domination'.[37] Lord Palmerston's government seriously contemplated intervening to support the South in 1861–2: according to Bourne, the Duke of Newcastle, the Colonial Secretary, 'talked of the regrettable necessity of having to burn New York and Boston'.[38]

The final crisis in Anglo-American relations came in 1895–6, when the administration of Grover Cleveland threatened Britain with war over the border between Venezuela and British Honduras, asserting US hegemony in the Western Hemisphere. Secretary of State Richard Olney famously wrote to the British Prime Minister, Lord Salisbury: 'Today the United States is practically sovereign in this continent and its fiat is law.'[39] Salisbury decided to reach a compromise with Washington, though he warned in January 1896: 'A war with America – not this year but in the not distant future – has become something more than a possibility.'[40] But British policy-makers subsequently moved towards appeasing the US by, for example, acquiescing in the building of the Panama Canal. This reorientation reflected the contradiction inherent in British strategy in North America: Britain had supported the Monroe Doctrine of 1823, in which the US declared the Western Hemisphere off-limits, because it conveniently excluded other European states from the Americas, but the unintended effect was to allow the US to expand in territory and power, while Washington's seizure of northern Mexico in 1846–8, and victory in the Civil War, effectively destroyed any possibility of regional balancing against the US. The decisive step in abandoning the option of war with the US came in 1905, when the Admiralty, against the opposition of the War Office (which in February 1898 approved a plan for seizing New York in the event of war), insisted that the need to concentrate naval forces in home waters to match the German fleet ruled out the use of British maritime power to defend Canada against attack from a US whose military capabilities were rapidly growing. The priorities of naval planning to deal with the more direct threat represented by Germany, not 'Anglo-Saxon solidarity' or the pacific orientation of liberal states towards one another, ruled out war with the US – or, as Henry Adams more colourfully put it at the time, 'the sudden appearance of Germany as the grizzly terror . . . frightened England into America's arms'.[41] Zakaria calls Britain's decision 'to accommodate itself to the rise of America rather than to contest it . . . a strategic masterstroke' that allowed London to 'focus its attention on other critical fronts'.[42]

But even after the US had joined Britain and the other Entente powers to defeat Germany in 1917–18, the tensions between London and Washington remained serious. Roskill subtitles the first volume of his study of British naval policy between the wars, devoted to the 1920s, *The Period of Anglo-American Antagonism*; at the Washington naval conference of 1921–2, the administration of Warren Harding forced the Lloyd George government to abandon Britain's strategically crucial alliance with Japan and to accept parity in capital ships with the US. This climb down was preceded by a clash between Lloyd George and Winston Churchill at the Committee of Imperial Defence in December 1920, when the Prime Minister argued that 'we could not fight the United States for economical as well as military reasons' but sought to preserve 'a defensive Alliance with Japan' in order to avoid the 'fatal policy' where 'we would be at the mercy of the United States'.[43] Writing in 1928, at another low point in Anglo-American relations (in this case provoked both by renewed disagreement over naval limitation and by US pressure on Britain to pursue deflationary economic policies), Robert Craigie, head of the American Department at the British Foreign Office, wrote: 'Except as a figure of speech, war is *not* unthinkable between the two countries. On the contrary, there are present all the factors which in the past have made for wars between states.'[44] Though Craigie went on to argue that a mixture of 'firmness' and 'judicious diplomacy' on London's part could lead to an improvement in relations with Washington, his analysis suggests that Trotsky was not simply mistaken when he argued in 1924 that '[t]he basic world antagonism occurs along the line of the conflict of interests between the United States and England'.[45]

4.2.3 Territorial expansion

In the end, of course, Britain did find itself 'at the mercy of the United States' during its second war with Germany (see §4.3.1 below). To understand why economic and geopolitical competition proved mutually reinforcing in this period, we need to look more closely at the interrelationship between capital accumulation and territorial expansion. Lenin placed this interrelationship at the centre of his theory of imperialism: 'capitalism's transition to the stage of monopoly capitalism, to finance capital, *is connected* with the intensification of the struggle for the partitioning of the world,' he wrote.[46] European colonial possessions rose from 2.7 million square miles and 148 million inhabitants in 1860, to 29 million square miles and 568 million inhabitants in 1914, and the process of expansion was not yet complete, since the Middle Eastern possessions of the Ottoman Empire were only partitioned between Britain and France at the end of the First World War. Colonial conquest was accompanied by a huge increase in European foreign investment, from £2 billion in 1862 to £44 billion in 1914.[47]

The significance of these figures needs to be set in context in two ways. First, in order properly to appreciate the extent of European territorial expansion, we need to take into account those cases that took the form of the extension of the borders of existing states rather than the annexation of overseas territories, and in particular that of the Russian Empire into Central Asia and the Amur region, and of the United States from the foothold occupied on the eastern seaboard by the Thirteen Colonies to the Pacific and the Rio Grande. As Gareth Stedman Jones puts it, 'American historians who speak complacently of the absence of the settler-type colonialism characteristic of European powers merely conceal the fact that the whole *internal* history of United States imperialism was one vast process of territorial seizure and occupation. The absence of territorialism "abroad" was founded on an unprecedented territorialism "at home".'[48] Secondly, subordination to capitalist imperialism did not necessarily involve formal annexation. John Gallagher and Ronald Robinson, in putting forward their famous thesis of the 'imperialism of free trade', stressed the importance of Victorian Britain's informal empire, for example, in Latin America, where the use of political and naval power reinforced the penetration of legally independent states by British trade and investment.[49] Similarly, Saul writes that 'Argentina and parts of China were more closely linked with Britain through trade and investment in 1913 than were Canada and the West Indies.'[50] Economic integration did not, however, generate the same political subordination as did formal annexation; unless directly subject to imperial military occupation or intervention (like Egypt, for example, and the central American republics), states that retained sovereignty enjoyed an important margin of manoeuvre thanks to their ability to play one Great Power off against another in an era of growing geopolitical rivalries.

What, then, was the economic function of empire, formal and informal? Gramsci writes: 'Capitalist Europe, rich in resources and arrived at the point at which the rate of profit was beginning to reveal its tendency to fall, had a need to widen the area of expansion of its income-bearing investment; thus, after 1890, the great colonial empires were created.'[51] Gramsci's dating is a bit late, but it is true that the world economy experienced between 1873 and 1896 what is commonly known as the Great Depression, which Arrighi compares to the 'long downturn' of the late twentieth century, both periods involving intensified competition and relative stagnation.[52] Chris Harman argues that in the last decades of the nineteenth century profitability was under pressure from a steadily rising organic composition of capital. Two different strategies were pursued out of the crisis.[53] In the US and Germany the concentration and centralization of capital rapidly accelerated, thanks to rationalization and cartellization that helped to produce the 'organized capitalism' on which Hilferding and Bukharin focused; these states thereby won a decisive lead in what Herman Schwartz calls 'the chemical/electrical cluster' of new technologies, facilitating a much larger scale of mass production that would be reflected, for example, in the development of the car industry.[54] Britain, by contrast, preserved the decentralized business structures that had developed in the Industrial Revolution, but hugely expanded its overseas investments. British overseas investment rose from £700 million in 1870 to more than £2 billion in 1900, and between £3.5 billion and £4 billion in 1913.[55] Saul argues that the expansion of US manufacturing exports, and growing American and German competition in Latin America made Britain in the years before 1914 ever more reliant 'upon building up her surpluses with India and the newly expanding countries of Asia and Africa'.[56]

It does not follow, as Lenin sometimes affirms, that the dynamic of imperialism was driven by the export of capital to exploit colonial slaves. Hobsbawm points out:

> Almost 80 per cent of all European trade throughout the nineteenth century, both exports and imports, was with other developed countries, and the same is true of European foreign investments. Insofar as these were directed overseas, they went mostly to a handful of rapidly developing countries mainly populated by settlers of European descent – Canada, Australia, South Africa, Argentina, etc. – as well, of course, to the USA.[57]

Table 4.2 confirms this pattern, but also highlights the growing importance of the formal Empire for British investors in the era of classical imperialism. It is worth pausing over the case of India, whose economic function is to some extent understated by these figures. This

153

Table **4.2** Area pattern of British overseas investment, 1860–1929 (percentages)

AREAS	1860–70	1881–90	1911–13	1927–9
British Empire				
Total	36	47	46	59
Canada	25	13	13	17
Southern Dominions	9.5	16	17	20
India	21	15	10.5	14
Other	3	3	5.5	8
Latin America	10.5	20	22	22
USA	27	22	19	5.5
Europe	25	8	6	8
Other	1.5	3	7	5.5

Source: M. Barratt Brown, *The Economics of Imperialism* (London, 1974), pp. 190–1, table 17

is particularly important because of the tendency of some contemporary Marxist theorists of imperialism to regard the British Empire in India as a case of non-capitalist domination. Wood, for example, writes:

> even capitalist states, well into the twentieth century, were not yet able to mobilize economic imperatives strong or expansive enough to dominate the colonial world and continued to depend to a great extent on modes of 'extra-economic' domination not fundamentally different from precapitalist forms. The British Empire in India is a dramatic case in point. Britain was certainly a capitalist economy, in fact the most developed capitalism in the world; but even here a commercial empire gave way to a tribute-extracting military dictatorship.[58]

Harvey apparently endorses this assessment, referring to 'the closed Empire of India'.[59] In case this kind of view becomes a new Marxist orthodoxy, it is important to stress that it is historically indefensible. It is true that the British East India Company initially expanded by inserting itself into existing commercial networks and exploiting the decline of Mughal power. It is also true that its position was transformed by the conquest of Bengal during the Seven Years War (1756–63) and that its efforts to reform the collection of the land revenue by attempting, through the Permanent Settlement of 1793, to turn the *zamīndārs* (hereditary owners of claims to a share of the agricultural surplus-product) into capitalist landowners had the effect instead of reinforcing pre-capitalist relations in the countryside.[60] The extraction of tribute from India, in the shape of the 'Home Charges', along with a trade surplus, interest on investments and other invisible earnings remained a constant during the two centuries that Britain dominated the subcontinent.[61] The nature and significance of this process of surplus-extraction, however, shifted significantly. As Irfan Habib puts it, 'during the period, about 1800 to 1850, the colonial objective changed from seizing Indian commodities to seizing the Indian market. The changed objective not only made the East India Company's monopoly over Indian internal commerce and overseas trade obsolete, but positively required free trade.'[62] The development of industrial capitalism in Britain, centred on the textile industry, made India important, not as an exporter of its own manufactures but as an importer of British manufactures. Economic competition and political intervention destroyed the Indian textile industry (see table 4.1). The revisions of the Company's charter in 1813 and 1833 scrapped its monopoly and the Company itself was abolished after the Mutiny of 1857. According to two firmly non-Marxist historians, P.J. Cain and A.G. Hopkins,

> Britain's export industries gained greatly from the extension of British sovereignty over India and in particular from the transfer from Company to crown rule in 1858 . . . The full value of British rule, the return on political investments first made in the eighteenth century, was not realized until the second half of the nineteenth century, when India became a vital market for Lancashire's cotton goods and when other specialized interests, such as jute manufacturers in Dundee and steel producers in Sheffield, also greatly increased their stake in the subcontinent.[63]

Harvey's reference to 'the closed Empire of India' is therefore particularly unfortunate. Free trade was an essential institutional condition of India's role as a captive market for British industrial exports; only after the British Government of India was given fiscal autonomy in 1919 were tariffs introduced that did severe damage to British textile exporters.[64] The growth of Indian protectionism even in the last decades of British rule reflects the development of locally based modern manufacturing industries, such as jute and textiles, from the 1870s onwards. This was one instance of how capitalist industrialization first developed in Asia, particularly in Japan and China, occurring with the framework of Western domination but stimulated by

Table 4.3 India's trade and bullion balances (annual averages £ million)

	1880/81–1882/3	1894/5–1896/7	1911/12–1912/14
United Kingdom	−10.7	−13.3	−52.3
Industrial Europe	+10.3	+9.9	+32.6
China and Japan	+8.0	+7.4	+18.6
United States	+0.25	+0.8	+1.8
Total	+15.3	+16.2	+20.1

Source: S.B. Saul, *Studies in British Overseas Trade 1870–1914* (Liverpool, 1960), p. 204, table LIX

trade within Asia itself and facilitated by indigenous networks of merchants and migrants.[65] The Indian version of this process, though it created a local protectionist lobby, also offered British capitalism very direct benefits. As international competition intensified in the 1890s and 1900s, Britain was able, through its political domination of the subcontinent, to maintain control of the Indian market while it was losing out to its rivals even in self-governing colonies such as Canada and Australia. Moreover, the developing Indian economy's export surpluses with the US, continental Europe and East Asia allowed Britain to cover its growing balance of trade deficit with the rest of the world (table 4.3). As Saul puts it:

> The importance of India's trade to the pattern of world trade balances can hardly be exaggerated. On the one side lay her heavy consumption of cottons and other exports from Britain as well as invisible services, on the other her diverse export trade in manufactures, raw materials and foodstuffs, giving her easy access to the markets of the great industrial countries, though not relying nearly so heavily on markets in Britain as did most other Empire countries.[66]

4.2.4 Military competition and state capitalism

The economic benefits that the hegemonic power derived from its empire, formal and informal, help to explain why other leading capitalist states were tempted to follow it on the path to territorial expansion. Thus, by the beginning of the twentieth century, many German state managers, intellectuals and industrialists were preoccupied by the fear that that they would be locked out of export markets and raw material supplies by the partition of the world among closed protectionist empires dominated by Britain, the US, France and Russia. They were divided over the most appropriate response: should Germany seek to construct its own colonial empire, which would bring it into conflict with Britain and France, or should it instead develop a zone of influence, perhaps even as the industrial lobbyist and National Liberal leader Gustav Stresemann put it in 1913, a 'closed economic area to secure our needs for raw materials and exports', in Central and Eastern Europe, an option that might produce a collision with Russia, and hence with Moscow's ally France? Both strategies had military consequences, respectively the development of a world-class navy and the further expansion of Germany's already formidable army. In effect, under Kaiser Wilhelm II (1888–1918), the Second Reich vacillated between both options, in the process antagonizing and therefore driving together Britain, France and Russia. The origins of the First World War are a notoriously tangled tale, and there were always German business interests (for example, in shipping) that opposed either strategy in favour of continued integration in an open world economy, but, particularly once Germany had opted to build a battle fleet the other side of the North Sea from Britain, confrontation between the two was likely to come, sooner and later.[67]

German military successes during the First World War allowed advocates of a formal empire in *Mitteleuropa* briefly to realize their dreams. The Treaty of Brest-Litovsk imposed by the Central Powers on the new Bolshevik republic in March 1918 deprived Russia of a third of its population, half its territory, and nine-tenths of its coal industry; Finland, the future Baltic states, Poland, Belorussia and the Ukraine fell under formal or informal German control. This triumph was, of course, short-lived, but Germany's military and political collapse in November 1918 served to underline the benefits of empire to Britain, as Avner Offer has shown in an outstanding study. Britain and Germany, as the two most industrialized of the European powers, had by the beginning of the twentieth century both developed highly specialized economies heavily dependent on imported food and raw materials. Britain, however, had what proved to be a decisive advantage, in that it controlled an extensive empire capable of supplying it with these commodities, while its naval superiority allowed it both to protect its own sea routes and to deny Germany access to the food and raw materials it needed to import. Planning for economic warfare therefore formed a major part of British preparations before 1914. The struggle over food and raw materials was an important factor in Germany's defeat, both because of the impact of the British blockade on the Central Powers and because the German submarine campaign in the Atlantic brought the US into the war and therefore helped to tip the balance in the Entente's favour.[68] Of course, the outcome of the Great War did nothing to remove the conflicts that had produced it – most fundamentally, the destabilizing impact on the Europe-centred state system of Germany's rise to the position of a world power. Moreover, as Cain and Hopkins put it, 'the period after 1914 was characterized by intense imperialist rivalries over the "unclaimed" regions of the world, the outstanding examples being South America and China'. Britain remained the largest foreign investor in both these regions in the interwar years, when its economic structures finally underwent a significant degree of corporate centralization; British state managers and business executives fought to maintain their position against challenges from the US, Germany and, in the Far East, Japan.[69]

As the dominant figure in Germany in the mid-1920s, when the Weimar Republic (1919–33) enjoyed a brief moment of stability, Stresemann pursued a strategy anticipating that adopted by Konrad Adenauer after 1945 – that of seeking to rebuild German power through reintegration in the world economy and, in particular, an orientation towards the US. But the viability of what Adam Tooze (somewhat anachronistically) calls this 'Atlanticist' strategy was drastically undermined by the onset in October 1929 of what proved to be the most serious economic depression in the entire history of capitalism.[70] Financial crisis developed into an industrial collapse that was especially severe for the two biggest manufacturing producers, the US and Germany, reflecting a low level of profitability that had been masked by the speculative boom of the 1920s. Moreover, the world market fragmented, causing a drastic contraction in international trade, as the leading states sought to preserve their individual economies by using politico-military power to carve out protectionist blocs. Probably the decisive step came when the Tory-dominated National Government formed in August 1931 first took Britain off the gold standard and then, a year later, negotiated a system of Imperial Preference with the self-governing Dominions and India at the Ottawa Conference a year later. In consequence, there was a massive decline in the level of global economic integration compared to that attained before 1914 (see table 4.4).[71]

One of Bukharin's most important insights was to recognize the relationship of mutual reinforcement between military competition and the tendency towards state capitalism that he highlighted when developing his theory of imperialism during the First World War: 'War is

Table 4.4 Ratio of merchandise trade to GDP

	1913	1950	1973	1995
France	35.4	21.2	29.0	36.6
Germany	35.1	20.1	35.2	38.7
Japan	31.4	16.9	18.3	14.1
Netherlands	103.6	70.2	80.1	83.4
UK	44.7	36.0	39.3	42.6*
US	11.2	7.0	10.5	19.0

*1994
Source: P. Hirst and G. Thompson, Globalization in Question (2nd edn, Cambridge, 1999), p. 27, table 2.3

accompanied not only by tremendous destruction of productive forces; in addition, it provides an extraordinary reinforcement and intensification of capitalism's immanent developmental tendencies.'[72] The reinforcement went both ways. The Great Depression saw a step-change in the statization of economic life, from the liberal democracies – Franklin Roosevelt's New Deal and the British National Government's extensive nationalizations and cartelization of industry and agriculture – to the 'totalitarian' dictatorships – the Five-Year Plans in Stalinist Russia, which were imitated by both National Socialist Germany and the Japanese Empire. The bureaucratic state capitalist regime that had emerged by the early 1930s in the Soviet Union represented the most extreme case of a general process.[73] But state capitalism did not offer a solution to the Great Depression. Indeed, the drive towards economic autarky by the Great Powers only exacerbated the tensions among them, since it gave those lacking ready access to colonial markets and raw materials a powerful incentive to use the military machines built up by these state capitalist policies to win a larger share of global resources for themselves. Mobilization for total war between 1939 and 1945 generated a further extension of state control of the economy in all the belligerent powers.[74]

Tooze writes: 'By 1936 at the latest it was abundantly clear that even with the most concerted management, it was simply impossible for Germany within the confines of its present territory to achieve anything like [food] self-sufficiency, certainly if the regime was determined to maintain the current standard of living and the current structure of German agriculture'; more broadly, an economic recovery driven by rearmament was hitting the buffers set by the scarcity

159

of raw materials and foreign exchange. Tooze argues that Hitler's decision to provoke a general war in the autumn of 1939 reflected short-term calculations in response to acute balance of payments difficulties and to a window of opportunity for the German military, as well as his strategic conception of an inevitable racial struggle with the two main arms of 'international Jewry' – the Soviet Union and the US. Similarly, Hitler saw the attack on the USSR in June 1941 as 'a campaign of economic conquest' that would give the Third Reich the resources to take on Britain and its American patron; German military planners assumed that the seizure of the Ukraine's grain would lead to death by starvation of (as Himmler put it) '30 million Slavs and Jews'.[75] Politics was clearly in command in this genocidal project of racial imperialism: under Göring's direction, after 1937 the Four-Year Plan office assumed increasing direction of the economy and the state-owned *Reichswerke* competed with private capital for industrial assets seized as war booty.[76]

But the Nazi military drive into Central and Eastern Europe dovetailed with the interests of significant sections of German capital, among whom, Volker Berghahn writes, '[c]onceptions of economic bloc-building . . . made a strong comeback' under the impact of the Great Depression. Carl Duisberg, head of the chemical combine IG Farben, declared in November 1931: 'Only a uniform economic bloc from Bordeaux to Sofia is going to give Europe the spine it needs to retain its importance in the world.'[77] Germany's pre-1914 European lead in chemicals, along with electrical engineering, was symptomatic of the cutting-edge industrial capitalism it had developed by the late nineteenth century. Firms in these sectors sought in the 1920s to revive their traditional export-oriented strategies, which made them (unlike the heavy steel and coal industries) uninterested in protectionism. But the Depression forced Farben, Siemens and AEG into efforts to cartelize their industries on a Europe-wide basis. After 1933 Farben found itself increasingly reliant on the state-dominated domestic market, which led it to campaign for the Reich to sanction its control of the chemicals industry in Occupied Europe and to build a synthetic chemicals plant at the SS camp complex at Auschwitz-Birkenau. In automobile manufacture, another advanced industry, the National Socialist regime systematically favoured a core of German firms – Volkswagen (its own creation), Daimler, BMW, Porsche and MAN – to the disadvantage of foreign corporations such as Ford and General Motors, a policy that the Federal Republic largely continued in the postwar years.[78]

Though operating in a substantially different context, during the 1930s Japanese imperialism also pursued the same logic of military expansion as the means of acquiring access to markets and raw materials. The Meiji Restoration of 1868 had allowed a process of revolution from above, promoting the capitalist modernization of a society that had already attained a high level of pre-capitalist industrial development. The relative success of this process made Japan by the 1890s a player in East Asia, which was then dominated by the informal empire imposed by Britain on China in the 1830s and 1840s. By the turn of the century, Britain was seeking to strike a balance between the system of treaty ports and other concessions forcibly extracted from the Qing state by outside powers and the Open Door in trade with China proclaimed by US Secretary of State John Hay in 1899–1900. Japan, having defeated China in the war of 1894–5, sought to insinuate itself into this system by accepting the Open Door and by allying itself to Britain in 1902, which enabled it to defeat Russia in the war of 1904–5. This policy allowed Japan to win control of Korea, Taiwan and parts of northern China, but it came apart in the 1920s, under the impact of the Russian and Chinese revolutions, growing American hostility to a rival in the Pacific, and the Great Depression. Military expansion – in particular, the seizure of Manchuria in 1931 and the outbreak of war with China in 1937 – was accompanied by the attempted development, within the framework of the Five-Year Plan (1937–41), of an integrated imperial economy in which Korea, Taiwan, Manchuria and northern China would function as markets and suppliers of food, raw materials and simple manufactures to Japan. The outbreak of the Second World War offered Japan an opportunity to expand southwards into the British, Dutch and French colonial empires – rendered highly vulnerable thanks to their governments' distraction by war in Europe, and containing key raw materials such as oil and rubber. Britain's increasing dependence on the US left the initiative in the hands of the Roosevelt administration, which responded to the Japanese occupation of Indochina in July 1941 by imposing an oil embargo. Teijiro Toyoda, the Japanese Foreign Minister, wrote: 'Our Empire must immediately take steps to break asunder this ever-strengthening chain of encirclement which is being woven under the guidance and with the participation of England and the United States, acting like a cunning dragon seemingly asleep.' The road to Pearl Harbor – and to the raw materials of Malaya and the Dutch East Indies – had been opened.[79]

4.2.5   Race and empire

The Second World War was marked by a paroxysm of racism. If the Nazi attempt to exterminate the Jews of Europe represented the most concentrated and extreme manifestation of this phenomenon, the Pacific War was marked by the mobilization of racial ideology on both sides to legitimize a vicious and brutal struggle, culminating in the indiscriminate US bombing campaign against the Japanese home islands and the nuclear attacks on Hiroshima and Nagasaki.[80] Racism permeated the thinking of state managers on both sides: 'the Negroes are in the lowest rank of human beings,' Under-Secretary of State Sumner Welles, perhaps the most fervent advocate of decolonization in the Roosevelt administration, told a committee in October 1942.[81] The role played by race in the constitution of modern imperialism has become the subject of close interrogation by postcolonial scholars probing how colonizers and colonized defined their relationship through discursive practices and ideological representations. Such studies have exposed a vast and complex domain, but one that no discussion of imperialism can ignore; as we have seen, racial ideology had become so pervasive by the end of the nineteenth century as to penetrate the discourse of even as trenchant a critic of the 'New Imperialism' as J.A. Hobson (§1.3). There is indeed a strong case for arguing that modern racism – discrimination against a group on the grounds of characteristics held to be inherent in members of that group – emerged in the historical process through which capitalism was formed, and in particular thanks to the development of systemic slavery in the plantation economies of the New World. Initially, the English colonies in North America and the West Indies relied on the labour of white indentured servants, who agreed to work for a particular master on a servile basis for three to seven years in exchange for free passage from Europe. As J.H. Elliott puts it, 'unfree white labour was vital for the peopling and exploitation of British America. Indentured servants constituted 75–85 per cent of the settlers who emigrated to the Chesapeake in the seventeenth century, and perhaps 60 per cent of the emigrants to all British colonies in America during the course of the century came with some form of labour contract.'[82]

   The difficulties of managing a servile labour force who had enjoyed and looked forward to regaining the liberties of 'freeborn Englishmen', together with the growing supply (and falling price) of African chattel slaves, encouraged the planters from the 1680s onwards to switch increasingly to exploiting the latter's labour to feed the growing markets for colonial products such as tobacco and sugar. This was the context in which the idea became entrenched that Africans, and other non-white 'races', are inherently inferior to Europeans. Though doctrines of natural inferiority pre-date modernity, they occupied less salience in pre-capitalist societies, where inequality of a visible, systematic, legally entrenched kind was the norm, reflecting their dependence on the coercive extraction of surplus-labour. In such hierarchical societies, slavery was one of a spectrum of unequal statuses, requiring no special explanation. Not so in capitalist societies, which rest on the exploitation of free wage-labour. The great bourgeois revolutions that entrenched the dominance of capitalism raised the banner of freedom and equality. The American Declaration of Independence of 4 July 1776 famously opens with the lines: 'We hold these truths to be self-evident: that all men are created equal; that they are endowed by their creator with certain inalienable rights; that among these rights are life, liberty, & the pursuit of happiness.'[83] These words were, of course, written by Thomas Jefferson, a Virginia slave-owner. The paradox was that capitalism, whose dominance involves the exploitation of free wage-labour, benefited enormously from racial slavery during critical phases of its development that, as we saw above, lasted well into the era of the Industrial Revolution. This reliance on slave labour became an anomaly requiring explanation. It was against this background that the idea began to take hold that blacks were subhuman, and therefore did not deserve the equal respect that was increasingly acknowledged as the right of human beings. Barbara Fields argues that 'racial ideology' became entrenched, especially among the white 'yeomanry' in the southern US – the small farmers and artisans who, representing nearly two-thirds of the population of the Old South, largely did not own slaves and sought to assert their claim to political and economic independence of the planters:

> Racial ideology supplied the means of explaining slavery to people whose terrain was a republic founded on radical doctrines of liberty and natural rights; and, more important, a republic in which those doctrines seemed to represent accurately the world in which all but a minority lived. Only when the denial of liberty became an anomaly apparent even to the least observant and reflective members of Euro-American society did ideology systematically explain the anomaly.[84]

Similarly, Peter Fryer has shown how racism emerged in eighteenth-century Britain 'as a largely defensive ideology – the weapon of a class whose wealth, way of life, and power were under mounting attack'.[85] Writers such as Edward Long, whose *History of Jamaica* (1774) was the most influential early articulation of racial ideology, sought to defend the West Indian planters and merchants from the growing political pressures to abolish, not just the slave trade, but the very institution of slavery itself. But, of course, the ideology survived abolition and indeed received further theoretical elaboration during the nineteenth century. The pseudo-scientific evolutionary biology of race that emerged, fusing together a bowdlerized version of Darwin's theory of natural selection and liberal conceptions of economic competition, continued to shape thinking till the mid-twentieth century.[86] The context of classical imperialism helps to explain this systematization of racial ideology. First, quite simply, the notion of a fixed hierarchy of races reflecting the outcome of a struggle for survival helped to legitimize both European colonialism and the growing competition among the Great Powers themselves. Secondly, the integration of the global South into the nineteenth-century world economy as a supplier of agricultural products and raw materials continued to involve different forms of coerced labour – the transnational spread of Indian indentured labourers to work in the plantation economies of the British Empire, the imposition of hut and poll taxes and of compulsory cash crops to force colonial peasantries to produce for the market, the migrant labour system and pass laws that developed to serve the needs of agricultural, mining and eventually manufacturing capitalism in southern Africa. Segregation and then apartheid in twentieth-century South Africa represented the most concentrated fusion of labour-repression and racial domination to emerge under classical imperialism, but the same elements were at work throughout the colonial world.[87] Thirdly, the global dominance of capitalism generated vast movements of people – in the course of the nineteenth century, 44 million Europeans (to the settler colonies of the Americas, Australasia and southern Africa), and nearly 50 million Indians and Chinese – but also the beginnings of the migration from the 'periphery' to the 'core' that is such an important feature of the contemporary world, as peasants from Ireland or Poland provided the industrial metropoles with cheap labour. The result, urban working classes where economic competition could fuse with cultural difference to constitute racial division, has survived the discrediting of biological racism thanks to the experience of National Socialism and the dismantling of the colonial empires after the Second World War.[88]

4.3 Superpower imperialism (1945–1991)

4.3.1 Open Door imperialism

Volker Berghahn writes: 'from an economic perspective and leaving aside Hitler's intolerant racist ideology and the power-political dimensions of the world conflict, the war amounted to a gigantic struggle between two diametrically opposed views on how to organize the world market: Closed Blocs vs. the Open Door'.[89] It was, more or less, the Open Door that won. We owe to William Appleman Williams the historical argument that the Open Door was more than a diplomatic initiative specific to China, and that indeed it has shaped the global strategy of the United States since the 1890s. Commenting on Hay's original Open Door notes in 1899–1900, Williams writes: 'Based on the assumption of what Brooks Adams called "America's economic supremacy", the policy of the open door was designed to clear the way and establish the conditions under which America's preponderant economic power would extend the American system throughout the world without the embarrassment or inefficiency of traditional colonialism.' Thus 'Hay's first note of September 6, 1899, asserted the proposition that American entrepreneurs "should enjoy perfect equality of treatment for their commerce and navigation" within all of China – *including spheres of interest held by foreign powers*.'[90] Here, then, there took shape the idea of a transnational expansion of capital accumulation that transcended politico-territorial demarcations. If the generalization of this idea was encouraged by practical considerations – in particular, the unhappy experience the US had of direct colonial rule in the Philippines after the Spanish–American War of 1898, the decisive stage in its ideological articulation came in 1917–19, when President Woodrow Wilson, in his Fourteen Points and intervention in the Paris Peace Conference, responded to the challenge thrown down to the existing order by the Russian Revolution and presented liberal democracy and free-market capitalism as the framework in which the world could attain peace and prosperity. As Neil Smith puts it,

> The brilliance of liberal US internationalists in this period, with Woodrow Wilson as their flag-bearer, . . . lay in the implicit realization that the wedding of geography and economics undergirding European capital accumulation was not inevitable; that the coming era could be organized differently; and that economic expansion divorced from territorial aggrandizement dovetailed superbly with US national

interests . . . With capital accumulation increasingly outstripping the scale of national boundaries and markets, and new colonialisms no longer feasible or practical, US internationalism pioneered a historic unhinging of economic expansion from direct political and military control over the new markets.[91]

This model of imperialism without colonies wasn't unprecedented: it had been anticipated by Britain's informal empire in Latin America and the Far East. But it was based on a very different kind of capitalism from the decentralized, transnational networks characteristic of the British hegemony; America's strength lay in mass-production industries organized by bureaucratically managed multi-branch corporations and supplying a continental economy insulated from the other major centres of economic and political power by the Pacific and Atlantic oceans.[92] Paradoxically, this combination of in-depth industrial strength and relative geopolitical isolation gave US capitalism the ability to establish global hegemony without creating its own formal territorial empire. But achieving this hegemony proved to require the projection of massive military power, as well as sustained political intervention in the key regions of Eurasia. Notoriously, Wilson's attempt to use the Paris peace settlement to institutionalize a transnational liberal capitalist order around the League of Nations ended in failure, critically because he was unable to achieve a compromise that would simultaneously provide France with the security guarantee it sought against a revived Germany and assure the American political elite that the US had not committed itself to participation in future European wars.[93]

Contrary to myth, however, the debacle of the Versailles Treaty did not lead to an American retreat into isolation. On the contrary, the Republican administrations that held office in Washington between 1921 and 1933 consistently pursued a strategy based on close collaboration with a network of central and investment bankers (including notably the Federal Reserve Bank of New York, J.P. Morgan & Co, and, on the other side of the Atlantic, the Bank of England) whose aim was to restabilize and reconstruct European capitalism by using the leverage that Washington had gained when it emerged from the Great War as the world's main creditor. While the immediate focus of these initiatives was to deal with the contentious issues of the war debts that Europe's allies had accumulated with the US and of the huge reparations imposed on Germany at Versailles (the object of two key US interventions, the Dawes Plan of 1924 and the Young Plan of 1928), there was also, particularly on the part of one key figure, Herbert Hoover (successively Commerce Secretary and President), a longer-term goal that would also figure in American planning for Europe in the 1940s. This was the aim of moving Europe towards what Michael Hogan calls

> an American political economy founded on self-governing economic groups, integrated by institutional coordinators and normal market mechanisms led by cooperating private and public elites, nourished but limited by positive government power, and geared to an economic growth in which all could share. These efforts married the older traditions associated with the localized and fragmented political economy of the nineteenth century, including individualism, privatism, competition, and anti-trust, to the twentieth-century trends towards an organized capitalism characterized by national economies of scale, bureaucratic planning, and administrative regulation.[94]

US efforts to reconstruct European capitalism in America's image were already under pressure before the Wall Street crash of October 1929, as a result of growing tensions between London and Washington and the destabilizing impact of huge inflows of short-term American capital into Germany. The onset of the Depression shattered the project, particularly after Britain abandoned the gold standard and free trade (and repudiated its American war debts in 1934). Hogan writes: 'A fair-weather approach, the theory of private and cooperative multinationalism could not stand the onslaught of hard times.'[95] The New Deal introduced a new inflection into the model of corporate capitalism championed by Hoover, inaugurating what Kees van der Pijl calls 'the corporate-liberal synthesis', where ' "progressive" state intervention was inserted into a revitalized liberal internationalism'.[96] As Hogan puts it, 'economic depression and New Deal activism led spokesmen for the capital-intensive bloc [of industrial capital] and great investment banks to redefine New Era formulations [dating from the 1920s] in a way that left more room for organized labour, conceded a larger role for the state, and included Keynesian strategies of aggregate economic management'.[97] But as a domestic programme the New Deal was insufficient to rescue American capitalism, which was hit by another severe recession in 1937–8. Charles Kindleberger writes: 'The steepest economic decline in the history of the United States, which lost half the ground gained for many indexes since 1932, proved that the economic recovery in the United States had been built on an illusion.'[98]

For American policy-makers, the solution lay in constructing a liberal international order where US capital and commodities could freely flow and from which European Great Power rivalries had been banished. The key obstacle to achieving this objective lay in the protectionist blocs established by the other leading capitalist states and most notably the British Empire. This diagnosis, which amounted to a reaffirmation of Open Door imperialism, was most strongly articulated by Cordell Hull, US Secretary of State through much of the Roosevelt administration, who described the 1932 Ottawa Agreement as 'the greatest injury in a commercial way that has been inflicted on this country since I have been in public life'.[99] David Reynolds suggests that Roosevelt himself 'might be called a "realistic Wilsonian", using the adjective in both the common-sense and the more technical meaning. That is to say he felt that Wilson had been generally naive about diplomacy and politics, and that he had neglected the centrality of great power relations,' but nevertheless saw the Second World War as an opportunity to construct an essentially Wilsonian global order underpinned by US and British military capabilities. The dilemma of successive British governments, confronted by the expansionist ambitions of German and Japanese imperialism, was naively summed up by the First Sea Lord, Sir Ernle Chatfield, in 1934: 'We are in the remarkable position of not wanting to quarrel with anybody because we have got most of the world already, or the best parts of it, and we only want to keep what we have got and prevent others from taking it away from us.' Neville Chamberlain and Winston Churchill, the great antagonists of British foreign policy debates in the late 1930s, shared this objective but pursued different strategies to achieve it. Chamberlain, believing that a Britain whose relative economic power was declining lacked the capabilities militarily to defend its Empire, sought to appease Germany, Italy and Japan. Even after this policy had failed, he rejected an alliance with the US, writing in January 1940: 'Heaven knows I don't want the Americans to fight for us – we should have to pay too dearly for that if they had a right to be in on the peace terms.'[100]

Chamberlain's fears proved prescient. Churchill's alternative strategy of confronting Hitler depended on American support, which became an existential question of survival after the fall of France to the German Blitzkrieg in May–June 1940. Initially, Roosevelt extended this support as an alternative to US entry into the war but the combination of British weakness and the prospect of a Eurasia closed to the US by victorious German and Japanese imperialisms set Washington towards mobilizing America's immense industrial power to defeat Berlin and Tokyo. Quite consistently, both before and after Pearl Harbor, the administration used the material and military resources that the US provided Britain as a means for extracting massive policy concessions from London. The most important American objectives were the abolition of Imperial Preference, which was included somewhat ambiguously in the February 1942 agreement on British repayment of the US Lend Lease programme, the dismantling of the British colonial empire, which was strongly pressed by Roosevelt and bitterly contested by Churchill, and greater US access to Middle Eastern oil.[101] The same pattern informed the protracted negotiations leading to the Bretton Woods agreement of July 1944, which established the International Monetary Fund and the World Bank. The US Treasury secured a postwar international monetary order based on a dollar gold-exchange standard and policed by a strong, American-dominated Fund; the efforts of Maynard Keynes, the chief British representative, to secure an international clearing union where creditors were given incentives to eliminate surpluses as well as debtors deficits were rebuffed for a system favouring the US in its position as global creditor. Keynes, embittered by his final struggle to secure an American loan to Britain after the administration of Harry Truman had cancelled Lend Lease when the Pacific War ended in August 1945, came back from the first meeting of the IMF and the World Bank at Savannah in March 1946, saying: 'I went to Savannah to meet the world and all I met was a tyrant.'[102]

4.3.2 The partial dissociation of economic and geopolitical competition

Once Germany and Japan had been defeated, and Britain more or less brought to heel, the most important obstacle to the liberal internationalist order sought by US state managers was constituted by the Soviet Union. This was less because of any direct military threat that it represented, particularly between 1945 and 1949, when the US enjoyed a monopoly of nuclear weapons, than because the survival of the state capitalist regime in the USSR and its expansion into Eastern and Central Europe in 1944–5, underpinned by Moscow's emergence from the Second World War as the greatest Eurasian land power, represented the persistence of the pre-war order of rival economic and geopolitical blocs. As Melvyn Leffler puts it,

> US officials feared a return to the conditions of the 1930s, when economic autarky perpetuated international depression, enhanced German and Japanese strength, and contributed to the outbreak of war. They worried that the compartmentalization of the world economy into the

169

Soviet and British blocs might again circumscribe the sphere of American trade, lead to economic stagnation, and jeopardize a full employment economy. Even more ominously, the Kremlin might use bilateral commercial agreements and joint stock companies to foster its economic growth and military power. Capitalizing on the prevailing chaos and economic dislocation, the Russians might lure additional countries into their orbit. They would seek to enhance their influence, improve their strategic position, and augment their abilities to mobilize resources and labour to wage war. Someday far in the future, the Kremlin might gain sufficient strength to contest America's position in the international system.[103]

Wartime US military planners had already identified the objectives of maintaining American military predominance in the Western Hemisphere and ensuring that no hostile power or coalition of powers emerged on the Eurasian landmass; to that end, detailed proposals for a global network of US military bases were developed.[104] Worries about the USSR's potential to disrupt the postwar order soon led to the adoption of the policy of containment, articulated by George Kennan in the famous 'Long Telegram' of February 1946, and the pursuit by the US of what Paul Nitze, Kennan's successor as Director of Policy Planning at the State Department, would call in 1952 'preponderant power'.[105] More significantly in the longer run, fears for the socioeconomic collapse of Western Europe and Japan, which might offer Moscow opportunities for political expansion, led Washington to engage in a much more concerted and ambitious version of the programme of restabilization and reconstruction that the administration had essayed in Europe during the 1920s. While geopolitical considerations were a powerful factor – and were stridently expressed by the Truman administration to win the political support of Congress ('we made our points clearer than truth', Secretary of State Dean Acheson subsequently admitted) – there were economic motives behind the policy as well. 'Indeed,' writes Thomas Borden,

it is useful to view postwar American foreign policy as shaped by the twenty-five year economic crisis which began in 1930. Overproduction, insufficient demand, and nationalistic policies all stifled commerce. The war simultaneously created great productive capacity in the United States and a limitless reservoir of demand elsewhere. There were, however, no means for the purchasers to compensate the producer.[106]

170

As economic reconstruction got under way in Western Europe and Japan, it ran up against a shortage of dollars required particularly to finance imports of capital equipment, food, and raw materials. The dollar gap amounted to $7.8 billion in 1946, $11.6 billion in 1947, and $6.9 billion in 1948. A division emerged between hard-currency areas (essentially the US and its economic extensions and Switzerland) and soft-currency areas, which included the British sterling bloc. Borden writes:

> The greatest American fear was the total breakdown of economic relations between the soft- and hard-currency areas, which would effectively close off European, African, and Asian markets to American manufacturing corporations and food and raw material producers. At times, the threat of a collapse of American exports and resulting economic depression was explicitly used as a rationale for aid.[107]

The aim behind the Marshall Plan (or European Recovery Programme), announced in June 1947, and equivalent policies adopted by the US-dominated occupation administration in Japan (the Supreme Command for the Allied Powers, SCAP), was therefore, according to Borden, 'to correct the massive structural disequilibrium in world trade by rebuilding the "workshop" economies of Europe and Japan and restoring their economic ties with primary producing areas in Asia, Africa, and Latin America,' and thereby to overcome 'the economic crisis which would have faced American officials even in the absence of a Communist threat'.[108] In the Japanese case, this involved SCAP reversing its initial policy of dismantling the oligopolies that had dominated the pre-war Japanese economy, facilitating the development of the *keiretsu*, corporate clusters each centred on a private bank, and maintaining the power of the state bureaucracy.[109] The European Cooperation Administration, the US agency administering Marshall Aid, pursued a more ambitious project of promoting European economic integration, in order both to create a continental market and to limit national antagonisms among the different European states, and of seeking to export American-style corporate liberalism. In Alan Milward's words, '[b]y creating a United States of Europe America could restore the equilibrium in world trade missing since 1914'. It met with consistent opposition from the British Labour government, which was anxious to preserve the state controls it regarded as essential if it was to pursue its programme of domestic social and economic reform, and which also sought to maintain Britain, though weakened by the abandonment of India in 1947, as

171

a world power at the centre of its Empire (rebranded as the Commonwealth) and the sterling area, overlapping with, but not subordinate to, the US and Western Europe. The financial crisis that forced Britain in August 1947 to give up its short-lived policy (a condition of the postwar American loan negotiated by Keynes) of restoring sterling to international convertibility highlighted the conflict between a US eager to reconstruct a multilateral trading order and European states using Keynesian demand management, exchange controls and bilateral agreements to rebuild their economies. Milward goes as far as to assert: 'If the "Bretton Woods system", as conceived in 1944, ever existed, it ended for European countries in 1947.'[110]

The intermeshing of geopolitical with economic interests was not simply driven by Washington's worries about Moscow: after all, the two world wars arose from the destabilizing impact of German expansion on the European state system. Commenting on Wolfram Hanreider's suggestion that 'America's post-World War II Western European grand strategy was one of *double* containment; that is, containment of both the Soviet Union and Germany', Christopher Layne argues that, 'had the United States not needed to pursue a European grand strategy based on double containment, the Open Door's logic would have impelled Washington to adopt a strategy of *single* containment'.[111] Any revival of European capitalism depended on that of Germany, the continent's leading industrial economy; an understanding of this was one factor in the decision of the US and Britain to merge their occupation zones in mid-1946, which proved to be an important step in the process of partitioning Germany and hence Europe between the two superpower blocs. France, on the other hand, wanted to keep Germany weak, and in particular to control the Ruhr (which it had briefly seized in 1923), Europe's key industrial region and the source of the coal and coke on which the Monnet Plan for industrializing France depended. The eventual outcome was the Schuman Plan, announced by Robert Schuman, the French Foreign Minister, in May 1950, which led to the establishment of the European Coal and Steel Community (ECSC), based on 'Little Europe' – France, West Germany, Italy and the Benelux countries. Essentially economic control over the Ruhr was pooled, thereby providing France with reassurance against a revival of German power and the new Federal Republic of Germany with a European framework in which to assert its interests and rebuild its standing in the state system.

This set-up – from which the European Economic Community (EEC) emerged in 1957–8 and ultimately the contemporary European

Union – presupposed the new pattern of economic growth that developed in continental Europe after 1945, in which West German expansion, driven by rising productivity and exports, offered a market for the manufacturing industries of the rest of 'Little Europe'; Britain, still oriented on imperial markets, and, particularly after the outbreak of the Korean War, committed to high levels of military spending to maintain its global position, found itself outside this virtuous circle. But European integration also rested on specific geopolitical conditions, in particular, the partition of the continent between the two superpowers, and the role played by the US in offering its Western Europe allies a security guarantee against Soviet invasion and France reassurance against German economic recovery developing into a renewed military threat. From Washington's perspective, European integration was a key element in the containment of Germany. As Kennan put it in March 1949, '[t]here is no solution of the German problem in terms of Germany; there is only a solution in terms of Europe'.[112]

But for continental European state managers, integration represented, not the dissolution of national interests, but a new means for their assertion, increasingly on the basis of a Franco-German understanding formalized by treaty in 1963. 'Europe will be your revenge,' Konrad Adenauer, the West German Chancellor, told the French Foreign Minister on 6 November 1956, the day that Britain and France caved in to American demands and ended their attempt to take the Suez Canal back from Egypt, a moment that marked the transition from British to US hegemony in the Middle East.[113] One of Adenauer's successors, Helmut Schmidt, wrote in a 1976 memorandum known as the 'Marbella paper' that West Germany's 'unwanted and dangerous rise to second world power of the West in the consciousness of other governments' could lead to 'a revival of memories not only of Auschwitz and Hitler but also of Wilhelm II and Bismarck . . . perhaps as much in the West as in the East'. It is consequently 'necessary for us, so far as at all possible, to operate not nationally and independently, but in the framework of the European Community and the [NATO] Alliance. *This attempt to cover [abdecken] our actions multilaterally will only partially* succeed, because we will (necessarily and against our own will) become a leadership factor in both systems.'[114] The higgling of national interests forced the US to make considerable compromises, for example, tolerating the high degree of protectionism involved in the EEC's Common Agricultural Policy. In the lead-up to the Treaty of Rome (March 1957), the Eisenhower administration overruled the objections of the Treasury, Department of Agriculture and Federal Reserve Board to the formation of a European common market that might damage US economic interests; this reflected the strategic commitment of the President and his Secretary of State, John Foster Dulles, to European integration.[115]

One final interaction between geopolitics and economics was decisive for shaping the US-dominated transnational order. Securing the preponderance over the Soviet Union desired by American policy-makers required a massive US military build-up, Nitze argued in a celebrated memorandum, NSC 68, drafted under Acheson's supervision and submitted to Truman in April 1950. The outbreak of the Korean War in July 1950 made the military spending involved – estimated at $50 billion, way above the ceiling set by Truman of $13.5 billion on the defence budget – politically feasible, and led to the transformation of the North Atlantic Treaty Organization (NATO) from a security pact between the US and its West European allies into a full-scale military alliance involving the long-term deployment of several American divisions in Europe. After warning that 'there are grounds for predicting that the United States and other free nations will within a period of a few years at most experience a decline in economic activity of serious proportions unless more positive governmental programs are developed than are now available', NSC 68 went on to offer a Keynesian justification for the mammoth rise in arms spending it proposed:

> From the point of view of the economy as a whole, the programme might not result in a real decrease in the standard of living, for the economic effects of the programme might be to increase the gross national product by more than the amount being absorbed for additional military and foreign assistance purposes. One of the most significant lessons of our World War II experience was that the American economy, when it operates at a level approaching full efficiency, can provide enormous resources for purposes other than civilian consumption while simultaneously providing a high standard of living.[116]

It would be silly to concoct a conspiracy theory in which, for example, the US provoked the Korean War in order to stabilize postwar capitalism: the geopolitical contest with the Soviet Union had its own dynamic. Nevertheless, it is clear that for senior US policy-makers the massive military build-up proposed in NSC 68 served a dual function – securing preponderance over the USSR and helping to avoid a return to the economic crisis of the interwar years. Borden writes 'The United States finally solved the dollar gap problem through the mechanism of "offshore procurement" or the purchase of military goods in dollars from Europe' as well as from Japan; according to Chalmers Johnson, '[t]he Korean War was in many ways the equivalent to Japan of the Marshall Plan'.[117] But, arguably, the development of what Michael Kidron dubbed the permanent arms economy played a larger stabilizing role. US military spending jumped from 4.3 per cent of gross national product in 1948 to a high of 13.6 per cent in 1953 and was still 9.0 per cent in 1969 – far above previous peacetime levels. Yet, as Chris Harman notes, '[t]hroughout this period the rate of profit seemed to defy Marx's "law"'. Indeed, between 1948 and 1973, global capitalism experienced its 'Golden Age', a long boom whose levels of sustained growth remain without historical parallel before or since (see table 1.1). One way to connect these facts without relying on the efficacy of Keynesian demand management (in fact very unevenly implemented in the postwar years) is on the basis of the theory pioneered by Henryk Grossman: that military expenditure is a form of unproductive consumption that, by diverting surplus-value from productive investment, slows down the rate of accumulation and hence the tendency for the organic composition of capital to rise, which in turn is responsible for the falling rate of profit (see §1.4). This explanation is supported by the evidence that the organic composition of capital rose only very slowly during the 1950s and 1960s from the low level it had reached at the end of the 1940s as a result of depression and war. Thus, according to Kidron and Harman, the postwar arms race – which led to the USSR striving to keep up with the US and Britain struggling to maintain a global role through its military expenditures – had the largely unforeseen effect of offsetting the tendency of the rate of profit to fall.[118]

In any case, however caused, the Long Boom of the 1950s and 1960s helped to cement the US system of alliances in Western Europe and East Asia, and thereby contributed to a long-term shift in the patterns of inter-capitalist competition. This is best summed up as the partial dissociation of geopolitical and economic competition.[119] In the first place, geopolitical competition continued, in the bipolar shape of the Cold War. In some respects this conflict was more intense than those in the past, since the rival blocs conceived themselves as not merely Great Power rivals but ideological enemies. But it did not result in a general war, partly because of the restraining effect of the two sides' nuclear arsenals, but also because both the US and the USSR, at least in the period of detente in the 1960s and 1970s, were willing to regard themselves and each other as status quo powers with no interest in revising the postwar settlement. Large-scale wars continued, but largely as proxy conflicts, at most involving directly only one of the superpowers in the periphery – Korea, Vietnam, Afghanistan. (The very bloody and destructive Iran–Iraq War of 1980–8 was a proxy conflict of a different kind, in which the US backed the Saddam Hussein regime as a means of containing the Iranian Revolution.)

Secondly, the advanced capitalist states were united under the political and military leadership of the US. Despite the importance of NATO and of the strategic partnership between the US and Japan, this represented more than a traditional system of alliances. The US was unable to achieve the liberal world order sought by the Roosevelt administration in the first half of the 1940s, but there nevertheless emerged a transnational liberal capitalist space embracing the three most economically advanced regions in the world – North America, Western Europe and Japan. The international financial institutions – the IMF, the World Bank and the General Agreement on Trade and Tariffs – provided a much denser political framework for this space than existed in the pre-1914 era and actively promoted the gradual liberalization of trade and investment. European currencies finally became internationally convertible in 1958–9, though in a very different context from that envisaged at Bretton Woods, as the booming continental European economies began to run up balance of payments surpluses with the US. A new liberal world economy took shape, initiating a process that Ronald Findlay and Kevin O'Rourke call 'reglobalization'.[120] The growing overhang of dollars in Europe, as well as efforts to bypass US exchange controls, gave birth to the Eurodollar market, the beginning of the vast offshore financial markets of the neoliberal era. Transnational production networks developed, pioneered by US multinationals, particularly during the Long Boom, as they sought to gain access to the huge but relatively protected market provided by the EEC, and these were soon imitated by European and Japanese corporations. The boom also reinforced the growing tendency of industrial firms to fund their investments from retained profits, thereby loosening the relationship between banking and productive capital that Hilferding had posited.[121]

Thirdly, as economic competition became more intense, it did not translate into geopolitical conflicts between the advanced capitalist states. This marked a fundamental difference from the era of classical imperialism when, as we have seen, economic and geopolitical competition tended to be mutually reinforcing. It is important to emphasize that the economic rivalries were (and remain) serious. From the

176

end of the 1950s onwards, the US grappled with increasingly pronounced balance of payments difficulties caused by the costs of America's informal empire (military spending abroad and foreign aid) and by first German and then Japanese competition in international trade in manufactured goods. Thanks to their politically subordinate positions, both German and Japanese capitalism enjoyed the advantage of relatively low levels of defence spending, which (together with the comparatively close institutional links between banks and industrial firms in both economies) allowed them to maintain very high levels of productive investment and therefore continually to raise the competitiveness of their exports. The final death agony of sterling's role as an international reserve currency during the 1960s masked a much more serious crisis facing the dollar, one that eventually led the Nixon administration to abandon the gold exchange standard in August 1971, and prompted a general shift to floating exchange rates in March 1973. The intensification of international economic competition in the late 1960s and the early 1970s (Ricardo Parboni describes the 1970s as 'an extended period of economic warfare between the United States and the other capitalist powers'), and the rundown of the Vietnam War, encouraged the administration to reduce military expenditure as a way of transferring investible resources to civilian industries. Whether or not this decline in the permanent arms economy was the cause, heightened economic competition was associated with a general fall in profitability in the leading capitalist states, from the late 1960s onwards, that marked the end of the Long Boom and the beginning of a protracted period of slower growth, punctuated by major recessions in the mid-1970s, the early 1980s and the early 1990s, and a weaker one at the beginning of the new millennium (see table 5.3).[122]

The 'long downturn' that began in 1973 did not see the kind of fragmentation of the liberal world economy that took place during the Thirty Years War of 1914–45. As table 4.5 shows, foreign direct investment flows increased through the great recessions of the mid-1970s and early 1980s. Transnational economic integration had by the 1990s achieved the levels of the late nineteenth century (see table 4.4). Of the two tendencies that Bukharin held to be constitutive of imperialism, the internationalization of capital was now prevailing over the trend to state capitalism (see §1.3). Moreover, despite recurrent political tensions between the US and its major Western allies – over, for example, Suez in 1956, France's attempt to pursue an independent foreign policy after Charles de Gaulle's return to power in 1958, the efforts of individual Western states to exploit detente

177

for their own advantage, and Germany's pursuit of *Ostpolitik* in the 1970s and 1980s – in no case did these threaten the break-up of the Western bloc. Three main causes can be identified for this relative harmony. First, the bipolar conflict with the USSR tended to act as a disciplining force on the advanced capitalist states. Secondly, the US sought aggressively to maintain its hegemonic position, intervening to subvert challengers.[123] Last, but not least, there were the benefits that other states obtained from participation in the transnational liberal space, particularly thanks to the increase in global economic integration; this is surely significant in explaining the relative weakness of protectionist pressures after 1973 in comparison with the collapse of international trade in the 1930s. In other words, despite the intensification of economic competition, US hegemony could still be plausibly represented as operating in the 'general interest' of the leading capital states (see §4.1 above). Whether this remains the case today – and will continue to be so in the future – is one of the main themes of chapter 5.

4.3.3 The Third World – malign neglect and partial industrialization

The place of what came to be called the Third World, or the developing countries, during the era of superpower imperialism was paradoxical. On the one hand, it provided the main theatre of the hot wars through which the US and the USSR tested their relative strengths. Moreover, the process of decolonization set the stage for a series of epic struggles for national liberation – in China, Indochina, Vietnam, Algeria and Portugal's African colonies. On the other hand, as I demonstrate below, in the postwar era the Third World was of diminishing economic importance to the advanced capitalist states. Decolonization wasn't a mechanical consequence of this fact: the dismantling of the European empires reflected American pressures, the impact of the Second World War in restricting the material capabilities and undermining the prestige of the colonial powers (in the latter respect, particularly as a result of Japan's rapid victories in the first phase of the Pacific War in 1941–2), and the upsurge of revolutionary nationalism in the 1940s and 1950s. In the British case, Bernard Porter writes, 'the empire had been "overstretched" for a long time: run on a shoestring and with very few personnel, inadequately defended by a second-rate military, and with little domestic commitment to it, especially if it involved serious repression. Its eventual collapse should come as no surprise'.[124] Even after the

178

abandonment of India in 1947, Labour and Conservative governments alike sought to hang on to a reconstructed Commonwealth, in
the process successfully fighting vicious counter-insurgency wars in
Malaya, Cyprus and Kenya, but the 1960s saw the definitive abandonment of empire and Britain's reorientation towards an EEC it had
initially shunned.[125]

The pain of decolonization – which in the case of France involved
two bloody wars in Indochina and Algeria before de Gaulle implemented an analogous reorientation in the early 1960s – was eased by
the transformation of postwar capitalism. The picture that Lenin had
painted of an imperialist system based on the export of capital to the
colonies – even in his time, as we have seen in §4.2, only a partial
truth – was completely at odds with the economic patterns that
developed after 1945. Summing up the immediate postwar experience, Kidron wrote in 1962: 'Capital does not flow overwhelmingly
from mature to developing capitalist countries. On the contrary,
foreign investments are increasingly made as between developing
countries themselves.'[126] As table 4.5 shows, this statement continued
to hold true for the world economy between 1965 and 1983, the
period when the Long Boom matured and collapsed. The World Bank
reported in 1985:

> about three quarters of foreign direct investment has gone to industrial
> countries since 1965. The remainder has been concentrated in a few
> developing countries, predominantly the higher income countries of
> Asia and Latin America. In particular Brazil and Mexico have received
> high volumes of direct investment. Within Asia Hong Kong, Malaysia,
> the Philippines, and Singapore have been the largest recipients; Singa-
> pore alone has accounted for nearly one-half of the total Asia receipts
> of foreign direct investment in recent years.[127]

These figures directly contradict the analyses of the world system
put forward at the time, by dependency theorists such as Andre
Gunder Frank, and theorists of unequal exchange such as Arghiri
Emmanuel and Samir Amin. The latter hold that the rich countries
exploit the poor ones, thanks to world prices reflecting the advantages the North gains from the high wages its well-organized workers
have secured, while the low wages of the South represent a higher
rate of profit for internationally mobile capital. But they cannot
explain the actual patterns of foreign direct investment, which are
the opposite of what the theory of unequal exchange would predict.
From the perspective of Marxist value theory, the critical error is not

Table 4.5 Direct foreign investment in selected foreign country groups, 1965–1983

Country Group	Annual average value of flows ($bn) (percentages)				Share of flows			
	1965–69	1970–74	1975–79	1980–83	1965–69	1970–74	1975–79	1980–83
Industrial countries	5.2	11.0	18.4	31.3	79	86	72	63
Developing countries	1.2	2.8	6.6	13.4	18	22	26	27
Latin America & Caribbean	0.8	1.4	3.4	6.7	12	11	13	14
Africa	0.2	0.6	1.0	1.4	3	5	4	3
Asia, inc. Middle East	0.2	0.8	2.2	5.2	3	5	4	3
Other countries & estimated unreported flows	0.2	–1.0	0.6	4.8	3	–8	2	10
Total	6.6	12.8	25.6	49.4	100	100	100	100

Source: World Bank, World Development Report 1985 (New York, 1985), p. 126, table 9.1

to take into account the significance of higher levels of labour productivity in the advanced economies. Nigel Harris makes the essential point: 'Other things being equal, the higher the productivity of labour, the higher the income paid to the worker (since his or her reproduction costs are higher) and *the more exploited he or she is* – that is, the greater the proportion of the worker's output [that] is appropriated by the employer.'[128] Far from the prosperity of capitalists (and workers) in the advanced countries depending on the poverty of the Third World, the main flows of capital and commodities passed the poor countries by. And the largest concentrations of wealth remained in the Western economies. As we saw in §4.2 above, one of the colonies' main roles under classical imperialism lay in the raw materials they provided for the increasingly specialized industrial economies of the metropoles. But the drive towards autarky during the Thirty Years War of 1914–45 involved sustained and successful efforts by the advanced economies to reduce their dependence on imported raw materials: thus synthetic substitutes were developed on a large scale, raw materials were used more efficiently and the agricultural output of the industrial countries vastly increased.[129]

Meanwhile, in the 1950s and 1960s, the developed countries were booming. Harris spells out the consequences:

> Rising real incomes in the advanced capitalist countries provided expanding markets for the increasingly sophisticated and highly priced output. And it ensured the profit rates on new investment that continuously sucked in an increasing proportion of the world's new savings. Both labour and capital were dragged out of the backward countries to service the economies of the advanced. The trade between advanced capitalist countries provided the dynamo for an unprecedented expansion in world trade and output in the period after 1948, and for an even greater concentration of capital in the hands of the rich countries. What had been seen by the imperialists as the division of labour between the manufacturing advanced and the raw material exporting backward countries was overtaken by a division between the relatively self-sufficient advanced enclave and a mass of poor dependents.[130]

It does not follow that the interventions by the US in the Third World never involved economic considerations. The Korean War of 1950–3 was partly motivated by the aim of securing Japan, a major centre of industrial capitalism. Initial American involvement in Indochina was prompted, not only by the decision to prop up the French colonial empire, but also by the strategy of deflecting Japan from the temptation of recovering its traditional market in China after the 1949 Revolution by offering it new markets in South-east Asia.[131] In the main, however, traditional geostrategic calculations, along with growing anxiety about American 'credibility', governed US interventions in the Third World at the height of the Cold War. As Gabriel Kolko puts it in his magisterial history of the Vietnam War, '[t]he American obsession with the successful application of power – "credibility" – is the inevitable overhead charge of its foreign policy after 1945 with its ambition to integrate a US-led international political and economic order'.[132] The mix is admirably captured in a paper by Assistant Defense Secretary John McNaughton, setting out US aims in South Vietnam (SVN), on the eve of President Lyndon Johnson's decision in spring and summer 1965 directly to engage in the ground war there:

70% – To avoid a humiliating US defeat . . .
20% – To keep SVN (and the adjacent) territory from Chinese hands.
10% – To permit the people of SVN to enjoy a better, freer way of life.[133]

When, in the 1960s, Kidron and Harris first analysed the changing relationship between advanced and developing economies, they noted one very important exception to the pattern of declining Western dependence on imported raw materials – oil.[134] Ensuring American hegemony in the Middle East has been a major dimension of US global strategy since the 1940s. Simon Bromley argues that Middle Eastern oil has been important to the US less because of its direct contribution to the American economy (which remained largely reliant on its own energy supplies till the late 1960s) than thanks to its function as a 'strategic commodity'. 'US control over world oil became a key resource in the overall management of its global leadership' after 1945, particularly given the greater dependence of the other main centres of Western capitalism – Europe and Japan – on imported oil.[135] Accordingly, in January 1980, in the wake of the Iranian Revolution and the Soviet intervention in Afghanistan, President Jimmy Carter announced what quickly came to be known as the Carter Doctrine: 'An attempt by any outside force to gain control of the Persian Gulf will be regarded as a vital interest of the United States of America, and such an assault will be repelled by any means necessary, including military force.'[136] Securing the Middle East has indeed proved to be the main axis of US military intervention in the past quarter-century.

Nevertheless, oil was precisely an *exception*. The norm in the Third World was not intensive exploitation by transnational corporations, but the effective exclusion of most poor countries from world trade and investment – what Michael Mann has more recently called 'ostracizing imperialism'.[137] The workers, peasants and urban poor of Africa, Asia and Latin America struggled in poverty, less because the fruits of their exploitation were the main source of imperialist superprofits than because their labour was irrelevant to the main centres of capital accumulation in North America, Western Europe and Japan – unless, as tens of millions from the Third World increasingly did, they followed this capital to its home bases. Despite the claims of dependency theorists, it did not follow, however, that the entire global South was condemned to permanent stagnation. On the contrary, some less developed countries were able to attain high levels of industrial growth. In particular, new, relatively independent centres of capital accumulation emerged during the 1960s and 1970s in East Asia (the 'Four Tigers' of Hong Kong, Singapore, South Korea and Taiwan, later followed by Indonesia, Malaysia, the Philippines and Thailand, and, more recently still, by Vietnam) and Latin America (Argentina, Brazil and Mexico).

Earlier phases of industrialization outside the imperialist centres had typically involved the production of previously imported consumer goods. The two world wars and the Great Depression allowed several major colonies and states in the South (for example, India, Egypt, South Africa and Argentina), where growth had hitherto been largely due to their exports of food and raw materials, to take advantage of the metropolitan manufacturing industries' diversion to military production to encourage local capitalists to produce for their own domestic markets.[138] After 1945, many Third World states sought to continue this process of import-substitution industrialization, the most ambitious – China under Mao, India under Nehru, Egypt under Nasser – copying the bureaucratic command methods of Stalinist Russia in order to build up their own heavy industrial base. These essays in autarkic state capitalism were generally unable to mobilize from within their own borders the resources necessary for the huge investments on which the heavy industries of the advanced countries rested. Thus Nasser's efforts in the late 1950s and early 1960s to build up state-owned heavy industry were made possible by the large reserves of foreign exchange accumulated during the boom in Egypt's main export, cotton, during the Korean War. These reserves financed the imports of machinery, components, and other inputs needed to build up Egypt's industrial base. But, when the foreign

183

exchange ran out, further imports could be financed either by exports, where Egyptian industry could not compete, or by Russian loans, which were paid for in exports of cotton and rice shipped to the USSR. The failure of Nasser's state-capitalist policies lay behind the adoption in the 1970s by his successor, Anwar Sadat, of *infitah*, the opening of Egypt to the world economy.[139]

The industrializing economies of East Asia and Latin America marked a significant divergence from this pattern. Whereas Mao, Nehru and Nasser had sought to follow Stalin in pursuing autarky, states such as South Korea and Brazil oriented themselves on the world market. They produced manufactured goods not necessarily (or even, in some cases, primarily) for the domestic market, but for export. And, particularly in the case of South Korea and Taiwan, which benefitted from the pre-war industrialization they had undergone as Japanese colonies, they were able to break into world trade in manufactured goods by rigorous state-capitalist methods. The South Korean state, for example, exercised centralized direction of private investment, not in an attempt to reproduce the kind of diversified industrial economy characteristic of the advanced countries, but to identify those international markets into which its capitalists could hope to break, provided that resources were concentrated on a limited number of industries. The interventionist state, operating frequently in defiance of the axioms of neoclassical economics, served as a battering ram into the world market, rather than a means of escaping it.[140] The Third World debt crisis that developed in the early 1980s as states and firms in the South found themselves unable to repay the loans that had been thrust on them by the Northern banks, eager for new customers as the recession of the mid-1970s cut investment in the advanced economies, gave the IMF and the World Bank the leverage to generalize the neoliberal economic policies pioneered by Ronald Reagan and Margaret Thatcher (what came to be called the Washington Consensus). The result of the crisis was a net financial transfer from South to North, and economic stagnation in large parts of Latin America and sub-Saharan Africa, though the transfer masked considerable capital flight to the advanced economies, as the propertied rich of the Third World sought to link themselves more closely with their Northern counterparts; the developmental state in East Asia proved, on the whole, more resilient.[141]

Benedict Anderson has identified broader geopolitical and historical conditions that allowed for the explosive growth of the East Asian capitalisms – the military security and economic aid provided by the US in a key region in the Cold War; proximity to the Japanese economic dynamo; the temporary introversion of China under Mao, removing a formidable potential competitor; and the role played by overseas Chinese business networks. [142] But the emergence of new centres of capital accumulation in the global South also had geopolitical effects, including the appearance of 'sub-imperialisms', Third World states aspiring to the kind of political and military domination on a regional scale that the superpowers enjoyed globally. This development underlay the 1982 Falklands/Malvinas War between Argentina and Britain as well as the longest conventional war of the twentieth century, between Iran and Iraq in 1980–8. Three factors were involved. First, decolonization meant that the exclusive control of colonial economies by individual metropolitan powers was now replaced by a more fluid state of affairs in which transnational corporations based in a variety of Western states invested in the same country, giving the local state room to manoeuvre between them and greater tax revenues to promote the expansion of native capital. In some cases the very process of postcolonial state-formation generated regional conflicts – for example, between India and Pakistan in South Asia, or between Israel and the Arab states in the Middle East.

Secondly, the uneven development of locally controlled industrial capitalisms could give rise to a version of the same dynamic that led to the emergence of capitalist imperialism in the first place. The expansion of these capitalisms (not always reflecting the process of industrialization discussed above, but sometimes the capabilities a state gained thanks to its access to oil revenues) might burst out of national borders, giving rise to regional conflicts between sub-imperialisms – between Greece and Turkey, India and Pakistan, Iran and Iraq – and sometimes, in the absence of such rivalries, to the growing regional dominance of a particular state – for example, South Africa in southern Africa. The post-Cold War era has seen the same dynamic at work most brutally in the interventions of rival coalitions of neighbouring states to extract resources and geopolitical advantage from the long agony of the Democratic Republic of the Congo.[143]

But, thirdly, despite the importance of specific regional economic and geopolitical dynamics, the policies of the superpowers played a major role in permitting certain medium-sized states to aspire to hegemony over their neighbours. Thus the very origins of the term 'sub-imperialism' can be traced to the strategy pursued by the US as part of the efforts of Richard Nixon's administration to extricate itself from the Vietnam catastrophe. Called the Nixon Doctrine, and first articulated in July 1969, it envisaged part of the burden of defending Western interests in the Third World being taken on by regional powers that would in exchange receive military and economic aid. Iran under the Shah is a good example of how industrializing Third World states sought to fill the vacuum left by a politically weakened imperialism – in this case, the Gulf after Britain's final withdrawal East of Suez in 1971.[144] More generally, sub-imperialisms were able to aspire to a regional role not merely by virtue of a certain level of capitalist development, but thanks to the support of one or other of the superpowers; thus Vietnam was able militarily to dominate Indochina after 1975 with the backing of the USSR. This did not make the sub-imperialisms mere puppets of their sponsors. The arrangements that permitted certain states to play regional roles typically rested on a convergence of interests rather than the patron's control of its client. But sub-imperialisms that crossed a line set by the biggest players could suffer severe consequences. Iraq under Saddam Hussein provides a classic example: promoted by Washington during the 1980s as a counterweight to revolutionary Iran, Saddam fatally misread the signals at the end of the Cold War, seizing Kuwait in August 1990, and suffering military defeat as a result, with economic blockade, the invasion and occupation of his country, and his own eventual execution. The global hierarchy of economic and military power that is a fundamental consequence of the uneven and combined development inherent in capitalist imperialism was not dissolved, but was rather complicated by the emergence of new centres of capital accumulation.[145]

The initial clash between the US and Ba'athist Iraq in 1990–1 occurred at the historical moment when the superpower partition of the globe was collapsing. The US responded to an apparent evening of the military balance with the Soviet Union during the 1970s, together with a series of setbacks in the Third World – most importantly defeat in Vietnam and the Iranian Revolution – by launching a massive build-up in arms expenditure that began under Carter but was accelerated after Reagan took office in 1981. Reagan also greatly extended the policy initiated under Carter of promoting right-wing guerrilla movements – first and most fatefully the *mujahedin* in Afghanistan, later the *contras* in Nicaragua and UNITA in Angola – as a means, alongside economic pressure, of subverting hostile Third World regimes.[146] It was, however, the ratcheting up of arms spending that proved decisive, eventually breaking the back of a Soviet economy considerably smaller and less productive than the American and denied by its very structure the advantages of integration in the world market. As the last Soviet leader, Mikhail Gorbachev, sought to end the nuclear arms race and thereby gain space for domestic reform, according to Raymond Garthoff, '[t]he US administration was unrelenting in pressing its advantage, so eager to "score" with its toughness, that little heed was given to the broader consequences of imposing one-sided compromises on Gorbachev and [his Foreign Minister, Eduard] Shevardnadze'.[147] The reunification of Germany on terms that kept it within NATO was rapidly followed by the collapse of the USSR itself. The US had won the Cold War. But what would be the geopolitical outcome of this upheaval? At the time I predicted a return *'to a world that is politically as well as economically multipolar'*.[148] This affirmation now seems to me, if not completely mistaken, then at very least requiring considerable qualification. What this involves will form the subject matter of chapter 5, where I attempt to answer Brenner's Question.

— 5 —

IMPERIALISM AND GLOBAL POLITICAL ECONOMY TODAY

5.1 The specificity of American imperialism

Robert Wade has suggested the following thought-experiment:

> Suppose you are an aspiring modern-day Roman emperor in a world of sovereign states, international markets, and capitalist economies. In order not to have to throw your military weight around more than occasionally, you need to act through hegemony rather than coercion and others must think that your predominance is the natural result of commonsensical institutional arrangements that are fair and just. If you – a unitary actor – could single-mindedly create an international framework of market rules to promote your interests, what kind of system would you create?[1]

Wade goes on to imagine an 'international financial architecture' involving no gold standard, the hegemon's currency serving instead as the main international reserve currency, its financial markets 'dominant in international finance', and 'a single integrated private capital market worldwide', with no barriers to entry or exit, all this supervised by 'a flotilla of international organizations that look like cooperatives of member states and confer the legitimacy of multilateralism, but that you [i.e., the hegemon] can control by setting the rules and blocking outcomes you don't like', and underpinned by 'a very large military, so as to be able to back your hegemony with coercion. The world financial architecture allows you to fund overwhelming military strength "on the cheap".' The upshot is that

> This international economic architecture allows your people to consume far more than they produce; it allows your firms and your

188

capital to enter and exit other markets quickly, maximizing short-run returns; it locks in net flows of technology rents from the rest of the world for decades ahead and thereby boosts incentives for your firms to innovate; and through market forces seemingly free of political power it reinforces your geopolitical dominance over other states. All the better if your social scientists explain to the public that a structure-less and agent-less process of globalization – the relentless technological change that shrinks time and distance – is behind all this, causing all states, including your own, to lose power vis-à-vis markets. You do not want others to think that globalization within the framework you have constructed raises your ability to have both a large military and prosperous civilian sector while diminishing everyone else's.[2]

This thought-experiment fits, of course, the contemporary American hegemony like a glove. The weakness of Wade's nicely ironic portrait is perhaps that it fixes too much of the present 'international economic architecture' in the cement of historical necessity. Thus, during the Bretton Woods era in the 1950s and 1960s, when arguably the pre-eminence of the United States in the advanced capitalist world was greater economically and geopolitically than it is today, the dollar was still backed by gold; the nineteenth-century British hegemony also involved the generalization of the gold standard. Moreover, as Wade acknowledges, the dollar's role as the main international reserve currency is a double-edged sword (see §5.2.3 below). Nevertheless, he is right to stress the extent to which contemporary transnational structures and institutions work to the specific advantage of American capitalism. Let's recall Robert Brenner's Question:

Why, with respect to the advanced capitalist world, did the imperialist expansion leading to inter-imperialist rivalry leading to war that prevailed before 1945 fail to obtain after that? Why, with respect to Europe, Japan, and indeed much of East Asia, did American hegemony for much of the postwar period fail to take an imperialist form, in Harvey's sense of the word – that is, the application of political power to consolidate, exacerbate, and make permanent already-existing economic advantage?[3]

Answering this question involves looking at the interests of both the US and the other advanced capitalist states. In the case of the US, the answer in a general sense is that the specific structure and global weight of American capitalism gave it the ability to dominate and lead the other major capitalist states without constructing a traditional territorial empire: the non-territorial imperialism of the Open Door suited US interests better (§4.3). But the way Brenner poses the question implies that American hegemony has not functioned to serve the interests of US capitals as opposed to those of the capitals based in the other advanced economies. In an unpublished paper he argues that US hegemony has operated to institutionalize the general conditions favourable to *all* capitals, American and foreign.[4] Simon Bromley, discussing the relationship between the invasion of Iraq and American oil strategy, argues along similar lines:

> the form of control that the United States is now seeking to fashion [in Iraq] is one that is open to the capital, commodities and trade of many states and firms. It cannot (yet?) be seen as an economically exclusive strategy, as part of a predatory form of hegemony. Rather, the United States has used its military power to fashion a geopolitical order that provides the political underpinning for its preferred model of the world economy: that is, an increasingly open liberal international order. US policy has aimed at creating a general, open international oil industry, in which markets, dominated by large multinational firms, allocate capital and commodities. The power of the US state is deployed, not just to protect the particular interests of the United States consumption needs and US firms, but rather to create the general preconditions for a world oil market, confident in the expectation that, as the leading economy, it will be able to attain all its needs through trade.[5]

It is important to distinguish three separate points here. First, as I have already argued, the US practises a non-territorial form of imperialism, working on the rule of thumb that an open liberal international order will generally benefit American-based capitals. Secondly, for its hegemony to function in a generally stable fashion, it would, in any case, have to secure significant benefits to other capitalist states (§4.1). But, thirdly, it does not follow in the least that the institutions that the US builds and the policies it pursues are neutral between the interests of capitals based in its territory and those based in other states. From a liberal internationalist perspective, John Ikenberry argues that at the two historical moments when American relative power was greatest, after 1945 and at the end of the Cold War, the US forewent temporary advantage and made significant concessions to other states in order to institutionalize an international 'constitutional order' that would maximize the long-term interests of all states. He writes: 'Stable orders are those in which the returns to power are relatively low and the returns to institutions are relatively high. These are precisely the circumstances that characterize the most fully developed constitutional orders.'[6]

But this argument fails sufficiently to address the question of how 'the returns to institutions' are distributed. Let's consider two instances where they have been high for the US relative to other states. The first concerns the international financial architecture, which Wade argues operates in the interests of American capitalism. Peter Gowan also contends that the US took advantage of the financial instability of the 1970s and 1980s, particularly after the 'Volcker shock' of October 1979, when Paul Volcker, Chairman of the US Federal Reserve Board, sharply raised interest rates, imposing a harsh monetary discipline on the US and world economies, to construct what he calls the Dollar-Wall Street Regime around a dollar that, though now purely fiat money unbacked by gold, remained the lynchpin of the international financial system, an advantage that Washington used to promote worldwide neoliberal policies favourable to the interests of US investment banks and transnational corporations.[7] Thus the Clinton administration caused severe tensions with Britain and Germany in particular when it responded to the Mexican financial crisis of 1994–5 by pressurizing the Group of Seven leading industrial countries to come up with a rescue package that bailed out mainly American investors. More spectacularly, the same administration during the East Asian crisis of 1997–8 blocked a Japanese proposal for an Asian Monetary Fund that would have limited the ability of the International Monetary Fund to manage the crisis, and in tandem with the IMF pressed on Asian governments policies of further economic liberalization designed both to weaken so-called 'crony capitalism' (the close links between the state, banks and private corporations, distinctive to the East Asian economic model) and to make the affected economies more permeable by American capital. In their analysis of this crisis Robert Wade and Frank Veneroso refer to 'the Wall Street-[US] Treasury-IMF complex' in order to highlight the nexus binding together the international financial institutions and specifically American interests.[8]

A second important example, also dating from the Clinton administration, involves the expansion of first NATO and then the European Union into Eastern and Central Europe. This policy represented a breach of the understanding reached between Mikhail Gorbachev, the last Soviet President, West German Chancellor Helmut Kohl and James Baker, the US Secretary of State, during the negotiations in 1990–1 that allowed a united Germany to remain in NATO in exchange for the assurance that, in Baker's words, '[t]here would be

191

no extension of NATO's current jurisdiction eastwards'.[9] The thinking behind the Clinton administration's violation of this promise was expressed very clearly by Zbigniew Brzezinski, the Democratic Party's leading geostrategic thinker. Brzezinski argues that the EU is 'the Eurasian bridgehead for American power and the potential springboard for the democratic global system's expansion into Eurasia'. Extending NATO and the EU in tandem into Central and Eastern Europe would accordingly extend American power: 'If the European Union is to become a geographically larger community . . . and if such a Europe is to base its security on a continued alliance with America, then it follows that its geopolitically most exposed sector, Central Europe, cannot be excluded from partaking in the sense of security that the rest of Europe enjoys through the transatlantic alliance'.[10] Stephen Cohen has described the 'real US policy' towards Russia as 'a relentless, winner-take-all exploitation of Russia's post-1991 weakness', involving the 'growing military encirclement of Russia, on and near its borders, by US and NATO bases, which are already ensconced or being planned in at least half the fourteen other former Soviet republics, from the Baltics and Ukraine to Georgia, Azerbaijan and the new states of Central Asia. The result is a US-built reverse iron curtain and the remilitarization of American–Russian relations', which has in turn provoked a more assertive foreign policy on Moscow's part under Vladimir Putin.[11] The dangers of Washington's strategy were amply illustrated by the war that broke out between Russia and Georgia in August 2008, following the attempt by the Georgian army, equipped and trained by the US and Israel, to seize back the Moscow-protected enclave of South Ossetia.

The examples of the Mexican and East Asian crises, and of NATO expansion, are particularly telling because they occurred under the Clinton administration, which is frequently praised by commentators for pursuing a multilateral approach subsequently, and disastrously renounced under George W. Bush. But even if these examples show how US institution-building served specifically American national interests, they do not address the second dimension that I suggested is required by an answer to Brenner's Question, namely the interests of the other advanced capitalist states. The fact that these states continue to participate in the international financial institutions and (in the case of the leading European states) in NATO, despite the evidence of US exploitation of these institutions to its own economic and political advantage, suggests prima facie that, on balance, it remains in their interest to do so. I look more closely at this issue, and at the geopolitical impact of the changing distribution of global

192

economic power in the next section. But, to gain a longer historical perspective, it may be helpful to get a better handle on what is distinctive about US imperialism by considering its affinities to and differences from its British predecessor.

Let's start with the affinities:

- First and foremost is the imperialism of free trade: the US has generalized the strategy of informal empire pioneered by Britain in the nineteenth century (§§4.2 and 4.3). It should, however, be stressed that American championing of free trade has always been pretty asymmetrical – more about opening other countries' markets than its own. In August 1949, during a row over trade with the British Labour government, the US Embassy in London admitted in words that are still true today: 'Sheer intellectual honesty compels us to say that the US favours multilateralism and non-discrimination in areas where we are in a strong competitive position; but resorts to subsidies, protectionism and discrimination in those areas where we are competitively weak.'[12]

- Both the British and the American hegemonies have depended heavily on control of the international financial system: indeed, Giovanni Arrighi argues that one symptom of hegemonic *crisis* is financialization, i.e., as returns on investment in industry and trade fall, 'capital *tends* to revert to more flexible forms of investment – above all, to its money form'.[13] This doesn't seem to be valid as a historical generalization: Britain reacted to its crisis of hegemony, exacerbated by a world slump in the 1930s, by going off the gold standard and seeking to construct a protectionist sterling bloc, which gravely *restricted* the scope of the City of London and helped to create the conditions for its being eventually supplanted by Wall Street (§§4.2 and 4.3). The recent reorientation of British capitalism around the City, which now rivals Wall Street as the world's most important financial centre, is indeed a response to relative economic decline, but it long postdates the end of London's hegemony. Arrighi's argument that 'the Reagan-Thatcher neoliberal counter-revolution . . . was not just, or even primarily, a response to the unsolved crisis of profitability but also – and especially – a response to the deepening crisis of [US] hegemony', in particular by 'competing aggressively for capital worldwide – through record-high interest rates, tax breaks, increasing freedom of action for capitalist producers and speculators and, as the benefits of the new policies materialized, an appreciating dollar – provoking the massive rerouting of capital flows towards the United States', has more going for it, but it should be treated as a specific historical interpretation rather than as a corroborating example for a cyclical theory of hegemonic decline.[14]

- Both Britain and the US have relied heavily on offshore naval and air capabilities, supported by a global infrastructure of bases, rather than on military land power; these bases indicate that even a non-territorial imperialism requires a minimal territorial extension to allow it to project power globally. The Royal Navy knitted together Britain's dispersed formal and informal empire. Britain's relative weakness as a land power set limits to its hegemony; at its height in the mid-nineteenth century, the powers that Lord Palmerston found hardest to manage were those sufficiently geographically insulated not to be particularly vulnerable to naval attack, above all Prussia and Russia. The development of air power during the First World War was seized on by British policy-makers as a way of controlling newly acquired territories such as Iraq without, as Winston Churchill put it, 'eating up troops and money'.[15] India's significance to the British Empire was not only economic; Lord Salisbury called it 'an English barrack in the Oriental Seas from which we may draw any number of troops without paying for them'.[16] The Indian Army significantly enhanced Britain's military capabilities in numerous colonial campaigns, as well as in the two world wars. The Second World War marked the definitive emergence of the US as a major land power, a position that it maintains today. But this difference from the British case shouldn't be overstated. The German offensive of July 1918, which turned into a successful Allied counter-offensive and the collapse of the Central Powers, was intended to seize victory by pre-empting the American mobilization that was still only building up. During the planning for US entry into the Second World War Franklin Roosevelt and the Army Chief of Staff, General George C. Marshall, decided to limit the American army to ninety divisions rather than the 215 estimated necessary to defeat Germany and Japan. Averell Harriman, a leading adviser to Roosevelt, explained: 'I believe he had in mind that if the great armies of Russia could stand up to the Germans, this might well make it possible for us to limit our participation largely to naval and air power.'[17] In the end, of course, a massive US-dominated expeditionary force was required to reconquer Western Europe, but it was indeed the Red Army that bore the brunt of destroying German military power. Subsequent land wars have not been a

Table 5.1   Defence expenditure of top fifteen economies, 2006 (ranked by GDP in current prices, 2007)

	Defence Expenditure (current US $, m)	Percentage of GDP
US	535,943	4.05
Japan	41,144	0.9
Germany	37,775	1.3
China	121,872	1.3*
UK	55,444	2.3
France	54,003	2.4
Italy	30,635	1.7
Spain	14,415	1.2
Canada	14,958	1.2
Brazil	16,206	1.5
Russia	70,000	4.11**
India	22,428	2.5
Korea, S.	24,645	2.8
Australia	17,208	2.4
Mexico	3,229	0.4

*Defence spending includes PPP estimates and extra budgetary expenditure. GDP figure refers to official budget only converted at official rates.
**PPP estimate.
Source: International Institute for Strategic Studies, The Military Balance 2008[18]

shining record of success for the Pentagon: the Korean War ended in a stalemate; Vietnam was a defeat; Iraq was overwhelmed in 1991 by a very broad coalition fighting a greatly inferior enemy that made the mistake of trying to wage the kind of conventional land war for which the Pentagon had been preparing since 1950; the Iraqi resistance has not repeated Saddam Hussein's error since the invasion of March 2003. Washington's unequalled naval and air capabilities remain its preferred forms of power projection. Evidently, as table 5.1 shows, the US today enjoys unprecedented military pre-eminence, but the Iraq War underlines the limits to which even this supremacy is subject.

There are, however, important differences between the British and American hegemonies:

• In the first place, as we saw in §§4.2 and 4.3, they were based on different economic structures – in the British case, a transnational, decentralized network of relatively small firms; in the American, a continental economy allowing bureaucratically managed large corporations to realize the economies of scale available to mass production. The latter structure is still important today: despite the intensification of international competition and the relative decline of America's share of global manufacturing output, US-based transnational corporations and banks enjoy the advantage of their vast home market. This strength in depth may help to explain the highly competitive position American firms retain in hi-tech industries and in services.

- Secondly, Britain and the US have had very different relationships to the other advanced capitalist states. Its emergence as the first industrial capitalism at the end of the eighteenth century allowed Britain to build up an advantage as a low-cost producer that (reinforced by the exercise of military power in the conquest of India and the opening up of China) allowed it to overwhelm the competition of artisanal industries; its hegemony after 1815 involved it dealing mainly with *ancien régime* monarchies still resting on a largely pre-capitalist economic base. It was the accelerating spread of capitalist industrialization across the Channel and the Atlantic in the second half of the nineteenth century that inaugurated the process of British decline, as it confronted the competition of manufacturing industries using the same (or more advanced) productive techniques and organizational forms as its own.[19] The US, by contrast, was the most important of these rivals, and has consequently always had to operate in an environment constituted by other advanced capitalist states whose industries have come to present an increasing competitive challenge. Consequently, managing the advanced capitalist world as a whole has been a key priority of the American hegemony.

- This helps to explain another distinctive feature of US hegemony, namely the specific role played in it by international institutions. The creation of the United Nations was very much an American project, reflecting Roosevelt's plans for an American-led global condominium of the 'Four Policemen' (the US, USSR, Britain and China), as was the establishment of the Bretton Woods institutions.[20] These, like the subsequent proliferation of other institutions – NATO, regional groupings such as the EU and the Asia-Pacific Economic Cooperation Forum (APEC) of which the US claims either patronage or membership, the G7, IMF, World Bank and the World Trade Organization – serve the common function of helping Washington to brigade together the leading capitalist states under its leadership. This doesn't mean that these institutions are simply instruments of American domination; their successful operation depends in part on their effectiveness in providing contexts in which conflicts can be articulated and compromises reached. Nevertheless, Barry Buzan is entirely right when he writes: 'The US is a superpower not just because of its material capability, but because of its institutionalized domination over the EU and Japan. If the US lost its institutional positions in Europe and East Asia, its material capability alone would not sustain its superpower status.'[21] The late nineteenth century did see a growth in international institutions playing a regulatory role in an increasingly economically integrated world, but these were marginal from the point of view of the British hegemony. The project of Imperial Federation promoted in the early twentieth century, in part by Unionists such as Leo Amery seeking to strengthen Britain against its challengers, foundered on the increasing divergences of interests between the metropolis and its settler colonies (which won effective political independence under the Statute of Westminster 1931), and in any case was directed against the other advanced capitalist states rather than intended as a means of integrating them as collaborators in the British hegemony.

- The final difference is, at least on the face of it, more in Britain's favour. British capital financed the global expansion of capitalism during the nineteenth century that gathered strength in the very period between 1870 and 1914 when Britain began to face serious competition (§4.2). The US began to take on the role of world creditor during and after the First World War, and American official aid and private overseas investment helped to fuel the economic recovery after 1945. Since the 1980s, however, the position has been reversed; the norm is now that the US runs a large balance of payments deficit with the rest of the world, closely associated with a large budget deficit, which are funded by a substantial inflow of foreign capital. Is this state of affairs, which is facilitated by the international financial system critically analysed by Wade and Gowan, a sign of American strength or a symptom of decline? Addressing this question requires that we look more closely at the global political economy.

5.2   Global capitalism at the Pillars of Hercules?

Discussing the tendency of the rate of profit to fall, and its countertendencies, Gramsci asks: 'When can one imagine the contradiction reaching its Gordian knot, a normally insoluble pass requiring the intervention of Alexander with his sword? When the whole world economy has become capitalist and reached a certain level of development, i.e., when the "mobile frontier" of the capitalist economic world has reached its pillars of Hercules.'[22] The idea that capitalism has indeed reached its Pillars of Hercules is commonplace today, for example, in the much more optimistic form of Thomas Friedman's claim that globalization 'is flattening and shrinking the world', and 'hence is going to be more and more driven not only by individuals but also by a much more diverse – non-Western, non-white – group of individuals. Individuals from every corner of the flat world are being empowered.'[23] The fact that a serious newspaper like the *Financial Times* should award such boosterism its prize for the Business Book of 2005 is explicable only by the euphoria surrounding the 'emergent markets' – and especially the BRICs (Brazil, Russia, India and China) – during the credit bubble of the mid-2000s.

Understanding the real contours of the world economy today is important if we are to gain an accurate measure of the future evolution of imperialism. Mainstream International Relations theory has been grappling with the problem of the shape of geopolitics since the end of the Cold War. Structural realists were quick to predict that the apparently unipolar form the state system assumed, after the collapse of the Soviet Union, would merely be a transitional phase as US predominance provoked the formation of a coalition seeking to balance against it. As Kenneth Waltz wrote in 1993, 'the response of other countries to one among them seeking or gaining preponderance is to try to balance against it. Hegemony leads to balance . . . This is now happening, but haltingly so'.[24] Confronted with the failure of such a coalition to emerge, he argues that his prediction was correct, but the timing of its fulfilment is impossible to determine: 'Realist theory predicts that balances disrupted will one day be restored. A limitation of the theory, a limitation common to social science theories, is that it cannot say when.'[25] Remaining faithful to structural realist premises, William Wolforth claims that the post-1991 unipolarity represents a stable resting point, rather than a passing moment, because US capabilities, both hard and soft, are so much greater than that of any of the other powers, and because the geopolitical fragmentation of Europe and East Asia makes it difficult for any other state to achieve the political centralization and concentration of resources required to challenge American hegemony.[26]

Economic relations figure in such explanations only insofar as they affect the material capabilities, and hence relative power of states. By contrast, liberal internationalists argue that the development of the modern capitalist world economy has made international trade a positive-sum game that gives states whose domestic sociopolitical structures are themselves liberal and capitalist an incentive to cooperate, and to institutionalize this cooperation, thereby greatly reducing the probability of war among them. As Andrew Moravcsik puts it in a sophisticated restatement of liberal International Relations theory, 'global economic development, over the past five hundred years has been closely related to greater per capita wealth, democratization, education systems that reinforce new collective identities, and greater incentives for trans-border economic transactions. Realist theory accords these changes no theoretical importance.'[27] There is an overlap here between liberal internationalism and classical Marxism, which also does not regard the capitalist world economy as a zero-sum game: the dynamic development of the productive forces under capitalism can, under appropriate conditions, raise both profits and real wages. These conditions obtained for much of the Long Boom of the 1950s and 1960s in the advanced economies. Moreover, it is an implication of the conception of capitalist world hegemony with which I have been working that the hegemon supplies public goods (for example, a stable international monetary system) that give other states an incentive to comply and cooperate. But the convergence between Marxism and liberalism is only very partial. Marxist political economy conceptualizes capitalism as an inherently contradictory and unstable process, constituted by the exploitation of wage-labour, liable to regular, destructive crises, and generating systemically uneven development. Any honest appraisal of the contemporary world economy would have to concede that it offers much to support this perspective on capitalism.

5.2.1   Entrenched uneven development

Pace Thomas Friedman, the world is not becoming flat. Table 5.2 shows the patterns of economic exclusion that developed after 1945 have persisted since the end of the end of the Cold War (see also §4.3): the average share of the developed countries in global flows of foreign direct investment (FDI) between 1992 and 2006 was 67.34 per cent. Of course, like all figures, these should be approached with care. FDI covers both greenfield investments in new productive facilities abroad and cross-border mergers and acquisitions. Fluctuations in the latter help to explain the gyrations in FDI flows into the US as the dotcom bubble reached its climax in the late 1990s and then

Table 5.2 Foreign direct investment inflows, 1992–2006 (billions of dollars)

Region/country	1992–7 (annual average)	1998	1999	2000	2001	2002	2003	2004	2005	2006
Developed countries	180.8	472.5	828.4	1,108.0	571.5	489.9	366.6	418.9	590.3	857.5
Western Europe	100.8	263.0	500.0	697.4	368.8	380.2	310.2	209.2	494.9	566.4
UK	19.5	74.3	88	118.8	52.6	27.8	14.5	56	193.7	139.5
Japan	1.2	3.2	12.7	8.3	6.2	9.2	6.3	7.8	2.8	–6.5
United States	60.3	174.4	283.4	314.0	159.5	62.9	29.8	135.8	101	175.4
Developing economies	118.6	194.4	231.9	252.5	157.6	157.6	172.0	283	314.3	379
South, East and South-East Asia*	69.6	92.1	109.1	142.7	102.2	86.3	96.9	149.2	167.2	199.5
China	32.8	45.5	40.3	40.7	46.9	52.7	53.5	60.6	72.4	69.5
India	1.7	2.6	2.2	2.3	3.4	3.4	4.3	5.8	6.7	16.9
Central and Eastern Europe**	11.5	24.3	26.5	27.5	26.4	31.2	21.0			
World	310.9	690.9	1,086.8	1,388.0	817.6	678.8	559.8	742.1	945.8	1305.9
Developed Countries as % of World	58.15	68.39	76.22	79.83	69.90	72.17	65.51	56.4	62.4	65.66

*Excluding Japan: FDI inflows to South Asia varied between $2.5 billion and $6.5 billion before rising sharply to $9.9 billion in 2005 and $22.3 billion in 2006.

**Now incorporated in figures for Western Europe (relabelled 'Europe')

Source: UNCTAD, *World Investment Report 2004, 2007:* ⟨www.unctad.org⟩

collapsed. But nevertheless the figures are indicative of the judgements of relative profitability made by those controlling internationally mobile capital: these continue massively to favour the advanced economies. China is of course the most important exception to this pattern, but here again the figures need to be treated with caution. As Alan Rugman points out, '[a] large percentage of foreign investment into China (in 2002 approximately 36 per cent) originates in Hong Kong, much of which is believed to be capital that was originally sent from China itself to avoid various government restrictions. Hong Kong and China together account for more than one third of the total inward stock of FDI held by developing countries.'[28] This is tribute to the vitality of Chinese capitalism, but it underlines the extent to which the global flows of capital favour the rich; in this, as in so many other respects, unto everyone that hath shall be given, and he shall have abundance.

The best explanation for this pattern is provided by the theoretical and empirical research that I cited in §2.2. Contrary to the neo-classical orthodoxy, there are rising returns to scale. In other words, improved profitability depends on large-scale investments in technological innovation that raises productivity. Where this strategy works, the scale of production is likely to continue growing. Supply firms will cluster around successful large enterprises. The result will be also large concentrations of workers, at least some of whom will be well paid because of their productivity-enhancing skills. Because these workers are also consumers, the resulting market for consumption goods and services will attract further investment in production, retailing, infrastructure and so on, further increasing employment and widening local markets. The implication is that in economically successful regions, success breeds success, tending to concentrate investment, production and consumption in certain areas. This doesn't mean that once successful, regions may not fail, a fact highlighted by the decline of the birthplace of the Industrial Revolution, the north of England. And new regions emerge – most notably, the Pearl and Yangtze River deltas in southeastern China. But these changes are more likely to lead to further unevenness than to smooth out economic differences.[29]

One key reason why the world isn't becoming flat is that, in part because of the advantages listed in the previous paragraph, labour productivity tends to be much higher in the advanced economies. The *Financial Times* reported in October 2006:

> Managers should take care not to be seduced into investing in emerging economies because their competitive advantage from low wages is

often exaggerated, says a report due out today by the Conference Board, the US business group.

When wages in China, India, Mexico, central and eastern Europe are adjusted for employees' low productivity, the cost advantage of locating there shrinks, sometimes dramatically . . . Mexico, for example, has average manufacturing wages almost 10 times lower than the US. However, an average Mexican worker produces 10 times less than a US manufacturing employee and wages have been rising, so unit labour costs are almost identical. China and India still maintain much lower unit labour costs because average manufacturing wages are even lower than productivity levels relative to the US. Chinese wages are just under 3 per cent of US levels, while the productivity of the country's manufacturing workers is 14 per cent of their US equivalents.[30]

Productivity differentials help to explain why Germany re-emerged in the mid-2000s as the world's largest exporter of manufactured goods, despite the high wage-costs constantly bewailed by employers and other proponents of neoliberal 'reforms'. The highly uneven nature of contemporary capitalist development casts light on the character of the transnational production networks that provide much of the organizational infrastructure of the world economy. Kees van der Pijl's research into the distribution of interlocking director-ships of major corporations identifies the crystallization in the course of the 1990s of two transnational corporate networks, one centred on the US, the other in continental Europe, with British and Scandi-navian companies spread across both.[31] On the basis of a study of multinational enterprises (MNEs), Rugman argues that much of what is called globalization is in fact regionalization:

writers on globalization often make three mistakes:

1 They often confuse international sales with globalization. In fact most of the sales of the world's largest MNEs are *within* their home regions.
2 They often argue that globalization is driven by US MNEs. In fact, there as many European as US MNEs and there are also many large Asian MNEs. Of the fifty largest MNEs in manufacturing, twenty five have their home region in North America, fifteen in Europe, and ten in the Asia-Pacific. In other words, there is a 'triad' of MNEs from North America, Europe, and Asia. No single region of the triad is dominant.
3 There is no evidence of commonality, that is, in the manufacturing sector there is no spread of production on a uniform, global basis. Rather, each set of triad-based MNEs develops and expands inter-national production, mainly within their home region of the triad.

202

Extremely few MNEs operate globally; nearly all are regionally based.[32]

Rugman distinguishes four kinds of MNEs (his figures date from 2001):

(i) Home-regional: over 50 per cent of sales in the corporation's home region: e.g. General Motors, NEC, Volkswagen, Ford, Total Fina Elf, Siemens, Philip Morris, Hitachi;

(ii) Bi-regional: at least 20 percent sales in two regions of the triad and more than 50 per cent of total sales made outside the home region: e.g. Toyota, BP, Nissan, Unilever, Motorola, Glaxo-SmithKline, Bayer, Ericsson;

(iii) Host-regional: bi-regional MNEs with more than 50 per cent sales in one region other than home region: e.g. Honda, DaimlerChrysler, AstraZeneca;

(iv) Global: MNEs with at least 20 per cent of sales in each of the triad regions but less than 50 per cent in any one region. There are nine of these: IBM, Sony, Philips, Nokia, Intel, Canon, Coca-Cola, Flextronics, Christian Dior. 'Seven of the nine . . . are in computer and electrical equipment. The high value to weight ratio of components and final products in this sector means they incur relatively few transport costs.'[33]

The idea, then, that capital has broken free of its geographical moorings remains a myth. An interesting American study of outsourcing notes that in 2002–4, there were 58 shifts of production sites from the US to China, 55 from Europe to China, and 33 from other Asian countries to China. But 'out of the 255 shifts [to all destinations] out of the US, 48 percent were simultaneous shifts to "near-shore" countries in Latin America (primarily to Mexico) and to China and other "off-shore" countries in Asia'. Moreover, the study 'found several cases where European countries simultaneously shifted production to Eastern Europe and China. This most likely occurred for the same reasons that a US company would shift to Mexico and China: to keep some production cross border but not off-shore, so it still can be quickly, cheaply, and easily accessed through ground transportation.'[34] This underlines the fact that a complex set of variables determines the location of investment – not just wage levels, but skills, labour productivity, proximity to markets and transport costs, which in turn are related to the nature of the product (as we see in the case of IT industries, the ratio of unit value to weight). Despite the controversial and partially reversed scrapping of EU tariffs on Chinese textiles in 2005, some European clothing retailers chose to switch production from China to sites closer to their home markets, in Turkey, Eastern Europe and India, in order to be able to respond quickly to changes in fashion.[35]

What has happened in the past few decades is that each of the three nodal points of the triad have spread somewhat – across the US border into Mexico; from the old Western core region of the EU into Central and Eastern Europe, Turkey and parts of the Maghreb; and, most importantly, from Japan into the rest of East Asia and, above all, China. This reconfiguration of the world economy has important implications for the distribution of power globally, as I discuss below. But it does *not* represent a break with the pattern of what Michael Mann calls 'ostracizing imperialism'. The commodities boom that developed in the mid-years of the present decade, thanks to rapid Asian growth and US economic recovery, led to a revival of investors' interest in sub-Saharan Africa, particularly in areas producing oil and strategic raw materials; the profound poverty and the political disarray of the region has made possible extraordinarily predatory practices.[36] But, however reminiscent of the nastiest forms of nineteenth-century imperialism this may be – particularly the looting of the Democratic Republic of the Congo, the site of King Leopold II of Belgium's notorious 'Congo Free State', the fact remains that this isn't the main locus of global capitalism. It is true that portfolio investment in corporate equity and bonds, as opposed to FDI, has in recent years been flooding into so-called 'emerging markets', and indeed initially provided, after the onset of the global credit squeeze in August 2007, one of the few forms of consolation for panicky investors But this development has to be kept in context. In the first place, it largely reflected a speculative movement comparable to the emerging markets boom of the early 1990s, which was punctured by the Mexican crisis of 1994–5 and the East Asian and Russian crashes of 1997–8. True to form, the inflows started to go into reverse when the financial markets crashed in autumn 2008. Secondly, by historical standards, they were still relatively small: according to Richard Cookson of HSBC, 'the average nineteenth century investor in Britain was likely to have had 25 percent of his money in emerging markets. By comparison, US institutional investors in recent years have had barely 10 percent invested in foreign securities, with a fraction of that devoted to emerging markets.' The total value of emerging market debt traded in London re-attained its 1905 level of 12 per cent of global GDP only in 2005.[37]

The most important implication of this jagged geographical distribution of economic power is the deep horizontal cut it makes in humankind. As table 3.1 indicates, the differences in per capita income between the rich core of global capitalism and the rest of the world remain enormous, and, from the long historical perspective, unprecedented. This is not to diminish the significance of the rapid economic growth experienced by China and, more recently, by India in taking hundreds of millions out of extreme poverty. Measuring poverty and inequality is an enormously complex and controversial matter. But, even on the World Bank's highly disputed estimates, 2.74 billion people lived on less than two US dollars a day in 2001, 44 per cent of the world's population.[38] Because uneven development is pervasive in contemporary capitalism, massive global economic poverty and inequality will persist. Moreover, the income differences between states fail to capture the enormous inequalities *within* societies. As is well known, the neoliberal era has seen a major redistribution of wealth and income to the rich in countries such as the US and Britain. The top one per cent of American households received on average 16.9 per cent of total household income between 1917 and 1940. Their share dropped to 8.4 per cent in 1973, but, after a generation of neoliberalism, soared to reach 19.6 per cent in 2001. Meanwhile, between the mid-1970s and 2000, the bottom 90 percent of households saw their share of total household income fall by 12 per cent.[39] In Britain inequality in incomes rose sharply during the Thatcher government, and has slightly exceeded this historically high level under New Labour.[40] The same pattern of chronic and growing inequality is to be found in those parts of the South that have grown fastest in the past generation. According to China's National Development and Reform Commission, the poorest 20 per cent of China's urban residents earn 3 per cent of urban income. The richest 10 per cent of urban dwellers control 45 per cent of urban assets, the poorest 10 per cent only 1.4 per cent.[41]

5.2.2 A persisting crisis of profitability

A second major feature of the contemporary global political economy is the protracted period of slow growth and low profitability that first gripped advanced capitalism in the late 1960s and early 1970s. The fact that, as table 5.3 shows, the rate of profit in the US remains in the doldrums compared to the levels it reached during the Long Boom of the 1950s and 1960s is all the more remarkable, given that that between 2000 and 2005 productivity in the business sector rose by 17 per cent, while the median real hourly wage increased only by 3 per cent, causing labour's share of national income to drop to 56.8

per cent in 2005 as profits rose to a near-record 13.6 per cent of GDP in the second quarter of 2006.[42] In other words, what in Marxist terms amounts to a substantial increase in relative surplus-value did not lead to a significant rise in the overall rate of profit. This chronic problem of profitability – which the research of Robert Brenner and other Marxist scholars shows is not confined to the US, but is general to advanced capitalism – suggests that successive economic crises have failed to eliminate the overhang of relatively inefficient capitals whose removal would be required to restore the return on investment to its levels of the 1950s and 1960s. So Preobrazhensky's argument that the more concentrated and centralized capitalism becomes, the greater the obstacles to the destruction of unprofitable capital become, seems still to have some leverage (§1.4) Indeed, from the late 1990s onwards, the US Federal Reserve Board sought to avoid a destabiliz-ing clearout of surplus capital by engaging in what Brenner calls 'asset price Keynesianism' – i.e., tolerating the development of speculative bubbles, first in stocks and shares in the late 1990s and then, after the double blow in 2000–1 of the collapse of the dotcom boom and 9/11, in real estate, that encouraged households whose net worth had risen with the prices of these assets to borrow and spend more. The global credit squeeze that began in the second half of 2007 represents the deflation of the latest of these bubbles; according to the IMF, it 'has developed into the largest financial shock since the Great Depres-sion, inflicting heavy damage on markets and institutions at the core of the financial system'.[43] The aggravation of this crisis in the financial crash following the collapse of Lehman Brothers on 15 September 2008 contributed to the rapid development of a global slump affect-ing all the major regions of the world economy.

Table 5.3 US non-financial corporate net profit rate by business cycle, 1948–2007

1948–1959	0.1327
1959–1969	0.1459
1969–1973	0.1137
1969–1979	0.1048
1979–1990	0.0979
1990–2000	0.1081
2000–2007	0.0951

Source: R. Brenner, Paper for *Historical Materialism* Conference, 11 November 2007, corrected and updated

This prolonged crisis of profitability provided the background against which neoliberalism replaced Keynesianism as the dominant economic policy regime. Critically, the objective of fiscal and monetary policy shifted from maintaining full employment to mimicking the kind of external discipline on economies that in the era of classical imperialism was provided by the gold standard.[44] David Harvey has described the installation of neoliberalism as a 'restoration of class power', in reaction to the workers' militancy and sociopolitical rebellions of the late 1960s and early 1970s.[45] But, though the role of the state in the advanced capitalist economies has in various respects been restructured, there has not been a dramatic retrenchment in the substantial share of economic activity that is taken by public expenditure.[46] More importantly, as the global recession precipitated by the financial upheavals of 2007–8 shows, neoliberalism has not succeeded in overcoming the contradictions that caused the collapse of the Long Boom and the protracted period of crises that have followed. Neoliberalism gave capitalists and state managers alike the ideological cohesion and self-confidence to force back organized labour; it legitimized the deregulation and global integration of financial markets; the more general drive to open up markets has provided capitals, whether industrial, commercial or financial, with the means to seek out every nook and cranny where there's a profit to be made; early in the neoliberal era Fredric Jameson wrote of 'a new and historically original penetration and colonization of Nature and the Unconscious'.[47] But neoliberalism hasn't succeeded in driving profitability back to the levels of the Long Boom. Indeed, its longer-term viability has been thrown into question by the massive state-mounted rescues of the banking system in response to the credit squeeze. This reality has important geopolitical implications. A global economy characterized, against the background of great instability, by the relatively slow growth of the advanced economies, and by (partly in consequence) intense international competition, is liable to be harder to manage cooperatively than one where a sustained and generalized expansion improves the situation of all the players. The difficulty is exacerbated if, as is true at present, significant changes in relative economic power are also taking place.

5.2.3   A redistribution of global economic power

A world that isn't economically flat isn't necessarily one where the bumps stay the same. Recall that Lenin's critique of ultra-imperialism rested not simply on uneven development, but on the fact that the

Table 5.4   Leading economies GDP, 1980–2007 (ranked by GDP in current prices 2007)

	1980			1992		
	GDP current prices $bn	GDP PPP $bn	% world GDP PPP	GDP current prices $bn	GDP PPP $bn	% world GDP PPP
US	2789.53	2789.53	22.467	6337.75	6337.75	22.807
Japan	1067.08	1039.39	8.372	3797.03	2552.04	9.184
Germany	826.142	752.905	6.11	2066.73	1635.38	5.885
China	307.599	249.113	2.006	483.047	1201.53	4.324
UK	537.776	486.488	3.918	1085.4	997.72	3.59
France	691.208	536.55	4.321	1374.29	1113.5	4.007
Italy	460.629	507.453	4.091	1271.91	1052.15	3.79
Spain	224.495	272.451	2.194	613.016	603.072	2.17
Canada	268.927	272.117	2.192	579.778	566.909	2.04
Brazil	162.615	443.959	3.576	426.519	831.599	2.992
Russia	N/A	N/A	N/A	85.572	1168.86	4.206
India	176.624	271.217	2.192	280.933	814.18	2.92
Korea, S.	64	94.806	0.764	329.928	405.251	1.458
Australia	160.643	144.439	1.162	313.419	319.63	1.149
Mexico	205.661	304.522	2.452	363.661	632.269	2.274

Source: International Monetary Fund, *World Economic Outlook Database*: ⟨www imf.org⟩

distribution of unevenness across the globe, and hence the relative power of states, is constantly changing as a result of the dynamic growth of capitalism (§1.5). This argument remains as valid as it was when Lenin wrote it. The shifting distribution of global economic power is, as I have already noted, the subject of much boosterism. A greater difficulty, however, which bedevils discussion of the size of contemporary economies, and of whether globalization is increasing or reducing global poverty and inequality, is how to measure national income. Using market exchange rates is liable to distortion because of inflation and currency fluctuations: thus the dollar's fall in early 2008 caused the economy of the euro-zone to become bigger, according to market exchange rates, than that of the US. This is one reason

2000			2007			
GDP current prices $bn	GDP PPP $bn	% world GDP PPP	GDP current prices $bn	GDP PPP $bn	% world GDP PPP	% world GDP current prices
9816.98	9816.98	23.603	13843.83	13843.83	21.363	25.50
4668.79	3205.51	7.707	4383.76	4289.81	6.607	8.80
1905.8	2160.69	5.195	3322.15	2809.69	4.344	6.12
1198.48	3006.52	7.229	3250.83	6991.04	10.827	5.99
1453.84	1485.92	3.573	2772.57	2137.42	3.303	5.10
1333.17	1531.09	3.681	2560.26	2046.9	3.166	4.71
1100.56	1393.51	3.353	2104.67	1786.43	2.762	3.88
582.377	897.721	2.158	1438.96	1351.61	2.088	2.65
725.158	886.025	2.13	1432.14	1265.84	1.956	2.64
644.283	1230.93	2.959	1313.59	1835.64	2.811	2.42
259.702	1120.53	2.694	1289.58	2087.82	3.176	2.37
461.914	1519.54	3.667	1098.95	2988.87	4.58	2.02
511.961	730.853	1.757	957.053	1200.88	1.853	1.76
389.983	514.853	1.237	908.826	760.812	1.181	1.67
580.791	953.462	2.291	893.365	1346.01	2.074	1.64

why the alternative measure of Purchasing Power Parity (PPP) is much favoured by international institutions, such as the IMF and the World Bank, and by historians of the world economy, such as Angus Maddison. The merit of PPP is that it adjusts exchange rates to take into account differences in national purchasing power, so that a PPP dollar would buy the same amount of goods and services anywhere in the world; because living costs are lower in the South, the effect is generally to increase the size of developing economies and to reduce that of advanced economies. One problem with this is that firms must buy hi-tech goods and state weapon-systems, not with ideal PPP dollars, but with real dollars fluctuating against other currencies day by day. Robert Wade offers a judicious summing up:

In principle, PPP adjustment is better for questions about relative domestic purchasing power or, more generally, access to material welfare.

But these are not the only questions for which we may be interested in income and its distribution. We may *also* be interested in relative income as a proxy for the relative purchasing power of residents of different countries over goods and services produced in *other* countries. If we are interested in any of the questions about the impacts of one state, economy or region on others . . . we should use FX [foreign exchange]. FX incomes are a better proxy for power and influence.[48]

Accordingly, in table 5.4, I have included both PPP and market exchange rate measures of national income (and, for 2007, shares of global GDP on both these measures). The figures serve to deflate some of the boosterism about the BRICs: even on the more favourable PPP measure, Brazil's and Russia's shares of world gross domestic product have fallen since the early 1990s. Nevertheless, five out of the fifteen biggest economies in the world in 2007 were in the global South. And the ascension of China as a major producer and exporter of manufacturing goods is undeniable. Arrighi sees in China's rise more than the emergence of a potential hegemon. He hopes for a reorientation of the Chinese Communist Party (CCP) that 'succeeds in reviving and consolidating China's traditions of self-centred market-based development, accumulation *without* dispossession, mobilization of human rather than non-human resources, and government through mass participation in shaping policies'.[49] It is hard to find more than wishful thinking in this. China's success in sustaining an average annual growth rate of 8–10 per cent for thirty years is undeniably a world-historic development. But in hard analytical terms it represents a particularly concentrated and harsh version of what Marx called the primitive accumulation of capital in which hundreds of millions of people, along with productive resources previously in the public domain, have been subordinated to the logic of global competition.[50]

The relevant question here is what implications China's rapid emergence as a major centre of world capitalism are likely to have for contemporary imperialism. Arriving at a clear answer is hard, in part because of the complexity of the relationship between China and the hegemonic power, the US. Economically, the two states are interdependent. The US runs a large current account deficit, equivalent to around 5 or 6 per cent of national income in the mid-2000s, while China, along with the other East Asian export economies, is in surplus. These payment imbalances reflect the massive flow of manufactured goods across the Pacific, from East Asia to the US. The sums add up, thanks to the lending back to the US of some of the dollars accumulated by the East Asian economies (China's foreign exchange reserves amounted to $1.81 *trillion* at the end of June 2008), thereby allowing American consumers to continue buying East Asian goods.[51] For some economists, this set-up – described by Fareed Zakaria as 'globalization's equivalent of the nuclear age's Mutual Assured Destruction' because its collapse would severely damage both the US and China – represents a revived version of the Bretton Woods system: the East Asian states reacted to the crisis of 1997–8 by avoiding foreign debt, and instead fixed their currencies against the dollar at rates that keep their exports internationally competitive, imposed restrictions on the export of capital and built up large foreign exchange reserves. On this analysis, the arrangement is a mutually beneficial and hence stable one, in which the East Asian economies can continue export-led growth so long as they underwrite American consumption.[52]

It is certainly true that the US–China circuit played a crucial role in powering the world economy during the boom of the mid-2000s. Some industrial economies – Japan, Germany, South Korea – reoriented themselves towards supplying plant and equipment and semi-finished goods for the Chinese assembly line; thus China has replaced the US as the largest recipient of Japanese exports, though the final destination of many of these goods is still the US, only now after final assembly in China. At the same time, raw material producers in Africa and Latin America discovered a voracious new consumer of and investor in their commodities. But how *stable* this circuit is is another matter. For one thing, the two ends of the circuit are hardly cases of balanced growth. At the US end, the 2000–1 recession precipitated by the dotcom boom was overcome largely thanks to the Fed's policy of slashing interest rates to the bone and flooding the US and world economy with cheap credit. The result wasn't simply the new bubble in the housing market, but the development of a classic speculative credit boom, complete with all sorts of scams and dodgy financial 'innovations' (collateralized debt obligations, structured investment vehicles and the like) and a stream of corporate takeovers by private equity firms using cheap credit whose main effect was, when the boom inevitably collapsed, to spread bad debts throughout the financial system, inducing a paralysis that precipitated a major global recession. At the Chinese end, a very rapid rate of accumulation has been sustained by the willingness of the banks, still controlled by the state, to make cheap loans to enterprises. This policy, combined with the banks' reluctance to drive firms into bankruptcy, has provided Chinese capitalists, usually closely allied with local officials and operating in conditions of intense competition, with incentives to continue to invest even when profit margins are declining, and to export, thereby building up increasingly powerful inflationary pressures. China's hybrid state and private capitalism has so far avoided a major economic crunch since slow growth and rising prices helped to precipitate the Tiananmen protests in 1989, but this doesn't mean the balancing act can continue forever, as the largely ineffectual warnings by the CCP leadership about the economy and rising inequality show it knows. Ho-fung Hung argues:

> The trends of overinvestment and underconsumption, when combined together, make China increasingly susceptible to a national overaccumulation crisis. With China's weight as the major territory for global surplus capital to park and realize their profits and as the major export market for raw materials producers as well as capital goods manufacturers, a national overaccumulation crisis in China, if it occurs, will surely generate widespread global repercussions.[53]

But there are more structural questions about the sustainability of Bretton Woods Mark II. The system depends on a relatively strong dollar, which, as we saw in §5.1 above, Robert Wade argues is one of the perquisites of effective hegemony. But he goes on to argue:

> In the real world the United States's ability to run large current-account deficits and maintain a large stock of dollar financial assets in foreign hands is a double-edged sword. It does give the United States an almost free lunch by allowing it to attract the necessary financing even while paying low interest rates. However, this 'hegemonic debtor's gain' can turn into a 'normal debtor's curse' if – as at present – the US domestic and external debt rises to the point where the United States has to plead with other countries to revalue their currencies and to go on holding dollar assets in the face of higher returns elsewhere and opportunities to diversify into an alternative international currency, such as the euro. A loss of foreign cooperation might lead to sudden falls in the value of the dollar, and even though this would not carry the normal debtor's curse of raising the burden of debt servicing it could still inflict costs on the U.S. economy. These costs could be serious, given that foreign official holdings of Treasury securities now [2003] amount to about one-third of the total Treasury-issued debt.[54]

In fact, certainly from an economic point of view, a strong dollar is even more double-edged than Wade suggests. The negative impact on the competitiveness of US manufacturing industry of the strong dollar that was a consequence of the monetary discipline imposed by the Fed under Paul Volcker in October 1979 forced a reversal of these policies in the mid-1980s. Though the Clinton administration returned to a strong-dollar policy a decade later, it was effectively abandoned during the younger Bush's first term.[55] But the danger of a major devaluation of the dollar is that, as in the 1970s, it could undermine US hegemony and destabilize the world economy. The onset of the global credit crisis in 2007–8 initially accelerated the dollar's decline (by about 25 per cent between early 2002 and 2008).[56] In a world economy where the fiat moneys of the leading states float freely, the beneficiary of a protracted fall in the dollar would be the euro. David McNally has argued that the emergence of the euro as a major reserve currency (with, in 2008, 27 per cent of total official reserves compared to the dollar's 63 per cent) represents a project on the part of the leading states in the euro-zone to develop a currency with the properties of world money and to liberate themselves from US seigniorage – that is, from the economic advantages the US gains from controlling the international reserve currency, in particular the ability to finance its balance of payments deficit simply by issuing dollars.[57] On one projection, the euro could overtake the dollar as early as 2015.[58] The complex evolution of the global economic crisis precipitated by the credit crunch caused the dollar's exchange rate to fluctuate dramatically. By September 2008, it had risen 10 per cent after dropping 7 percentage points in the early part of the year, and the immediate impact of that month's financial crash was to make it a haven of safety for frightened investors.[59] Such gyrations are likely to continue. Sufficient financial and economic instability could produce a sudden and chaotic flip in the international monetary system from one state to another. The world economy may be entering a period of prolonged currency instability comparable to that accompanying the replacement of the pound by the dollar as the leading reserve currency between the 1920s and the 1950s.

5.2.4   Continuing geopolitical competition

What are the likely consequences of continuing economic instability and relative US decline for the state system? Barry Buzan offers a useful framework for conceptualizing that system. He proposes 'a three-tiered scheme: *superpowers* and *great powers* at the system level, and *regional powers* at the regional level'. A superpower must posses 'broad-spectrum capabilities right across the whole of the international system', while 'what distinguishes great powers from merely regional ones is that they are responded to by others on the basis of system-level calculations as well as regional ones, about the present and near future distribution of power'. The post-Cold War 'global power structure' has been what Buzan calls '1 + 4' – the US as the sole superpower and China, the European Union, Japan and Russia as great powers. Finally, as Buzan notes, 'the US has adopted a *swing-power* strategy in which it positions itself as a member of three macro-regions (Asia-Pacific, North Atlantic, Western Hemisphere) as a way of legitimizing its actual presence as an outside power in Europe, East Asia and Latin America'.[60] Buzan's analysis invites us to look pair-wise as the relationship of the US with each of the great powers.

Thanks to its expansion into Eastern and Central Europe, the EU boasts a larger GDP than that of the US. But, as we saw in §5.1 above, the historic achievement of the Clinton administration was to preserve the position of the US as the hegemonic power in Europe, in particular by linking the enlargement of the EU to that of NATO as an integrated process of extending the 'Euro-Atlantic' world deep into Eurasia. This doesn't mean either that there are no conflicts of interest between the US and the leading European states, or that the present situation can be maintained indefinitely. France and Germany opposed the invasion of Iraq and ostentatiously refused to help the Bush administration extricate itself from the subsequent mess. Washington's successful campaign in 2005 to block an EU decision to end the arms embargo it had imposed on China after the Tiananmen massacre of June 1989 was another major moment of trans-Atlantic tension.[61] The disgrace and removal of the leading neoconservative ideologue Paul Wolfowitz from the presidency of the World Bank, in May 2007, was at the insistence of the Grand Coalition government in Germany, which vetoed various compromises.[62] In April 2008 France and Germany blocked the Bush administration's drive to admit Ukraine and Georgia to NATO.

But there are structural reasons for doubting that the EU is likely in the short term to develop into a major 'peer competitor' of the US. Such a change would depend on the EU developing military capabilities to match its economic power. The idea, encouraged by the concept's author, Joseph Nye, that the US should concentrate on the exercise of soft power – ideological and cultural influence – fails to take into account that, to put it in Gramscian terms, hegemony and domination are interdependent.[63] The crisis of legitimacy that the US is generally acknowledged to have experienced thanks to the invasion

of Iraq would have been much less severe had the occupation succeeded. But Europe's development of capabilities comparable to those
of the US in projecting power confronts formidable obstacles. In the
first place, the necessary and very large increases in military expenditure would be extremely hard to secure politically, at a time when
the pursuit of neoliberal 'reforms' has provoked massive social resistance in defence of the welfare state. Secondly, the US has shown
itself to be highly suspicious of even the most modest attempts by the
EU to create its own military capabilities, and could be expected to
react in an extremely hostile manner to any serious steps towards
European security independence. Finally, as Donald Rumsfeld's notorious invocation of 'New Europe' on the eve of the Iraq War indicates, the EU's political structure offers Washington plenty of
opportunities for divide and rule (and not just Washington: over
energy supplies and the Caucasus, Moscow has been able to play
some European states against others). The EU is what Claude Serfati
has admirably called a 'hybrid configuration': though it has developed in some dimensions the functions of a federal state (perhaps
most importantly with respect to international trade), the EU still
takes most of its major decisions through a process of institutionalized interstate bargaining marked by the assertion of national interests that often diverge significantly. Britain has a particularly
important part to play here, since its military capabilities and strategic position in the international financial system would almost certainly make it indispensable to any attempt to transform the EU into
a superpower, but its state managers continue to pursue the strategy
first embraced by Churchill in 1940–1 of seeking to maintain a global
role through close alliance with the US. None of this means that the
EU may not play a more actively imperial role, assuming greater
military responsibilities particularly on its own peripheries and in
sub-Saharan Africa; Herfried Münkler affirms as much, predicting
that 'Europe's future will not be able to do without borrowing from
the imperial model'. But this development is more likely to be in
tandem with than in opposition to the US.[64]

It seems even less probable that Japan will break loose from the
American hegemony any time soon. Taggart Murphy argues that the
current Bretton Woods II system, binding together the US and East
Asia, is in fact just the latest version of a much longer-term strategy,
pursued by Japanese state managers since the Meiji Restoration, of
aligning themselves with the dominant power – Britain till the 1930s;
the US after 1945, particularly since the 1955 party merger that
inaugurated the domination of the Liberal Democratic Party:

The merger was taken to forestall any possibility of leftists coming to power, something that the US had effectively insisted on as a condition for ending the Occupation. But the 1955 system also included the sublimation of all other national goals into single-minded devotion to economic growth and acquiescence in the US-Japan 'alliance'. The aim was to build an industrial superpower under American military protection and within a stable dollar-centred global financial frame-work . . . The US needs Japan today to a far greater degree than Britain ever did. Japan's companies manufacture a range of both high value-added components and finished products on which American techno-logical and military supremacy totally depend. Japan's continued central role in financing the US trade and government deficits and propping up a dollar-centred international order is . . . the key expla-nation for Washington's ability to project and sustain a vast global military establishment without crushing domestic tax burdens. Since the mid '70s, at every crisis point when it has looked as if upheavals in the foreign-exchange market might force the US to live within its means, it has been the Japanese elite that has acted to support the dollar, the Bretton Woods II regime and, by extension, the continua-tion of American hegemony . . . Any alternative would demand a fun-damental reconsideration of the assumptions of the 1955 system, and thus risk fostering another dangerous and debilitating intra-elite strug-gle [such as the inter-war conflicts that sent Japan into its disastrous collision with the US].[65]

But if Tokyo's strategic subordination to the US has provided Japan's state managers and capitalists with the security and financial condi-tions permitting them to sustain an economic model based on export-led accumulation, its maintenance has also been pursued by Washington, and not only for the reasons highlighted by Murphy. Japan has a pivotal role to play in what seems to be the dominant US strategy towards China, namely to encircle it with powers aligned to the United States. The same motivation underlay the Bush admin-istration's decision in March 2006 to abandon the long-standing US policy of opposing India's development of nuclear weapons, and to sign a deal providing New Delhi with assistance in upgrading its nuclear energy programme. According to the *Washington Post*, 'sup-porters of the approach said it was an important part of a White House strategy to accelerate New Delhi's rise as a global power and as a regional counterweight to China. As part of the strategy, the administration is also seeking ways to bolster Japan's posture in the region.'[66] As we saw in §5.1, Russia has been contained through an analogous strategy of encirclement. The confidence of Russian state managers has been boosted by the revenues generated by the energy boom of the present decade and by Putin's recapture of political control over key export industries and more general policy of national self-assertion. Nevertheless, Russia, with a shrinking population and share of global GDP, and deprived of economically and strategically crucial regions such as Ukraine and Azerbaijan, is in no position to mount a global challenge to the US – though, as the August 2008 war with Georgia showed, Moscow is ready to assert its military power ruthlessly to exploit US preoccupation with Iraq and Afghanistan, and to limit Western encroachment on its borders.[67]

Continuing US hegemony over the other regions of advanced capitalism provides considerable support for Serfati's conclusion that 'there is no risk that the inter-capitalist economic rivalries among the countries of the trans-Atlantic zone will develop into military confrontations, as was the case with the inter-imperialist rivalries of the twentieth century that ended up in the world wars'. Serfati identifies three factors making inter-imperialist war improbable: the overwhelming military superiority of the US; the interdependence of the advanced economies; and the political solidarity binding together the leading states of the Atlantic world.[68] One might add also the development of nuclear weapons as, to put it mildly, a further disincentive to going to war as a means of resolving economic or geopolitical disputes. US military power continues to be projected outwards, in the name of the 'international community', beyond the frontiers of advanced capitalism into dangerous border zones. These wars and the protectorates they have produced – Bosnia, Kosovo, Afghanistan and Iraq – represent efforts to manage what Brzezinski calls the 'the Eurasian Balkans' – the vast, unstable, but energy-rich region extending from South-eastern Europe and the Horn of Africa, through the Middle East, into Central Asia, Afghanistan and Pakistan.[69] The 'war on terrorism' (which has survived the administration of the younger Bush), legitimized by the blowback produced by earlier interventions in this region, now provides a framework for further interventions, which will no doubt generate new forms of blowback, in an infernal cycle.

Perry Anderson suggests that the resulting set-up represents a global Concert of Powers comparable to that established in Europe by Metternich and Castlereagh at the end of the Napoleonic Wars:

American primacy imposes a series of *faux frais* on its partners that are unlikely to diminish. But just because there is no automatic coincidence between the particular interests of the US and the general interests of the system, a consciously managed Concert of Powers is

217

required for the adjustment of tensions between them. That adjustment will never be perfect, and the mechanisms for achieving it have yet to be fully formalized: pressure and counter-pressure intertwine within a bargaining process that is unequal but not insubstantial. To date, however, the gaps and rough edges in the system have not seriously threatened the emergent legitimacy of the 'international community' as a symphony of the global capitalist order, even with a somewhat erratic conductor.[70]

This seems much too strong. In the first place, it underestimates the extent of conflict among the leading capitalist states. The combined impact of continuing slow growth in the core of the system and of a shifting global distribution of economic power is likely to create significant centrifugal pressures on the major blocs of capital that, it should never be forgotten, are in competition with each other. Maintaining both the political cohesion of the advanced capitalist world and US hegemony over it is not (as Anderson concedes) an automatic effect of a self-equilibrating system. It requires a continuous creative political effort on the part of the US, and in particular the successful pursuit of divide-and-rule strategies at the western and eastern ends of the Eurasian landmass where the two zones of advanced capitalism outside North America are to be found. Numerous texts by American policy intellectuals bear witness to this reality and to the extent that it preoccupies US state managers. The Bush administration's 2002 *National Security Strategy* contains the following celebrated passages: 'We are attentive to the possible renewal of old patterns of great power competition. Several potential great powers are now in the midst of internal transition – most importantly Russia, India, and China;' 'Our forces will be strong enough to dissuade potential adversaries from pursuing a military build-up in hopes of surpassing, or equalling, the power of the United States.'[71] This is no mere neocon braggadocio but represents the settled view of American policy-makers of all political backgrounds. Zbigniew Brzezinski is a particularly clear example: an outspoken critic of the younger Bush's unilateralism, he is the author of *The Grand Chessboard* (1997), which reads like a handbook of imperial rule, less in its detailed prescriptions than in the general strategic outlook that it represents, with the attention devoted to maintaining US hegemony in Europe and, in the Far East, preventing an alignment between China and Japan from developing.[72]

Secondly, there is of course the case of China, which Serfati acknowledges to be an exception to the general cohesion of the advanced capitalist world. China's economic expansion is likely in the course of the next couple of decades to make it the most powerful state in the most dynamic region of world capitalism. It is outside the US system of alliances; the strategic partnership between Washington and Beijing against Moscow in the final decades of the Cold War is a historical memory now. The CCP leadership has defined national objectives, in particular with respect to the reabsorption of Taiwan into the People's Republic of China, that are a potential source of conflict with the US. Moreover, China's rise is already destabilizing the existing pattern of global relationships. The Wall Street-US Treasury-IMF complex has become increasingly restive about the spread of Chinese investments and loans through the global South, which gives poorer countries access to capital that doesn't require confinement within the neoliberal conditionalities demanded by the World Bank in exchange for its loans. Moreover, Beijing has given Moscow greater elbow room: China and Russia work together in the Shanghai Cooperation Organization, which has shown some success in limiting US expansion in Central Asia, for example, enticing Uzbekistan out of the American sphere of influence (though their interests are far from identical in this region or indeed elsewhere). Some International Relations analysts have detected the development of what they call 'soft balancing' against the US – diplomatic manoeuvring designed to block American initiatives but falling well short of the formation of a balancing coalition; over time, such tactics are likely to depend heavily on Beijing's existence as an alternative centre of gravity to Washington.[73]

None of this means that the Chinese leadership is set on a path of challenging US hegemony. It presides over a country most of whose population remains very poor, despite the economic growth of the past generation: only 3 per cent own a motor vehicle.[74] The build-up of Chinese military capabilities, on which the US Congress now requires the Pentagon to submit an annual report, is no doubt partly to ensure the eventual return of Taiwan to Beijing's rule and partly, and entirely rationally from the CCP's leadership's perspective, as a hedge against American bullying. Nevertheless, quite independently of the intentions of China's state managers, the revival of Chinese economic and military power threatens to destabilize US hegemony. Moreover, as the annual reports indicate, their American counterparts perceive China as a threat. This is entirely in line with traditional US strategic thinking. 'Intentions tend to grow with the capability to carry them out,' Paul Nitze, an architect of American grand strategy at the height of the Cold War, told the Senate

Intelligence Committee in 1980.[75] One of the themes of the Pentagon's last Quadrennial Defense Review in 2006 was 'Shaping the
Choices of Countries at Strategic Crossroads'. The Review notes:
'Of the major and emerging powers, China has the greatest potential
to compete militarily with the United States and field disruptive
military technologies that could over time offset traditional US
military advantages absent US counter strategies.' After expressing
concern at the rapid rate of Chinese military modernization, the
Review continues:

> The United States will work to ensure that all major and emerging
> powers are integrated as constructive actors and stakeholders into the
> international system. It will also seek to ensure that no foreign power
> can dictate the terms of regional or global security. It will attempt to
> dissuade any military competitor from developing disruptive or other
> capabilities that could enable regional hegemony or hostile action
> against the United States or other friendly countries, and it will seek
> to deter aggression or coercion. Should deterrence fail, the United
> States would deny a hostile power its strategic and operational
> objectives.[76]

Once again, US perception of China as a threat to its hegemony does
not imply that a collision is inevitable. As I have already indicated,
American strategy in Asia involves seeking, in particular, to maintain
Japan's strategic subordination and, more generally, developing a
coalition of states capable of containing China. The fragmented and
competitive geopolitical structure of the region works to Washington's advantage. As Buzan notes:

> China's regional position bears some resemblance to that of Germany
> between 1870 and 1945. Although it is a big and relatively powerful
> state within its region, many of its neighbours are formidable powers
> in their own region . . . Given China's lack of soft power resources
> among its neighbours . . . , and the generally weak international society
> in East Asia, China faces the (neo) realist logic that its neighbours
> would balance against it if its material power began to look preponder-
> ant. Such balancing could well mean that China faced serious obstacles
> within its region to any bid for superpower status. Given the historical
> fears it attracts, its lack of leadership legitimacy in the region, and the
> actual and potential military and economic strength of its neighbours,
> China might well expect to remain trapped within its region.[77]

But it is not good enough to argue, as Anderson does, that the
tensions I have been outlining can be contained by the economic

interdependence of the leading capitalist states: 'In such a Concert, interstate relations can be expected to remain below the threshold of antagonism, as defined in the classical theory of contradictions, because of the universal interlocking of financial and commodity markets in a post-nuclear age.'[78] Such arguments have a pedigree, dating back even before Kautsky's theory of ultra-imperialism to Norman Angell's best-seller of 1909, *The Great Illusion*, which argued that global economic integration had rendered war obsolete. The Thirty Years War of 1914–45 shattered such hopes. Britain was Germany's most important export market before 1914, while the City of London benefited massively from the services (loans, insurance, shipping, etc.) that it provided Germany; this did not prevent an epochal conflict developing between the two states.[79] As Japan's industrialization began to mature after 1900, the US became its key trading partner, supplying both advanced industrial goods and raw materials, and taking 35 per cent of Japanese exports during the 1920s; the very intimacy of US–Japanese economic relations proved in the end to be a destabilizing factor, since the Roosevelt administration's imposition of an oil embargo on Japan in July 1941 played an important role in Tokyo's decision to launch a preventive war.[80] More generally, a careful empirical study suggests that greater economic interdependence between states makes them more rather than less prone to engage in militarized disputes with one another.[81] Nor is it persuasive, as Anderson and others do, to cite the prevalence of the neoliberal economic policy regime as a force cementing together the leading powers. In the first place, China and to some extent all the East Asian capitalisms remain something of an anomaly within this regime; their participation in Bretton Woods II implies the rejection of floating exchange rates, in violation of neoliberal nostrums; moreover, as we have seen, China's accumulation path continues to rely on a powerful dose of state capitalism. Secondly, the regime is loose enough to accommodate significantly different strategies; the divergent reactions of the Fed and the European Central Bank to the 2007–8 credit squeeze – one slashing interest rates, the other lowering them only slightly for fear of stoking inflationary expectations – is the latest instance of a much more long-standing pattern, dating back at least to Washington's attempt to persist with Keynesian policies and aggressively to devalue the dollar during the onset of economic crisis in the 1970s, while Bonn stuck to a counter-inflationary strong *Deutschmark* policy.[82] Finally, the fact that states share an economic policy regime doesn't prevent them developing the most serious antagonisms: all the belligerent powers in 1914 pursued the orthodox fiscal and monetary policies demanded by the gold standard; similarly, the generalized shift to state capitalism in response to the Great Depression of the 1930s was a factor making for war rather than preventing it (§4.2).

Of course, there is no reason to assume that history will repeat itself. But any understanding of contemporary imperialism that fails to take into account the tensions and potential fractures among the leading powers is dangerously one-sided. This is particularly so when it comes to assessing the global strategy pursued by the US. Recent discussion has focused, of course, on the policies pursued under Bush *fils* after 9/11, and particularly the Iraq War. As Anderson correctly notes, '[v]irtually all commentary in Europe, not to speak of much in the US itself, now regards the war as a thoroughly irrational aberration, the product of either one-eyed special interests (oil companies, or corporations at large) or unhinged ideological zealots (a neoconservative cabal) in Washington'. He goes on to offer his own version of this kind of diagnosis by endorsing John Mearsheimer's and Stephen Walt's invocation of the influence of the Israel lobby in the US to explain this aberration:

> Historically, however, a circumstantial irrationality – typically, some gratuitous yet fatal decision, like Hitler's declaration of war on the US in 1941 – is nearly always the product of some larger structural irrationality. So it was with Operation Iraqi Freedom. Putting it simply, the reality was – and remains – this. The Middle East is the one part of the world where the US political system, as presently constituted, *cannot* act according to a rational calculus of national interest, because it is inhabited by another, supervening interest. For its entire position in the Arab – and by extension Muslim – world is compromised by its massive, ostentatious support for Israel . . . [thanks to] the grip of the Israeli lobby, drawing strength from the powerful Jewish community in the US, on the American political and media system. Not only does this lobby distort 'normal' decision-making processes at all levels where the Middle East is concerned. Until recently . . . it could not even be mentioned in any mainstream arena of discussion: a taboo that, as with all such repressions, injected a further massive dose of irrationality into the formation of US policy in the region.[83]

The influence of the Israel lobby in distorting, and, to a significant degree, preventing serious public debate of the Arab and Muslim world in the US is undeniable. But to conclude that the tail wags the dog and that Israeli interests dictate American policy, in an area whose oil reserves make it the most important region of the world

222

economy outside the triad itself, seems pretty wild. Establishing US hegemony in the Middle East was one of the key objectives of successive administrations in the 1940s and the 1950s; maintaining that hegemony led to the adoption of the Carter Doctrine in 1980 (§4.3.3). The alliance with Israel has provided Washington with the dual advantage of possessing a formidable military ally in containing the threat to US interests in the region represented by Arab nationalism and, more recently, radical Islamism, and, as Gilbert Achcar puts it, of providing the US with 'political benefits in Arab countries' eyes by showing that it had a grip on the watchdog's leash'. Where American and Israeli interests have diverged, Washington has been ready to exert pressure, as, for example, the administration of Bush *père* did in the early 1990s to lever a reluctant Israeli government into the 'peace process' with the Palestinians, and as the Pentagon has done under both Clinton and the younger Bush to force Israel to cancel arms sales to China. The neocons who made the running in formulating US global strategy under Bush *fils* had a particularly intimate relationship with the Israeli right, but even here it is important to highlight the convergence of interests, as both governments faced a deteriorating situation in the Middle East, arising from the outbreak of the second Palestinian *intifada* in September 2000 and the increasing difficulties Washington found in sustaining international support for its policy of dual containment directed at both the Islamic Republican regime in Iran and Iraq under the Ba'ath.[84]

George W. Bush's eventual response to this situation – to impose regime change on Iraq by invading and occupying the country – must also be set in the context of US global strategy after the Cold War. A drift towards achieving foreign policy objectives by the unilateral use of military force was perceptible under the Clinton administration in the 1990s. Despite Clinton's commitment to 'strategic partnership' with Beijing, when the People's Liberation Army carried out missile tests in the Taiwan Strait in March 1996, he sent two aircraft carrier groups close to Taiwan; the aerial bombardment of Iraq in 1998 was carried out by the US and Britain alone, prefiguring the 2003 invasion; the NATO bombing campaign against Serbia in 1999 was mounted without the authorization of the UN Security Council. The global network of five US unified combatant commands (the best known is Central Command, covering the Horn of Africa and western Asia) increasingly assumed a political role, with the chiefs of these commands partially usurping the diplomatic functions of a weakened State Department. One way of understanding this process of militarizing US foreign policy is to see it as an attempt to use one of

America's main comparative advantages – its overwhelming military lead over all the other powers combined – as a way of maintaining Washington's hegemony in an increasingly pluralistic global economy. Already in the mid-1990s, at the height of elite celebrations about neoliberal globalization, the Pentagon's strategic doctrine was oriented on maintaining US military supremacy over all other powers and preparing for war against China and Russia. It is striking to note the extent to which a concern with handling rising economic powers, most particularly China, informed the thinking of Wolfowitz, the most important neocon ideologue and one of the main architects of the Iraq War. The conquest of Iraq thus played a triple function. First, by demonstrating US military supremacy, it would serve as a reminder of the costs of challenging American hegemony. George Friedman argues that, after 9/11, '[t]he United States needed a military victory of substantial proportions. This was not driven by bloodlust or some cowboy mentality. It was a matter of credibility.'[85] Secondly, seizing Iraq would entrench US domination of the Middle East, the region whose oil reserves numerous studies showed to be of growing economic importance in coming decades, particularly to the EU, Japan, China and India – that is, to all 'the major and emerging powers' whose 'choices' Washington is eager to shape. Apart from the direct economic benefits specific American (and British) oil companies might gain from occupying Iraq, the tighter grip on what David Harvey calls the 'global oil spigot' that the invasion would give the US would enhance its influence over its potential hegemonic rivals.[86] Thirdly, and most speculatively, installing liberal capitalism in Iraq would be the start of a 'democratic revolution' in the Middle East that could give secure sociopolitical roots to the local regimes' alignment with the West.[87]

All this is, of course, now in ruins, thanks to the determined resistance with which the US-British occupation of Iraq was met. The 'surge' of US troop numbers in Iraq in 2007–8, and the tactics such as local alliances with Sunni militias that accompanied it, may have brought a degree of stability to a military situation that, particularly after the bombing of the Shia Golden Mosque in Samarra in February 2006, had been deteriorating disastrously. But there is no evidence that the US has thereby significantly enhanced its ability to achieve a sustainable long-term political settlement in Iraq that would be favourable to its interests.[88] The broader design of 'democratic revolution' in the Middle East perished in 2006, with Hamas's victory in the Palestinian parliamentary elections and Hezbollah's defeat of the Israel Defence Forces' invasion of Lebanon. But the failure of the policy, while indicative of the hubris with which it was conceived, doesn't mean that it was simply irrational; nor does the fact it was widely contested within the American ruling class. As I argued in §2.3, the articulation of a state's interests is necessarily a disputed process, in which different groups articulating varying balances between what Max Weber called material and ideal interests offer rival representations of how best to advance them. Moreover, the parameters of disagreement have been set relatively narrow in the case of Iraq. Brzezinski has been a particularly stringent establishment critic of the Bush administration, but the main thrust of his polemic was directed less at the resort to force than at the failure to carry the EU as a whole along, on the grounds that American primacy requires Europe as junior partner (Brzezinski dismisses the idea of 'a perfectly balanced 50–50 partnership' as 'a myth'): 'Europe can reinforce US military power, while the combined economic resources of the United States and the EU would make the Atlantic Community omnipotent.' Brzezinski also displays precisely the understanding of the geopolitical significance of Middle East oil that, Harvey and I argued, informed the decision to invade Iraq: 'Not only does America benefit economically from the relatively low costs of Middle Eastern oil, but America's security role in the region gives it indirect but politically critical leverage on the European and Asian economies that are also dependent on energy exports from the region.'[89] The differences within the American policy elite are more ones of tactics or emphasis than of principle or strategy.

The implication of this analysis is that, despite the adventurism and incompetence surrounding the American seizure of Iraq, the episode revealed deep-seated structural features of what it is still correct to call the imperialist system. The United States remains the dominant capitalist power, but it retains this position as a result of the considerable efforts it has to undertake to maintain its hegemony in three key regions – Europe, East Asia and the Middle East. There are three reasons for believing that this situation is unstable. First, the changing global distribution of economic power may limit American resources and expand the options of other leading states. It is important to stress that this is a long-term process and that the US remains, by comparison with any other power, well ahead in both economic and military capabilities. But, once one has discounted the hype, the fact remains that an increasingly centrifugal world is going to become progressively harder for Washington to manage. Secondly, the world economy is not, as neoliberal ideologues claim, a source of limitless growth and prosperity. As the credit crunch and its aftermath have shown, reflecting the structural tendencies of the capitalist mode of production, it can be a powerfully destabilizing force in its own right, with incalculable consequences on the global geopolitical configuration. Finally, the propensity of the US to succumb to the temptation to perpetuate its hegemony by exploiting two of its key advantages – its military superiority and its role as the orchestrator of the main international and regional institutions – can badly rebound. Iraq is the most obvious example, but the international crisis that developed as a result of the war between Russia and Georgia in August 2008 is another. The reckless pursuit of NATO expansion to extend Washington's influence deep into Eurasia and encircle Russia provoked an entirely predictable response from a Moscow whose resources had been boosted by the boom in energy prices and its military capabilities rebuilt since the humiliations of the Yeltsin era. The crisis highlighted how invading Iraq had weakened the US, tying down most of its military assets and depriving its denunciations of Russia's violation of Georgian national sovereignty of much plausibility. The episode also demonstrated that what classical Marxists called inter-imperialist rivalries remain a feature of the contemporary international system, even if the form they take is, as I have tried to show, not the same as it was in the first half of the twentieth century. As George Friedman put it, '[a]ll this basically means is that Russia emerges as a great power. Not a global power like it used to be, but a power that has to be taken very seriously.'[90]

So the world in the twenty-first century is unlikely to be characterized by a consensual Concert of Powers basking in neoliberal prosperity. Moreover, this is not because of a timeless cyclical process in which empires rise and fall. On the contrary, it reflects the specific imprint that capitalism has given to modern geopolitics. The remedy, therefore, lies not (as liberal apologists would claim) in more capitalism, but in replacing capitalism with a democratic and progressive alternative. This study of imperialism and how to theorize it has systematically viewed the world from above. I make no apology about having done this. Capitalist imperialism is a system of domination and exploitation that works to the advantage of a relatively narrow stratum at the top, especially of the advanced capitalist states. The strategies for maintaining this system or altering it to the advantage of one particular state or coalition of states are, once again, conceived and executed from the top. The idea, articulated by the Italian workerists of the 1960s and 1970s, and still affirmed by Toni Negri, that the structures and transformations of capitalism depend on creative initiatives from below by the exploited and oppressed is, alas, untrue.[91]

None of this is intended to discount resistance to imperialism. On the contrary, this book is written by a participant in the contemporary international movement against the 'war on terrorism' and the occupations of Iraq and Afghanistan. Any acquaintance with the historical record will confirm the significance of resistance, both to specific imperial adventures and to the system itself. The conclusion of both world wars was deeply marked by the interaction between rebellion in the colonies and upsurges of the revolutionary and radical left in Europe; on a spectacular but lesser scale, something similar happened during the Vietnam War at the end of the 1960s. The same dynamics are still at work today. The stubborn power of nationalist resistance to humble even the mightiest states has asserted itself once again in Iraq – albeit under very different banners from those of the secular anti-colonial movements of the mid-twentieth century. And, quite unexpectedly, a new convergence of anti-imperialism and anti-capitalism emerged as the new international movements of resistance to neoliberal globalization that became visible in the demonstrations at Seattle and Genoa. These provided the launching pad for the giant transnational protests against the invasion of Iraq in the early months of 2003.[92]

The history of past struggles and the trajectory of contemporary movements pose many important questions of principles, strategy and tactics. It has not been my aim to address these here. But I believe that those seeking a different social world may be assisted in their efforts by a better understanding of the nature of the system they confront. I have sought in this book to contribute towards such an understanding. In doing so, I hope also to have shown the kind of analytical purchase Marxist social theory still has in the twenty-first century. How well I have succeeded in attaining these objectives I am happy to leave to others to judge, but the importance of the issues discussed in this book seems undeniable. Knowing empire is part of fighting it.

NOTES AND REFERENCES

INTRODUCTION: EMPIRE OF THEORY, THEORIES OF EMPIRE

1   This introduction is based on my inaugural lecture at King's College London, 15 October 2007.
2   R. Suskind, 'Without a Doubt', *New York Times Magazine*, 17 October 2004.
3   Z. Brzezinski, *The Grand Chessboard* (New York, 1998), p. 10.
4   N. Ferguson, *Empire: How Britain Made the Modern World* (London, 2003), p. xxi.
5   N. Ferguson, *Colossus: The Rise and Fall of the American Empire* (London, 2004), pp. 183, 193.
6   F. Cooper, *Colonialism in Question* (Berkeley and Los Angeles, 2005), p. 5; see also ibid., ch. 2, 'The Rise, Fall, and Rise of Colonial Studies, 1951–2001'. I am grateful to Sharad Chari for this reference.
7   M.W. Doyle, *Empires* (Ithaca, 1986), p. 30. Unless there is some specific reason for doing otherwise, I shall use the terms 'imperialism' and 'empire' interchangeably.
8   Cooper, *Colonialism in Question*, pp. 26–7. Cooper offers an extended discussion of empire as a political form in ibid., ch. 6, 'States, Empires, and Political Imagination'. C. Calhoun et al., *Lessons of Empire* (New York, 2006) seek to bring the historiography of past empires to bear on the current situation. See also H. Münkler, *Empires* (Cambridge, 2007), criticized in B. Teschke, 'Imperial Doxa from the Berlin Republic', *New Left Review*, I/40 (2006). For Marxist discussions of pre-capitalist empires, see E.M. Wood, *Empire of Capital* (London,

2003), chs 2 and 3, and K. Van Der Pijl, *Nomads, Empires, States* (London, 2008), ch. 3.

9 V.I. Lenin, *Imperialism, The Highest Stage of Capitalism*, in id., *Collected Works*, XXII (Moscow, 1964), p. 267.

10 F. Halliday, 'The Persistence of Imperialism', in A. Rupert and H. Smith, eds, *Historical Materialism and Globalization* (London, 2002), p. 76. This judgement is all the more remarkable in the light of Halliday's political hostility to contemporary anti-imperialism, which he dismisses as 'a coalition of the romantic and the authoritarian', ibid., p. 85.

11 P. Patnaik, 'Whatever Has Happened to Imperialism?', *Social Scientist*, 18/6–7 (1990): 73, reprinted as 'Whatever Happened to Imperialism?', in *Monthly Review*, November 1990.

12 N. Geras, 'Reductions of the Left', *Dissent*, winter 2005 ⟨www.dissentmagazine.org⟩.

13 See Nigel Harris's brilliant, if overstated, *The End of the Third Word* (London, 1986).

14 P. Clarke, *The Last Thousand Days of the British Empire* (London, 2007), p. 280. On the Great Bengal Famine, see A.K. Sen, *Poverty and Famines* (Oxford, 1981), ch. 6.

15 For a survey, see R.J.C. Young, *Postcolonialism: An Historical Introduction* (Oxford, 2001), and, for a more critical response from a historian, Cooper, *Colonialism in Question*.

16 J. Darwin, *After Tamerlane* (London, 2007), p. 491.

17 Ibid., p. 505.

18 M. Hardt and A. Negri, *Empire* (Cambridge, MA, 2000) and *Multitude* (New York, 2004).

19 P. Anderson, 'European Hypocrisies', *London Review of Books*, 20 September 2007.

20 N. Chomsky, *Hegemony or Survival: America's Quest for Global Dominance* (London, 2003), pp. 182, 232.

21 B. Porter, *Empire and Superempire* (New Haven, 2006). Linda Colley makes some perceptive and partly parallel observations, in 'The Difficulties of Empire: Past, Present and Future', *Historical Research*, 79 (2006).

22 J. Gallagher and R. Robinson, 'The Imperialism of Free Trade', *Economic History Review*, 2/VI (1953): 6.

23 W.A. Williams, *The Tragedy of American Diplomacy* (New York, 1991).

24 Quoted in R. Wiggershaus, *The Frankfurt School* (Cambridge, 1994), p. 256. Halliday offers a related paraphrase of Horkheimer: 'those who do not want to talk about capitalism,

should not talk about international relations, or globalization', 'The Persistence of Imperialism', in A. Rupert and H. Smith, eds, *Historical Materialism and Globalization*, p. 77.

25 M. Kidron, 'Imperialism – Highest Stage but One', *International Socialism*, 9 (1962) and 'International Capitalism', ibid.: 20 (1965), both reprinted in *Capitalism and Theory* (London, 1974) and available at: ⟨www.marxists.org⟩.

26 A. Callinicos, *Althusser's Marxism* (London, 1976).

27 R.J.C. Young, *White Mythologies* (London, 1990).

28 D. Harvey, *Spaces of Hope* (Edinburgh, 2000), ch. 1.

29 L. Althusser and E. Balibar, *Reading Capital* (London, 1970), p. 180.

30 See A. Callinicos, *The Resources of Critique* (Cambridge, 2006), esp. chs 3 and 4.

31 D. Harvey, *The New Imperialism* (Oxford, 2003), and A. Callinicos, *The New Mandarins of American Power* (Cambridge, 2003). For some reservations about Harvey's treatment of accumulation by dispossession, see S. Ashman and A. Callinicos, 'Capital Accumulation and the State System', and B. Fine, 'Debating the "New Imperialism"', *Historical Materialism*, 14:4 (2006).

32 See the symposia on *The New Imperialism* in *Historical Materialism*, 14:4 (2006) and around my article 'Does Capitalism Need the State System?', in the *Cambridge Review of International Affairs*, 20/4 (2007), and subsequent issues.

33 Hardt and Negri, *Empire* and *Multitude*, and W. Robinson, *A Theory of Global Capitalism* (Baltimore, 2004).

34 E. Wood, 'Global Capital, National States', in Rupert and Smith, eds, *Historical Materialism and Globalization*.

35 L. Panitch and S. Gindin, 'Global Capitalism and American Empire', in Panitch and Colin Leys, eds, *The New Imperial Challenge: Socialist Register 2004* (London, 2003), 'Finance and American Empire', in Panitch and Leys, eds, *The Empire Reloaded: Socialist Register 2005* (London, 2004), and 'Superintending Global Capital', *New Left Review*, II/35 (2005).

36 Perry Anderson offers a very similar view of contemporary imperialism as an American-led Concert of Powers in 'Jottings in the Conjuncture', *New Left Review*, II/48 (2007). See, for a critique of Hardt and Negri in line with this perspective, A. Boron, *Empire and Imperialism* (London, 2005).

37 R. Kiely, 'Capitalist Expansion and the Imperialism–Globalization Debate', *Journal of International Relations and*

Development, 8 (2005), pp. 32–4. See, in addition to the texts by Harvey and me cited above, W. Bello, *Dilemmas of Domination* (New York, 2005), P. Gowan, *The Global Gamble* (London, 1999), C. Harman, 'Analysing Imperialism', *International Socialism*, 2/99 (2003), J. Rees, *Imperialism and Resistance* (London, 2006), and C. Serfati, *Imperialisme et militarisme* (Lausanne, 2004).

38 For example, G. Arrighi, *The Long Twentieth Century* (London, 1994), and *Adam Smith in Beijing* (London, 2007).

39 R. Brenner, 'What is, and What is Not, Imperialism?', *Historical Materialism*, 14.4 (2006), and 'Imperialism and Neoliberalism', paper given at *Historical Materialism* conference, London, 10 November 2007. Aijaz Ahmad occupies a broadly similar theoretical position: *Iraq, Afghanistan and the Imperialism of Our Time* (New Delhi, 2004).

40 B. Sutcliffe, 'How Many Capitalisms?', in Rupert and Smith, eds, *Historical Materialism and Globalization*, p. 50.

41 B. Sutcliffe, 'Imperialism Old and New', *Historical Materialism*, 14/4 (2006): 74.

42 Among my earlier efforts are: A. Callinicos, 'Imperialism, Capitalism, and the State Today', *International Socialism*, 2/35 (1987), 'Marxism and Imperialism Today', *International Socialism*, 2/50 (1991), and 'Periodizing Capitalism and Analysing Imperialism', in Robert Albritton et al., *Phases of Capitalist Development* (Basingstoke, 2001). For the International Socialist tradition, in addition to the texts by Harman, Kidron, and Rees cited above, see T. Cliff (1957), 'The Economic Roots of Reformism', in id., *Marxist Theory after Trotsky* (London, 2003), N. Harris (1971), 'Lenin and Imperialism Today', in id., *India-China: Underdevelopment and Revolution* (Delhi, 1974), J. Rees, 'The New Imperialism', *International Socialism*, 2/48 (1990), and Callinicos et al., *Marxism and the New Imperialism* (London, 1994). I have incorporated fragments from the first two articles cited, and from 'Bourgeois Revolutions and Historical Materialism', *International Socialism*, 2/43 (1989), albeit altered, and surrounded by much new material, in chapters 1, 3 and 4.

43 Callinicos, 'Does Capitalism Need the State System?', p. 542, and, in response, G. Pozo-Martin, 'Autonomous or Materialist Geopolitics?', *Cambridge Review of International Affairs*, 20/4 (2007).

1   THE CLASSICAL LEGACY

1   B. Sutcliffe, 'How Many Capitalisms', in M. Rupert and H. Smith, eds, *Historical Materialism and Globalization* (London, 2002), p. 50. Study of the history of Marxist political economy in general and of the classical theory of imperialism in particular is greatly facilitated by the existence of two outstanding works: A. Brewer, *Marxist Theories of Imperialism* (2nd edn; London, 1990), and M.C. Howard and E. King, *A History of Marxian Economics* (2 vols; London, 1989, 1992); despite the authors' neo–Ricardian intellectual allegiances, both books are first-rate pieces of intellectual history.

2   R. Hilferding, *Finance Capital* (London, 1981), pp. 22–3.

3   P. Anderson, *Considerations on Western Marxism* (London, 1976), esp. ch. 1.

4   Brewer, *Marxist Theories of Imperialism*, pp. 88–9.

5   Howard and King, *A History of Marxian Economics*, I, chs 2 and 3.

6   Hilferding, *Finance Capital*, p. 21.

7   R. Luxemburg [1913], *The Accumulation of Capital* (London, 1971), p. 417.

8   Among the most helpful treatments of Marx's economic manuscripts are R. Rosdolsky [1968], *The Making of Marx's Capital* (London, 1977), E. Dussel [1988], *Towards an Unknown Marx* (London, 2001), and 'The Four Drafts of *Capital*', *Rethinking Marxism*, 13 (2001), and M. Heinrich, review of *MEGA*, Bd. 15, *Historical Materialism*, 15.4 (2007). In addition to these, I am indebted for my understanding of *Capital* in particular to the following (in rough historical order): I.I. Rubin [1928], *Essays on Marx's Theory of Value* (Detroit, 1972), E.V. Ilyenkov [1960], *The Dialectics of the Abstract and the Concrete in Marx's* Capital (Moscow, 1982), L. Althusser and E. Balibar [1965], *Reading Capital* (London, 1970), G. Duménil , *Le Concept de loi économique dans 'Le Capital'* (Paris, 1978), J. Weeks, *Capital and Exploitation* (Princeton, 1981), D. Harvey, *The Limits to Capital* (Oxford, 1982), and J. Bidet [1985], *Exploring Marx's* Capital (Leiden, 2007). My own views were first presented in 'The Logic of *Capital*' (DPhil thesis, University of Oxford, 1978) and are available, albeit in the form of critique, in 'Against the New Dialectic', *Historical Materialism*, 13.2 (2005). I hope, before too long, to devote a book to the subject.

9   K. Marx, [1867], *Capital*, I (Harmondsworth, 1976), p. 90 (italics added).
10 R. Brenner, 'The Economics of Global Turbulence', *New Left Review*, I/229 (1998): 23. Aside from *Reading Capital*, the most important discussion of the basic concepts of historical materialism is G.A. Cohen, *Karl Marx's Theory of History* (Oxford, 1978). I offer my own take in *Making History* (2nd edn, Leiden, 2004).
11 K. Marx, [1939] *Grundrisse* (Harmondsworth, 1973), p. 657. See, on Ricardo, Piero Sraffa's superb Introduction to D. Ricardo, *Works and Correspondence* (11 vols, Cambridge, 1951–73), I (available at ⟨www.oll.libertyfund.org⟩). The disputes over Marx's value theory can be traced in B. Rowthorn, 'Neo-Classicism, Neo-Ricardianism, and Marxism', *New Left Review*, I/86 (1974), I. Steedman, *Marx after Sraffa* (London, 1977), B. Fine and L. Harris, *Rereading Capital* (London, 1979), ch. 2, I. Steedman et al., *The Value Controversy* (London, 1981), C. Harman, *Explaining the Crisis* (London, 1984), pp. 160–2, E. Mandel and A. Freeman, eds, *Ricardo, Marx, Sraffa* (London, 1984), B. Fine, ed., *The Value Dimension* (London, 1986), D.K. Foley, *Understanding Capital* (Cambridge, MA, 1986), G. Carchedi, *Frontiers of Political Economy* (London, 1991), A. Saad-Filho, *The Value of Marx* (London, 2002), and A. Kliman, *Reclaiming Marx's Capital* (Landham, MD, 2007).
12 Marx, *Capital*, I, p. 739.
13 Marx, *Capital*, I, p. 166 (italics added). Marx's theory of fetishism and its pitfalls are discussed in A. Rattansi, ed., *Ideology, Method and Marx* (London, 1989). I take a perhaps overly negative view in *Making History*, chs 4 and 5.
14 F. Moseley, 'Hostile Brothers: Marx's Theory of the Distribution of Surplus-Value in Volume III of *Capital*', in M. Campbell and G. Reuten, eds, *The Culmination of Capital* (Houndmills, 2002).
15 K. Marx, *Capital*, III (Harmondsworth, 1981), p. 117.
16 Ibid., p. 967.
17 Marx, *Grundrisse*, p. 101.
18 Duménil, *Le Concept de loi économique dans 'Le Capital'*, p. 89; see also ibid., p. 373ff.
19 F. Engels, 'Law of Value and Rate of Profit', Supplement and Addendum to *Capital*, Volume III. For critiques, see Weeks, *Capital and Exploitation*, pp. 50–62, and C. Arthur, *The New Dialectic and Marx's* Capital (Leiden, 2002), ch. 1.

20 Marx, *Grundrisse*, p. 100.
21 Bidet, *Exploring Marx's* Capital, chs 6 and 7.
22 L. Althusser, Avant-propos, Duménil, *Le Concept de loi économique dans 'Le Capital'*, pp. 17–18. See, on the difference between the Hegelian and Marxist dialectics, L. Althusser, 'Marx's Relation to Hegel', in id., *Politics and History* (London, 1972).
23 K. Marx, letter to Ludwig Kugelmann, 11 July 1868, in Marx and Engels, *Collected Works* (50 vols, London, 1975–2005), XLIII, p. 69.
24 K. Marx [1956], *Theories of Surplus-Value* (3 vols, Moscow, 1963–72), II, p. 174.
25 Though this interpretation follows that of 'The Logic of *Capital'*, ch. IV, Chris Arthur has persuaded me that my argument, expressed both in my thesis and in various published works, notably *The Revolutionary Ideas of Karl Marx* (London, 1983), that the structure of *Capital* is organized according to the distinction that Marx draws in the *Grundrisse* (e.g., p. 449) between 'capital in general' (*Capital*, Volume I and Volume II, Parts 1 and 2) and 'many capitals' (Volume II, Part 3, and Volume III) is mistaken, and that *Capital* as a whole takes as its object 'capital in general': see especially C.J. Arthur, 'Capital, Competition and Many Capitals', in Campbell and Reuten, eds, *The Culmination of Capital*.
26 For a fine brief treatment, see M. Campbell, 'The Credit System', in Campbell and Reuten, eds, *The Culmination of Capital*. The role of the credit system in both extending and undermining the accumulation process is a major theme of Harvey's '"second-cut" at the theory of crisis', in *The Limits to Capital* (quotation from p. 326).
27 Marx, *Capital*, III, p. 515. Bidet has an excellent discussion of Marx's functional conceptualization of ideology in *Capital*: *Exploring Marx's* Capital, ch. 8.
28 K. Marx, letter to Friedrich Engels, 2 April 1858, in Marx and Engels, *Collected Works*, XL, p. 298.
29 Hilferding, *Finance Capital*, p. 21.
30 I. Lakatos, *Philosophical Papers* (2 vols, Cambridge, 1978).
31 I discuss objections to the very idea of phases of capitalist development in A. Callinicos, 'Periodizing Capitalism and Analysing Imperialism', in R. Albritton et al., eds, *Phases of Capitalist Development* (Basingstoke, 2001).
32 Hilferding, *Finance Capital*, pp. 366, 367.

33   R. Luxemburg [1921], 'The Accumulation of Capital – an Anti-Critique', in id. and N.I. Bukharin, *Imperialism and the Accumulation of Capital* (London, 1972), p. 77.
34   Luxemburg, *The Accumulation of Capital*, Part One.
35   Ibid., pp. 350, 352.
36   Luxemburg, 'The Accumulation of Capital', p. 64.
37   Id., *The Accumulation of Capital*, pp. 364–5, 371.
38   Ibid., p. 446.
39   R. Luxemburg [1916], 'The Junius Pamphlet', in M.A. Waters, ed., *Rosa Luxemburg Speaks* (New York, 1970), p. 269. See N. Geras, *The Legacy of Rosa Luxemburg* (London, 1976), ch. I.
40   Howard and King, *A History of Marxian Economics*, I, p. 112 (see §1.4 for the distinction between constant and variable capital). See ibid., ch. 6, M. Bleaney, *Underconsumption Theories* (London, 1976), ch. 9, Brewer, *Marxist Theories of Imperialism*, ch. 3, and T. Cliff [1959], *Rosa Luxemburg*, in id., *Marxist Theory after Trotsky* (London, 2003), for good critical discussions of Luxemburg.
41   Luxemburg, *The Accumulation of Capital*, pp. 334–5.
42   N.I. Bukharin [1925], 'Imperialism and the Accumulation of Capital', in Luxemburg and Bukharin, *Imperialism and the Accumulation of Capital*, pp. 163ff.
43   Brewer, *Marxist Theories of Imperialism*, p. 62.
44   Ibid., p. 63.
45   Luxemburg, *The Accumulation of Capital*, pp. 348–9.
46   Bukharin, 'Imperialism and the Accumulation of Capital', pp. 239, 202. See also ibid., chs 1 and 2.
47   D. Harvey, *The New Imperialism* (Oxford, 2003), pp. 138, 141, 144. Strictly speaking, Luxemburg offers her theory of the impossibility of realizing capitalized surplus-value, not as an explanation of economic crises, but of the general tendency of capitalist development. Thus she poses the problem of reproduction 'leaving cycles and crises out of consideration', *The Accumulation of Capital*, p. 36. Hardt and Negri also draw somewhat ambivalently on Luxemburg in their discussion of imperialism: *Empire* (Cambridge, MA, 2000), ch. 3.1.
48   Luxemburg, *The Accumulation of Capital*, chs XXVI and XXX (quotation from p. 361).
49   E.M. Wood, *Empire of Capital* (London, 2003), pp. 126, 125, 127.

50 Bukharin, 'Imperialism and the Accumulation of Capital', p. 253. Lenin makes a similar point: [1917] *Imperialism, the Highest Stage of Capitalism*, in id., *Collected Works*, XXII (Moscow, 1964), pp. 268–9.

51 E.V. Preobrazhensky [1931], *The Decline of Capitalism* (Armonk, NY, 1985), p. 18.

52 Lenin, *Imperialism*, pp. 276–85.

53 Sutcliffe, 'How Many Capitalisms?', pp. 49–50.

54 Lenin, *Imperialism*, p. 266.

55 Ibid., pp. 266, 298.

56 G. Arrighi, *The Geometry of Imperialism* (London, 1978), pp. 10–11.

57 Ibid., p. 20.

58 Note from the Editors, *Monthly Review*, January 2004.

59 Lenin, *Imperialism*, p. 269.

60 J.A. Hobson [1902], *Imperialism: A Study* (3rd edn; London, 1938), p. 6.

61 Arrighi, *The Geometry of Imperialism*, p. 38.

62 Hobson, *Imperialism*, p. 55.

63 Ibid., pp. 59, 56–7.

64 J.A. Hobson, *The South African War* (London, 1900), Part II.

65 Id., *Imperialism*, p. 191, and see more generally ibid., Part II, ch. II, 'The Scientific Defence of Imperialism', and Part II, ch. IV, 'Imperialism and the Lower Races'.

66 Ibid., pp. 85–6. See generally ibid., Part I, ch. VI, 'The Economic Taproot of Imperialism', and, for a detailed critical discussion of Hobson's version of under-consumptionism, Bleaney, *Underconsumption Theories*, ch. 8.

67 Hobson, *Imperialism*, p. 88.

68 Lenin, *Imperialism*, p. 242.

69 Arrighi, *The Geometry of Imperialism*, p. 117.

70 Ibid., pp. 24–5. See also the discussion of this ambiguity in C. Harman, 'Analysing Imperialism', *International Socialism*, 2/99 (2003): 9–18.

71 Lenin, *Imperialism*, p. 277.

72 Hobson, *Imperialism*, p. 314. See also ibid., p. 265.

73 Lenin, *Imperialism*, p. 281.

74 Good critiques of Lenin's theory of the labour aristocracy can be found in T. Cliff [1957], 'The Economic Roots of Reformism', in id., *Marxist Theory after Trotsky*, H. Weber, *Marxisme et conscience de classe* (Paris, 1975), pp. 235–69, Brewer, *Marxist Theories of Imperialism*, pp. 128–33, and C. Post,

'The Myth of the Labour Aristocracy', *Against the Current*, 123, July/August 2006, and 124, September/October 2006. Studies of the early Communist movement that support the historical claim made in the text include J. Hinton, *The First Shop Stewards' Movement* (London, 1973), S. Smith, *Red Petrograd* (Cambridge, 1985), and P. Broué, *The German Revolution, 1917–1923* (Leiden, 2005).

75 Hobson, *Imperialism*, p. 311.

76 Brewer, *Marxist Theories of Imperialism*, p. 107. Ibid., ch. 6, and Howard and King, *A History of Marxian Economics*, I, ch. 13, provide excellent general treatments of Lenin and Bukharin; see also M. Haynes, *Nikolai Bukharin and the Transition from Capitalism to Socialism* (London, 1985).

77 N.I. Bukharin, *Selected Writings on the State and the Transition to Socialism* (Nottingham, 1982), pp. 16–17.

78 Id. [1920], *Economics of the Transformation Period* (New York, 1971), p. 37.

79 Id. [1917], *Imperialism and World Economy* (London, 1972), pp. 25–6, 125.

80 Id., 'Imperialism and the Accumulation of Capital', p. 256. On the circuits of capital, see K. Marx, *Capital*, Volume II (Harmondsworth, 1978), Part 1.

81 Brewer, *Marxist Theories of Imperialism*, p. 111.

82 Bukharin, *Selected Writings on the State and the Transition to Socialism*, p. 31; id., *Imperialism and World Economy*, pp. 17–18.

83 Marx, *Capital*, I, pp. 92, 799, 783.

84 Marx, *Capital*, III, pp. 343, 357. The theory of the tendency of the rate of profit to fall is another area of great controversy. For a survey, see S. Cullenburg, *The Falling Rate of Profit*. Simon Clarke offers in *Marx's Theory of Crisis* (London, 1994) a valuable examination of the evolution of Marx's thinking, though, out of an attempt to correct for deterministic 'orthodox Marxist' distortions, he plays down the importance of the theory of the tendency of the rate of profit to fall.

85 Howard and King, *A History of Marxian Economics*, I, p. 316. For the very rich debates among Bolshevik economists in the 1920s and 1930s, see Richard Day's fascinating study *The 'Crisis' and the 'Crash'* (London, 1981).

86 See Luxemburg's dismissal of the theory in 'The Accumulation of Capital', pp. 76–77n. Though the focus of Gramsci's thought is political and philosophical, his writings mark an exception

to this neglect: e.g., *Further Selections from the Prison Note-books* (ed. D. Boothman; London, 1995), pp. 428–35.

87 Hilferding, *Finance Capital*, Part IV, and Bukharin, 'Imperialism and the Accumulation of Capital', ch. 3.

88 Bukharin, *Selected Writings on the State and the Transition to Socialism*, p. 22.

89 Quoted in Howard and King, *A History of Marxian Economics*, I, p. 272.

90 Ibid., pp. 273–5.

91 Bukharin, *Economics of the Transformation Period*, p. 19. Bukharin's use of the term 'organization' to refer to the conscious transcendence of the market, very much present in his philosophical essay [1921], *Historical Materialism* (Ann Arbor, 1969), is a reflection of the influence of A.A. Bogdanov's philosophy of 'organization'. It aroused the suspicions of Lenin, who wrote: 'Commodity production is also "organized" economy,' Marginal Notes to Bukharin, *Economics of the Transformation Period*, p. 212. On Bogdanov, see the appendix to D. Lecourt, *Proletarian Science?* (London, 1977).

92 Bukharin, 'Imperialism and the Accumulation of Capital', p. 226. Tony Cliff discusses this text in his examination of the problem of crisis under state capitalism and predicts (correctly, as it proved) that arms production would postpone the tendency towards economic stagnation intrinsic in this form of capitalism: [1948] 'The Nature of Stalinist Russia', in Cliff, *Marxist Theory after Trotsky*, ch. 8.

93 Bukharin, 'Report on the Programme of the Communist International', *International Press Correspondence*, 8/56, 27 August 1928: 986.

94 Id., 'The International Situation and the Tasks of the Comintern', *International Press Correspondence*, 8/41, 30 July 1928: 729.

95 Id., *Economics of the Transformation Period*, p. 19.

96 Id., 'The International Situation and the Tasks of the Comintern': 729.

97 N. Stone, *Europe Transformed, 1878–1919* (London, 1983), p. 246.

98 Harman, *Explaining the Crisis*, p. 69.

99 B. Warren, *Imperialism: Pioneer of Capitalism* (ed. J. Sender; London, 1980), p. 79. See the discussion of oligopolistic competition in Carchedi, *Frontiers of Political Economy*, ch. 7.

100 Preobrazhensky, *The Decline of Capitalism*, pp. 5, 51.
101 Ibid., pp. 29, 15–16. Marx deals with turnover times and fixed capital in *Capital*, II, Part 2. For recent attempts to integrate these topics into a broader account of capital accumulation and crises, see Harvey, *The Limits to Capital*, *passim*, and M. Itoh and C. Lapavitsas, *Political Economy of Money and Finance* (London, 1999), ch. 6.
102 Preobrazhensky, *The Decline of Capitalism*, p. 16.
103 J. Steindl [1952], *Maturity and Stagnation in American Capitalism* (New York, 1976), and P. Baran and P. Sweezy, *Monopoly Capital* (Harmondsworth, 1968). For the reception of Preobrazhensky's book, see Day, *The 'Crisis' and the 'Crash'*, pp. 229–47.
104 Brewer, *Marxist Theories of Imperialism*, p. 142. See also on Baran and Sweezy, Howard and King, *A History of Marxian Economics*, II, ch. 6.
105 H. Grossman [1929], *The Law of Accumulation and Breakdown of Capitalism* (ed. J. Banaji; London, 1992), p. 95.
106 Ibid., pp. 122–3, 157. See O. Bauer [1913], 'The Accumulation of Capital', *History of Political Economy*, 18 (1986), and Luxemburg, 'The Accumulation of Capital', pp. 107–35. For detailed discussions of Grossman, see Howard and King, *A History of Marxian Economics*, I, ch. 16, and Rick Kuhn's excellent biography, *Henryk Grossman and the Recovery of Marxism* (Urbana and Chicago, 2007).
107 K. Kautsky (1914), 'Imperialism', in J. Riddell, ed., *Lenin's Struggle for a Revolutionary International* (New York, 1984), p. 181.
108 Ibid., p. 180.
109 A.J. Mayer, *Why Did the Heavens Not Darken?* (New York, 1990), p. 31.
110 B. Rowthorn, 'Imperialism in the 1970s – Unity or Rivalry?', *New Left Review*, I/69 (1971): 31–2. This and the other contributions to this debate were reprinted in H. Radice, ed., *International Firms and Modern Imperialism* (Harmondsworth, 1975).
111 Compare H. Magdoff, *The Age of Imperialism* (New York, 1969), and E. Mandel, *Europe vs. America* (New York, 1970).
112 M. Hardt and A. Negri, *Empire* (Cambridge, MA, 2000), p. xii. See also W. Robinson, *A Theory of Global Capitalism* (Baltimore, 2004).

113 H. Lacher and B. Teschke, 'The Changing "Logics" of Capital-ist Competition', *Cambridge Review of International Affairs*, 20 (2007): 574, 576.

114 Ibid., p. 576. The passages cited by Lenin and Bukharin are to be found in the latter's *Imperialism and World Economy*, pp. 13–14, 142.

115 Arrighi, *The Geometry of Imperialism*, p. 24.

116 Lenin, *Imperialism*, p. 272, 295. See also ibid., p. 253.

117 Howard and King, *History of Marxian Economics*, I, p. 249. They note also the absence of the concepts of either uneven or combined development from Bukharin's version of the theory of imperialism.

2 CAPITALISM AND THE STATE SYSTEM

1 B. Sutcliffe, 'Imperialism Old and New', *Historical Material-ism*, 14/4 (2006): 60.

2 Ibid., pp. 60, 61.

3 M. Kidron [1962], 'Imperialism: Highest Stage but One', in id., *Capitalism and Theory* (London, 1974), p. 127.

4 R. Hilferding [1910], *Finance Capital* (London, 1981), p. 307.

5 L.D. Trotsky, *The History of the Russian Revolution* (3 vols, London, 1967), I, p. 22.

6 G. Arrighi, *The Geometry of Imperialism* (London, 1978), p. 130.

7 Bob Jessop's *The Capitalist State* (Oxford, 1982) remains the most important single critical survey of Marxist state theory. He discusses Marx and Engels and 'Stamokap' theory in chap-ters 1 and 2 respectively.

8 N.I. Bukharin, *Selected Writings on the State and the Transition to Socialism*, pp. 30, 31. See, on Bukharin's influence on Lenin's mature theory of the state, M. Sawyer, 'The Genesis of *State and Revolution*', in R. Miliband and J. Saville, eds, *The Socialist Register 1977* (London, 1977). I am grateful to Chris Harman for pointing out that I was wrong to attribute to Bukharin an instrumentalist theory of the state in 'Imperialism and Global Political Economy', *International Socialism*, 2/108 (2005): 110.

9 D. Harvey, *The New Imperialism* (Oxford, 2003), pp. 183, 30.

10 G. Arrighi, *The Long Twentieth Century* (London, 1994), p. 33; italics added.

11 Id., *Adam Smith in Beijing* (London, 2007), p, 212 n.2.

12   D. Harvey, 'Last Days of Empire', *Socialist Worker*, 30 July 2005.

13   A. Callinicos, 'The Grand Strategy of the American Empire', *International Socialism*, 2/97 (2002), pp. 4–5, and *The New Mandarins of American Power* (Cambridge, 2003), pp. 99–106.

14   C. Barker, 'A Note on the Theory of Capitalist States', *Capital and Class*, 4 (1978): 118. Somewhat parallel considerations were raised by some German Marxists in the 1970s: see O. Nachtwey and T. den Brink, 'Lost in Transition: The German World-Market Debate in the 1970s', *Historical Materialism*, 16/1 (2008). Holloway now concedes Barker's point: for example, *Change the World without Taking Power* (London, 2002), p 95. Some of the most important contributions to the state-derivation debate will be found in J. Holloway and S. Picciotto, eds, *State and Capital* (London, 1978) and S. Clarke, ed., *The State Debate* (Basingstoke, 1991).

15   See above all K.N. Waltz, *Theory of International Politics* (Reading, MA, 1979).

16   A. Giddens, *A Contemporary Critique of Historical Materialism* (London, 1981), M. Mann, *The Sources of Social Power* (2 vols, Cambridge, 1986, 1993), W.G. Runciman, *A Treatise on Social Theory* (3 vols, Cambridge, 1983, 1989, 1997), T. Skocpol, *States and Social Revolutions* (Cambridge, 1979).

17   M. Hardt and A. Negri, *Empire* (Cambridge, MA, 2000), p. 182. See ibid., ch. 3.5, 'Mixed Constitution', on the institutional structure of Empire.

18   E.M. Wood, 'The Separation of the Economic and the Political in Capitalism', *New Left Review*, I/127 (1981): 78.

19   Ibid.: 78–9, 80, 82. Compare K. Marx, *Capital*, I (Harmondsworth, 1976), p. 899.

20   J. Hirsch, 'The State Apparatus and Social Reproduction', in Holloway and Picciotto, eds, *State and Capital*.

21   J. Holloway and S. Picciotto, 'Capital, Crisis, and the State', *Capital and Class*, 2 (1977). A relevant collection of Open Marxist essays can be found in W. Bonefeld and J. Holloway, eds, *Global Capital, National State and the Politics of Money* (Basingstoke, 1996). Their treatment of the problem of the state system is, however, purely descriptive: for example, Holloway, 'Global Capital and the National State', and P. Burnham, 'Capital, Crisis and the International State System', both in the collection just cited.

22 B. Tesckhe, *The Myth of 1648* (London, 2003), pp. 145–6. See esp. ibid., chs 4 and 5 for supporting historical arguments.

23 H. Lacher, 'Making Sense of the International System', in M. Rupert and H. Smith, eds, *Historical Materialism and Globalization* (London, 2002), pp. 156–7, 161, 159, 162. This argument is effectively endorsed by Brenner: 'What is, and What is Not, Imperialism?', *Historical Materialism*, 14/4 (2006): 84.

24 E.M. Wood, 'Global Capital, National States', in Rupert and Smith, eds, *Historical Materialism and Globalization*, pp. 22, 25, 29, 30. Brenner developed the notion of '*politically constituted forms of private property*' to denote the dependence of feudal lords on 'forms of state, of political community, whether local or national, that had as one of their central functions the economic support of the members of the dominant class . . . – either by making possible direct lordly levies from the peasants, based on lordship, or by constituting property in central or local offices, based largely on taxation', *Merchants and Revolution* (Princeton, 1993), p. 652. See also ch. 3 of this volume.

25 E.M. Wood, 'Logics of Power', *Historical Materialism*, 14/4 (2006): 26.

26 Id., 'Global Capital, National States', p. 32 (italics added). Here again Wood echoes Lenin's and Bukharin's response to Kautsky – to admit ultra-imperialism as a theoretical possibility but then to explain why it is unlikely to be realized: see §1.5 of this volume.

27 Id., *Empire of Capital* (London, 2003), p. 141.

28 Id., 'Logics of Power', p. 25.

29 V. Chibber, 'Capital Outbound', *New Left Review*, II/36 (2005): 156–7, 157. The dangers of seeking to derive form from function (or the reverse) were highlighted in the state-derivation debate: e.g., Hirsch, 'The State Apparatus and Social Reproduction', and B. Blanke et al., 'On the Current Marxist Discussion on the Analysis of Form and Function of the Bourgeois State', in Holloway and Picciotto, eds, *State and Capital*.

30 R. Brenner, 'The Economics of Global Turbulence', *New Left Review*, I/229 (1998): 23. In a discussion of this article, Wood herself acknowledges the significance of competition, but even here competition is considered primarily as a presupposition of capitalist exploitation: the vertical relationship between capital and labour remains, in other words, the focus of her argument: E.M. Wood, 'Horizontal Relations: A Note on Brenner's Heresy', *Historical Materialism*, 4 (1999).

31 K. Marx, *Grundrisse* (Harmondsworth, 1973), p. 414.
32 A. Callinicos, 'Does Capitalism Need the State System?', *Cambridge Review of International Affairs*, 20 (2007).
33 Compare R. Rosdolsky, *The Making of Marx's* Capital (London, 1977) and E. Dussel, 'The Four Drafts of *Capital*', *Rethinking Marxism*, 13/1 (2001).
34 I owe to Colin Barker a recognition of the lacuna in Marx's theory of the capitalist mode that arises from his failure to discuss taxation from various conversations over the years, but the point comes up in two important unpublished manuscripts of his, 'The Force of Value', and 'Industrialism, Capitalism, Value, Force, and States'.
35 E.M. Wood, 'A Reply to Critics', *Historical Materialism*, 15/3 (2007): 155.
36 Id., *Empire of Capital*, pp. 119–20.
37 Id., 'Global Capital, National States', p. 24.
38 Callinicos, 'Does Capitalism Need the State System?', p. 542. Justin Rosenberg has written the classic Marxist critique of realism, *The Empire of Civil Society* (London, 1994).
39 G. Pozo-Martin, 'Autonomous or Materialist Geopolitics?', *Cambridge Review of International Affairs*, 20 (2007): 558, 560.
40 Callinicos, 'Does Capitalism Need the State System?', p. 543 n.11.
41 But see A. Callinicos and J. Rosenberg, 'Uneven and Combined Development: The Social-Relational Substratum of the International?', *Cambridge Review of International Affairs*, 21 (2008).
42 Pozo-Martin, 'Autonomous or Materialist Geopolitics?', p. 556.
43 Holloway, *Change the World without Taking Power*, pp. 92, 94.
44 P. Burnham, 'Class Struggle, States and Global Circuits of Capital', in Rupert and Smith, eds, *Historical Materialism and Globalization*, pp. 122, 124, 126. World systems theory is discussed in §3.1 of this volume.
45 Specifying these mechanisms meets the legitimate demand of analytical Marxists that historical materialist explanations provide micro-foundations that make irreducible reference to the beliefs and desires of individual actors, though they were mistaken in reducing such explanations to their micro-foundations: see A. Callinicos, *Making History* (2nd edn; Leiden,

2004), esp. ch. 2, and 'G.A. Cohen and the Critique of Political Economy', *Science and Society*, 70 (2006).

46 F. Block [1977], 'The Ruling Class Does Not Rule', in id., *Revising State Theory* (Philadelphia, 1987), p. 54. See C. Offe, and V. Ronge [1975], 'Theses on the Theory of the State', in A. Giddens and D. Held, eds, *Classes, Power, and Conflict* (Berkeley/Los Angeles, 1982), R. Miliband, 'State Power and Class Interests', *New Left Review*, I/138 (1983), and C. Harman, 'The State and Capitalism Today', *International Socialism*, 2/51 (1991).

47 Block, 'The Ruling Class Does Not Rule', p. 58.

48 Ibid., pp. 58–9.

49 Ibid., p. 66. See also F. Block [1980], 'Beyond Relative Autonomy: State Managers as Historical Subjects', in id., *Revising State Theory*, esp. pp. 87–9.

50 Harman, 'The State and Capitalism Today', p. 13. Sam Ashman and I have used Brenner's concept of the rules of reproduction that specific groups of actors must follow to maintain their socioeconomic position to restate Block's argument: 'Capital Accumulation and the State System', *Historical Materialism*, 13/4 (2006): 112–15. The argument as it stands assumes that state managers are a relatively unified group, which may well not be the case. It is a merit of Nicos Poulantzas's definition of the state as 'the specific materialized condensation of a relationship of forces between classes and class fractions' that it is open to the possibility, indeed the probability, of conflicts between different branches of the state apparatus: *State, Power, Socialism* (London, 1978), and J. Martin, ed., *The Poulantzas Reader* (London, 2008). But (i) these conflicts need not be a passive reflection of external class antagonisms, but may involve quite active alliances between the state managers in specific branches and other social forces of the kind studied in mainstream policy network analysis; (ii) to function effectively, a state needs to have mechanisms for overcoming or at least regulating these conflicts; (iii) Poulantzas tends to bracket the agency of the state managers themselves; as Block puts it, '[a] condensation cannot exercise power', 'Beyond Relative Autonomy', p. 83. Hirsch has a good discussion of what he calls '[t]he heterogeneous and increasingly chaotic structure of the bourgeois state apparatus', 'The State Apparatus and Social Reproduction', pp. 100–2.

51 Brenner, 'What is, and What is Not, Imperialism?', p. 82. Brenner has developed his analysis of the Bush strategy most

fully in 'Imperialism and Neoliberalism', paper given at *Historical Materialism* conference, London, 10 November 2007.

52 Brenner, 'What is, and What is Not, Imperialism?', p. 83.
53 K. Marx, *Grundrisse* (Harmondsworth, 1973), p. 414.
54 Ibid., pp. 83–4.
55 L.D. Trotsky, *The Third International after Lenin* (New York, 1970), pp. 18, 19–20. Uneven and combined development has come under increased attention from Marxist IR theorists in recent years, particularly as a result of Justin Rosenberg's effort to make the concept the basis of a transhistorical theory of the international: see, for example, 'Why Is There No International Historical Sociology?', *European Journal of International Relations*, 12 (2006), our exchanges, Callinicos and Rosenberg, 'Uneven and Combined Development', and the section devoted to the subject in the *Cambridge Review of International Affairs*, 22/1 (2009).
56 K. Marx, *Capital*, III (Harmondsworth, 1981), pp. 373–5.
57 Alan Freeman uses Marx's theory of differential profits in a very similar way in 'Explaining National Inequality', paper given at *International Socialism* Political Economy Day School, 29 September 2007, available at: ⟨www.repec.org⟩.
58 R. Storper and R. Walker, *The Capitalist Imperative* (Oxford, 1989), and S. Ashman, 'Globalization as Uneven Development' (PhD thesis, University of Birmingham, 2006).
59 R.H. Wade, 'On the Causes of Increasing World Poverty and Inequality,' *New Political Economy*, 9 (2004): 172. In a very important but as yet unpublished paper, Peter Gowan has highlighted the importance of the tendency (excluded by neo-classical economics, which assumes constant returns to scale) for increasing returns to scale (that is, for expanded scale of production and distribution to reduce average and marginal costs of production) in explaining economic and interstate competition: (2005), 'Industrial Dynamics and Interstate Relations in the Core'. For a powerful critique of Hardt's and Negri's portrayal of the 'smooth world' of Empire, see G. Arrighi, 'Lineages of Empire', *Historical Materialism*, 10/3 (2002).
60 Harman, 'The State and Capitalism Today', pp. 9–10.
61 Harvey, *The New Imperialism*, pp. 103, 105, 106.
62 For a Marxist example, see B. Jessop, *The Future of the Capitalist State* (Cambridge, 2002).

63 H. Lacher and B. Teschke, 'The Changing "Logics" of Capital-
    ist Competition', *Cambridge Review of International Affairs*,
    20 (2007): 574.
64 Ibid., p. 577.
65 F. Cooper, *Colonialism in Question* (Berkeley/Los Angeles,
    2005).
66 Lacher and Teschke, 'The Changing "Logics" of Capitalist
    Competition', pp. 579, 570, 571.
67 For further discussion of Lacher and Tesche and other critics
    of my original article, see A. Callinicos, 'How to Solve the
    Many-State Problem: A Reply to the Debate', *Cambridge
    Review of International Affairs*, 22 (2009).
68 A. Wendt, *Social Theory of International Politics* (Cambridge,
    1999), pp. 96, 97, 107, 111. See also ibid., ch. 6, 'Three Cul-
    tures of Anarchy', and id., 'Anarchy is What States Make of
    It', *International Organization*, 46 (1992).
69 Wendt, *Social Theory of International Politics*, pp. 111,
    94–5. It is presumably because of this reduction of relations
    to ideas that Wendt claims that G.A. Cohen seeks 'to
    derive relations of production from the forces' (ibid., 252 n.
    18), an interpretation that involves a complete misunderstand-
    ing of the functional relationship that Cohen posits between
    the forces and relations: *Karl Marx's Theory of History*
    (Oxford, 1978).
70 See, for example, S.B. Greenberg, *Race and State in Capitalist
    Development* (New Haven, 1980).
71 See Wendt, *Social Theory of International Politics*, ch. 2.
    Opposition to reductive treatments of relations is a major
    theme of the version of scientific realism that I defend in *The
    Resources of Critique* (Cambridge, 2006), Part 2. Wittgen-
    stein's discussion of rule-following in the *Philosophical Inves-
    tigations* undermines any attempt to treat rules as 'shared
    ideas': C. McGinn, *Wittgenstein on Meaning* (Oxford, 1986).
72 J.J. Mearsheimer and S.M. Walt, 'The Israel Lobby', 23 March
    2006, extended into *The Israel Lobby and US Foreign Policy*
    (London, 2007). Their critique of the Iraq adventure is set out
    in 'An Unnecessary War', *Foreign Policy*, 134 (January 2003).
    Mearsheimer develops his version of 'offensive realism' most
    fully in *The Tragedy of Great Power Politics* (New York,
    2001).
73 F. Zakaria, *From Wealth to Power* (Princeton, 1998), quota-
    tions from pp. 38, 39.

74 C. Layne, *The Peace of Illusions* (Ithaca, 2006), pp. 3, 28, 30, 201.

75 See esp. ibid., chs 1 and 8, and, for the US as an offshore balancer outside the Western Hemisphere, Mearsheimer, *The Tragedy of Great Power Politics*, ch. 7. Williams first set out his interpretation of the Open Door in [1959] *The Tragedy of American Diplomacy* (New York, 1991). Peter Gowan offers a sympathetic Marxist critique of Layne's argument in 'A Radical Realist', *New Left Review*, II/41 (2006).

76 Pozo-Martin, 'Autonomous or Materialist Geopolitics', p. 554.

77 *Inter alia*, K. van der Pijl, *The Making of an Atlantic Ruling Class* (London, 1984), *Global Rivalries from the Cold War to Iraq* (London, 2006), and 'Capital and the State System: A Class Act', *Cambridge Review of International Affairs*, 20 (2007).

78 For a good critical introduction, see T. Eagleton, *Ideology* (London, 1991).

79 Wendt, *Social Theory of International Politics*, ch. 5 (quotations from pp. 230, 231–2, 237). I offer extended treatments of interests, ideologies and identities in *Making History* (2nd edn; Leiden, 2004), chs 3–5.

80 See, *inter alia*, R.W. Cox, 'Gramsci, Hegemony and International Relations', *Millennium*, 12 (1983), 'Social Forces, States and World Order', in R.O. Keohane, ed., *Neorealism and its Critics* (New York, 1986), and *Production, Power and World Order* (New York, 1987), A. Morton, *Unravelling Gramsci* (London, 2007), and 'Disputing the Politics of the States System and Global Capitalism', *Cambridge Review of International Affairs*, 20 (2007), A. Bieler and A. Morton, 'The Gordian Knot of Agency-Structure in International Relations', *European Journal of International Relations*, 7 (2001), and, for a critique, R.M. Germain, and M. Kenny, 'Engaging Gramsci: International Relations Theory and the New Gramscians', *Review of International Studies*, 24 (1998).

3 CAPITALISM AND *LA LONGUE DURÉE*

1 B. Buzan and R. Little, *International Systems in World History* (Oxford, 2000), p. 295.

2 E.J. Hobsbawm, *The Age of Revolution 1789–1848* (London, 1962), *The Age of Capital* (London, 1975), and *The Age of Empire 1875–1914* (London, 1987).

3   Id., *The Age of Empire*, p. 56.
4   E.M. Wood, 'A Reply to Critics', *Historical Materialism*, 15/3 (2007): 145.
5   M. Dobb, *Studies in the Development of Capitalism* (London, 1946), p. 126; see generally ibid., chs 2–4.
6   R.H. Hilton, ed., *The Transition from Feudalism to Capitalism* (London, 1976).
7   A. Brewer, *Marxist Theories of Imperialism* (2nd edn; London, 1990), p. 18.
8   Ibid., p. 163. See A.G. Frank, *Capitalism and Underdevelopment in Latin America* (Harmondsworth, 1971).
9   I. Wallerstein, *The Modern World-System*, I (New York, 1974), pp. 7, 15.
10 Ibid., pp. 91, 127.
11 F. Braudel, [1979] *Civilization and Capitalism, 15th–18th Century* (3 vols; London, 1981, 1982, 1984), III, p. 39, II, p. 230.
12 Ibid., II, pp. 231–2, III, pp. 256, 34.
13 G. Arrighi, *The Long Twentieth Century* (London, 1994) pp. 9, 6. See also G. Arrighi, B. Silver, et al., *Chaos and Governance in the Modern World System* (Minneapolis, 1999) and G. Arrighi, *Adam Smith in Beijing* (London, 2007).
14 Arrighi, *The Long Twentieth Century*, pp. ix–x, 214–15, *Adam Smith in Beijing*, Part 3. For more on Arrighi's theory of capitalist hegemony, see §4.1 of this volume.
15 R. Brenner, 'The Origins of Capitalist Development', *New Left Review*, I/104 (1977), and 'The Social Basis of Economic Development', in J. Roemer, ed., *Analytical Marxism* (Cambridge, 1986; quotations from pp. 24, 26, 27). Brenner's concept of 'social-property relations' is identical in content to Marx's production relations, though he has an unpersuasive argument that they are different: ibid., p. 46. A recent, comprehensive restatement of Brenner's interpretation of capitalist development will be found in 'Property and Progress: Where Adam Smith Went Wrong', in C. Wickham, ed., *Marxist History-Writing for the Twenty-First Century* (Oxford, 2007).
16 Ibid., pp. 32, 34, 33. In more recent work, Brenner has underlined the implicit distinction drawn here between separation from the means of subsistence – above all, land – and separation from the means of production, which comprises tools and other instruments of production as well: according to him, only the latter constitutes proletarianization in Marx's sense (the

transformation of small producers into wage-labourers), but the former is sufficient for the market-dependence required to support a capitalist economic dynamic 'because it implies subjection to competition'; 'The Low Countries in the Transition to Capitalism', in P. Hoppenbrouwers and J.L. Van Zanden, eds, *Peasants into Farmers?* (Brepols, 2001) p. 278 n.1.

17   For Marx's own explanation of why the wage-form facilitates higher productivity on the worker's part, see 'Results of the Immediate Process of Production', appendix to *Capital*, I (Harmondsworth, 1976), pp. 1026–34.

18   Brenner, 'The Origins of Capitalist Development', pp. 70–1. See, for a detailed study of early modern Poland that tends to substantiate this argument, W. Kula, *An Economic Theory of Feudalism* (London, 1976).

19   R. Brenner, 'Agrarian Class Structure and Economic Development in Pre-Industrial Development', *Past & Present*, 70 (1976).

20   G. Bois, 'Against the Neo-Malthusian Orthodoxy', *Past & Present*, 79 (1978): 67. See generally T.H. Aston and C.H.E. Philpin, eds, *The Brenner Debate* (Cambridge, 1985). For a powerful critique of Brenner's account of the origins of capitalism, see C. Harman, 'From Feudalism to Capitalism', *International Socialism*, 2/45 (1989).

21   E.M. Wood, *Empire of Capital* (London, 2003), pp. 62, 63.

22   K. Marx, *Capital*, III (Harmondsworth, 1981), pp. 442, 444, 445, 452.

23   Ibid., p. 453 (italics added).

24   R. Blackburn, *The Making of New World Slavery* (London, 1997), pp. 376–7. The concept of transitional forms is developed and applied with great subtlety by Lenin in *The Development of Capitalism in Russia* (Moscow, 1967), ch. III. Wood seems to go some way towards this kind of position: 'The growth of slavery in the British colonies is a striking example of how capitalism has, at certain points in its development, appropriated to itself, and even intensified non-capitalist modes of exploitation,' *Empire of Capital*, p. 104.

25   R. Brenner, *Merchants and Revolution* (Princeton, 1993), quotations from pp. 83–4, 114.

26   Ibid., pp. 652, 668–70, 685–6. Jairus Banaji forcefully argues for a revaluation of the role played by merchant capital in the development of capitalism in 'Islam, the Mediterranean and the Rise of Capitalism', *Historical Materialism*, 15/1 (2007).

27 For example, C.A. Bayly, *The Birth of the Modern World 1780–1914* (Oxford, 2004), and J. Darwin, *After Tamerlane* (London, 2007).

28 K. Pomeranz, *The Great Divergence* (Princeton, 2000).

29 J.L. Abu-Lughod, *Before European Hegemony* (New York, 1989). Ronald Findlay and Kevin O'Rourke have written an excellent history of the world economy over the past thousand years, *Power and Plenty* (Princeton, 2007); intellectually orthodox in its reliance of neoclassical assumptions and positively provincial in its refusal to engage with pertinent Marxist research, it is more adventurous in the stress it lays on interstate violence. Theoretically much more catholic, Herman Schwartz's *States versus Markets: The Emergence of a Global Economy* (2nd edn; Basingstoke, 2000) is quite outstanding. See also P.M. Kennedy, *The Rise and Fall of the Great Powers* (London, 1988).

30 Ibid., p. 361.

31 On ancient slavery, see, above all, G.E.M. de Ste Croix, *The Class Struggle in the Ancient Greek World* (London, 1981).

32 C. Wickham, 'The Uniqueness of the East', *Journal of Peasant Studies*, 12 (1985): 170, 168, 187, 185.

33 Ibid., pp. 185–6. Honesty compels me to report that Wickham has now retreated from this position and regards 'tax-based systems' and 'land-based systems' as 'sub-types of the same mode of production, in that both are based on agrarian surplus extracted, by force if necessary, from the peasant majority', *Framing the Early Middle Ages* (Oxford, 2005), p. 60. A similar stance is taken by Samir Amin, who seems to have been mainly responsible for giving the concept of what he calls 'the tribute-paying mode of production' wide currency on the left – see *Unequal Development* (Brighton, 1976), and by a number of leading Marxist historians: for example, H. Berktay, 'The Feudalism Debate: The Turkish End', *Journal of Peasant Studies*, 14 (1987), J.F. Haldon, *The State and the Tributary Mode of Production* (London, 1993), and C. Harman, 'The Rise of Capitalism', *International Socialism*, 2/102 (2004). I am nevertheless unpersuaded by the idea that most pre-capitalist class societies were dominated by a single, undifferentiated mode of production, called (according to taste) feudal or tributary: Wickham precedes his retraction of his earlier views with a summary of the significant differences between tax-based and land- (or rent)-based economic systems, which is

substantiated in much detail in his magisterial history of the passing of Late Antiquity: *Framing the Early Middle Ages*, pp. 57–60. There are two main arguments I have encountered for abandoning the distinction between the tributary and feudal modes. The first highlights the tendency of one to shift into the other, depending critically on the power of the state and its independence from the landed aristocracy. This is only to be expected given that both modes involved the same exploited class – a peasantry that typically would be paying tax to the state and rent to the landowners – and given also the relative fragility of pre-modern states; it does not alter the fact that the difference in the form of surplus-extraction implies distinct rules of reproduction for exploiters and (hence) for the exploited. Secondly, Chris Harman has made the more *ad hominem* objection that recognition of a distinct tributary mode implies that 'absolutist France was not feudal, since the exploitation of the peasantry and enrichment of the nobility was mainly through the tax system of the monarchy', a position taken by Political Marxists such as Benno Teschke (see *The Myth of 1648* [London, 2003], ch. 5): Harman, 'The Rise of Capitalism', p. 85 n.57. But this conclusion in no way follows from my position: see the discussion of early modern European statebuilding in §3.3 below. As Neil Davidson's comment on Harman [2004], 'Asiatic, Tributary or Absolutist?', at ⟨www. isj.org.uk⟩, indicates, the development of the concept of the tributary mode of production was intended partly to extract something historically defensible from the mess that is Marx's discredited idea of the Asiatic Mode of Production, on which see P. Anderson, *Lineages of the Absolutist State* (London, 1974), pp. 462–549, A.M. Bailey and J. Lobera, eds, *The Asiatic Mode of Production* (London, 1981), and B. O'Leary, *The Asiatic Mode of Production* (Oxford, 1989).

34   I. Habib [1963], *The Agrarian System of Mughal India 1556–1707* (2nd edn; New Delhi, 1999), pp. 367–8. Habib has been criticized for overstating the coherence and effectiveness of the Mughal system; see the studies collected in M. Alam and S. Subrahmanyam, eds, *The Mughal State 1526–1750* (New Delhi, 1998), though these seem to qualify rather than to refute Habib's great synthesis. I am grateful to John Game for guiding me through the historiographical thickets surrounding this subject.

35   M. Elvin, *The Pattern of the Chinese Past* (London, 1973), p. 28. While denying the distinction between feudal and

tributary modes, John Haldon has shown that, under both the Byzantine and Ottoman Empires, a tendency developed for the control exercised over the distribution of the surplus-product by the imperial court to decline in favour of private landowners (in the Byzantine case, the growing power of landlords and holders of *pronoiai*, territorially delimited assignments of rent and revenue, from the eleventh century onwards; in the Ottoman case the emergence in the mid–seventeenth century of the *a'yan* class of provincial landowners to challenge the dominance of the central *devşirme* elite of state slaves): Haldon, *The State and the Tributary Mode of Production*, pp. 109–39, 158–88.

36   Wickham, *Framing the Early Middle Ages* (quotation from p. 82); see id., 'The Other Transition', *Past & Present*, 103 (1984), for an earlier version of the same interpretation, and n.33 above for his change of mind.

37   Wickham, *Framing the Early Middle Ages*, chs 3 and 11 (quotations from pp. 709, 790). Keith Hopkins highlights the formative role of military conquest in the political economy of the Roman Empire: *Conquerors and Slaves* (Cambridge, 1978), ch. 1. See also Michael Mann's analysis of the Roman 'legionary economy': *The Sources of Social Power* (2 vols, Cambridge, 1986, 1993), I, ch. 9.

38   Habib, *The Agrarian System of Mughal India*, esp. ch. II.

39   A. Das Gupta [1970], 'Trade and Politics in Eighteenth-Century India', in Alam and Subrahmanyam, eds, *The Mughal State*.

40   Elvin, *The Pattern of the Chinese Past*, p. 69.

41   Ibid., *passim* (quotation from pp. 281–2).

42   Arrighi, *Adam Smith in Beijing*, pp. 314–36 (quotations from pp. 314, 316, 324).

43   K. van der Pijl, *Nomads, Empires, States* (London, 2008), pp. 89–109.

44   Elvin, *The Pattern of the Chinese Past*, pp. 312, 314.

45   R. Brenner and C. Isett, 'England's Divergence from the Yangtze Delta: Property Relations, Microeconomics, and Patterns of Development', *Journal of Asian Studies*, 61 (2002) (quotations from pp. 615, 616, 631). Angus Maddison's interpretation of pre-colonial Chinese macroeconomic trends seems consistent with this argument: *Contours of the World Economy, 1–2030 AD* (Oxford, 2007), pp. 157–65. Mainstream historians such as Bayly and Darwin sometimes generalize the pattern diagnosed by Brenner and Isett in China, arguing that the Old

World experienced in the seventeenth and eighteenth centuries an 'industrious revolution' based on the intensification of labour that was of far greater importance than the Industrial Revolution till the nineteenth century; the effect, as Vivek Chibber points out, is 'to sideline the advent of industrial capitalism as a framework for understanding the nineteenth century': 'Sidelining the West?', *New Left Review*, II/47 (2007): 141. Mark Elvin has an interesting discussion of these issues in his review of *Adam Smith in Beijing*: 'The Historian as Haruspex', *New Left Review*, II/52 (2008).

46 Arrighi, *Adam Smith in Beijing*, p. 320.

47 Wickham, 'The Uniqueness of the East', p. 169.

48 G. Bois, *La Mutation de l'an mil* (Paris, 1989). The idea of the Feudal Revolution *c.*1000 seems to have been coined by Georges Duby: see, for example, *The Three Orders* (Chicago, 1980), ch. 13.

49 Mann, *The Sources of Social Power*, I, ch. 5 (quotation from p. 170). Herfried Münkler stresses both the unbounded and the hierarchical character of empire as a political form: *Empires* (Cambridge, 2007), ch. 1. For Hardt and Negri, by contrast, postmodern Empire is unbounded but centre-less: *Empire* (Cambridge, MA, 2000). For good treatments of the relationships between empires and nomads, see Buzan and Little, *International Systems in World History*, ch. 8, and Van Der Pijl, *Nomads, Empires, States*, ch. 3.

50 Brenner, 'The Social Basis of Economic Development', pp. 31–2.

51 R. Bartlett, *The Making of Europe* (London, 1993).

52 G. Bois, *The Crisis of Feudalism* (Cambridge, 1984).

53 R. Brenner, 'The Agrarian Roots of European Capitalism', *Past & Present*, 97 (1982): 81. The logic of Brenner's argument is that absolutism 'expresses a *transformed* version of the old system' – i.e., feudalism; this is also the position taken by Anderson in *Lineages of the Absolutist State*. This is different from Teschke's argument that 'absolutism cannot be subsumed under feudalism or the "feudal mode of production" . . . It was a *sui generis* social formation, displaying a specific mode of government and determinate pre–modern and pre–capitalist domestic and international "laws of motion"', *The Myth of 1648*, p. 191. The apparent tying of this '*sui generis* social formation' to 'a specific mode of government' etc. contradicts Lacher's and Teschke's correct argument that the same

253

economic system – in this case capitalism – may 'co-vary' with different forms of territorial state (see §2.2 of this volume). Why feudalism should be denied such 'co-variance' is not obvious. Chris Harman argues such a denial is forced on anyone who distinguishes the tributary and feudal modes (see n.33 above); but this argument is also not compelling. Given the intensity of early modern interstate rivalries, the entrenched position of the landed aristocracy – with which the French monarchy had difficulties right up to 1789, and the porousness that integration in the developing capitalist world economy gave European societies, the possibility of a tributary empire emerging in Europe remained a fantasy – despite the dreams of the Habsburgs and Bourbons. The success, noted below, of the feudal lords in colonizing the absolute state helps to explain the strategies pursued by tributary rulers – the Mughals' changing *jāgirs* (revenue allocations) every few years or the reliance of the Ottoman sultans in the classical era on state slaves to staff the bureaucracy and the army. The structural problem of how pre-modern rulers could prevent their agents appropriating the state is one of the main themes of Weber's discussion of patrimonialism: *Economy and Society* (Berkeley/Los Angeles, 1968), II, pp. 1010ff.

54   C. Tilly, 'Reflections on the History of European State-Making', in id., ed., *The Formation of National States in Western Europe* (Princeton, 1975), p. 15. In recent work Brenner himself has generalized the vertical/horizontal distinction: 'Property and Progress', p. 58.

55   Mann, *The Sources of Social Power*, I, p. 490; see ibid., I, chs 13, 14, II, chs 11–14.

56   C. Wickham, 'Productive Force and the Economic Logic of the Feudal Mode of Production', *Historical Materialism*, 16/2 (2008).

57   C. Harman, *A People's History of the World* (London, 1999), p. 155.

58   The fact that '[t]he superstructures in mediaeval Europe were weak and fragmented' compared to those in India and China plays an important part in Harman's explanation of why capitalism first became dominant in Europe, though he refuses to relate this difference to one between modes of production: 'The Rise of Capitalism', p. 68.

59   See, for a Marxist synthesis of early modern economic history that lays great stress on proto-industrialization, P. Kriedte,

Peasants, Landlords and Merchant Capitalists (Leamington Spa, 1983), and, for a critical take, D.C. Coleman, 'Proto-Industrialization: One Concept Too Many', *Economic History Review*, XXXVI (1983).

60   C.R. Boxer, *The Portuguese Seaborne Empire 1415–1825* (Harmondsworth, 1973).

61   J.H. Elliott, *Empires of the Atlantic World* (New Haven, 2006), p. 411. Fred Anderson and Andrew Catton contrast French and English patterns of colonization and war in North America in *The Dominion of War* (London, 2005), ch. 1.

62   Wood, *Empire of Capital*, p. 68.

63   E.J. Hobsbawm, 'The Crisis of the Seventeenth Century', in T. Ashton, ed., *Crisis in Europe 1560–1660* (London, 1965), p. 42. See, on the Dutch Revolt, G. Parker, *The Dutch Revolt* (Harmondsworth, 1979), J. Israel, *The Dutch Republic: Its Rise, Greatness, and Fall* (Oxford, 1998), Part I, and P. Brandon, 'The Dutch Revolt: A Social Analysis', *International Socialism*, 2/116 (2007).

64   J. Israel, *Dutch Primacy in World Trade, 1585–1740* (Oxford, 1989), pp. 12, 13.

65   Ibid., esp. chs 2–5, and, more generally, K.N. Chaudhuri, *The Trading World of Asia and the English East India Company 1660–1760* (Cambridge, 1978).

66   J. de Vries and A. van der Woude, *The First Modern Economy: Success, Failure, and Perseverance of the Dutch Economy, 1500–1815* (Cambridge, 1997), pp. 667, 232, 243, 609, 633.

67   Brenner, 'The Low Countries in the Transition to Capitalism', p. 332.

68   Israel, *Dutch Primacy in World Trade*, pp. 411, 188–9.

69   C. Trebilcock, *The Industrialization of the Continental Powers 1780–1914* (London, 1981), pp. 112, 114.

70   Israel, *Dutch Primacy in World Trade*, pp. 307–13. See, on Dutch decline, ibid., chs 7–11, de Vries and van der Woude, *The First Modern Economy*, ch. 13, and I. Wallerstein, *The Modern World-System II* (New York, 1980).

71   C. Hill, 'A Bourgeois Revolution?', in J.G.A. Pocock, ed., *Three British Revolutions* (Princeton, 1980), pp. 134–5. The best Marxist account of the English Revolution is provided by Brian Manning in *The English People and the English Revolution 1640–1649* (London, 1976), to which Brenner's *Merchants and Revolution* provides a valuable complement.

72   Hill, 'A Bourgeois Revolution?', p. 120.

73 C. Hill, 'Braudel and the State', in id., *Collected Essays*, III (Brighton, 1986), pp. 132, 140.

74 Mann, *The Sources of Social Power*, I, pp. 483–5.

75 P. Mathias and P. O'Brien, 'Taxation in Britain and France, 1715–1810', *Journal of European Economic History*, 5 (1976). Two important recent studies of Britain's eighteenth-century geopolitical struggles, focusing respectively on the American and European theatres, are F. Anderson, *Crucible of War* (London, 2000), and B. Simms, *Three Victories and a Defeat* (London, 2007), quotation from p. 71.

76 J. Brewer, *The Sinews of Power* (London, 1989), ch. 4.

77 Wallerstein, *The Modern World System II*, pp. 274–88.

78 G. Ardant, 'Financial Policy and Economic Infrastructure of Modern States and Nations', in Tilly, ed., *The Formation of National States in Western Europe*, p. 213.

79 For a fine study of the seventeenth-century Anglo–Dutch antagonism, see C. Wilson, *Profit and Power* (London, 1957).

80 B. Simms, *Three Victories and a Defeat*, pp. 246, 366. For a symmetrical French view, see ibid., pp. 368–9.

81 W.H. McNeill, *The Pursuit of Power* (Oxford, 1983), pp. 211–12.

82 Blackburn, *The Making of New World Slavery*, ch. XII (figures from p. 542); E. Williams [1944], *Capitalism and Slavery* (New York, 1966) p. 105. See, for an analysis that also stresses the importance of the triangular trade to the Industrial Revolution, this time from a neoclassical perspective, Findlay and O'Rourke, *Power and Plenty*, pp. 330–45, and, on the Haitian Revolution and Anglo-French efforts to seize St Domingue from the rebels, R. Blackburn, *The Overthrow of Colonial Slavery 1776–1848* (London, 1988), ch. VI.

83 De Vries and van der Woude, *The First Modern Economy*, p. 129; see more generally ibid., pp. 91–129.

84 N.A.M. Rodger, *The Command of the Ocean: A Naval History of Britain 1649–1815* (London, 2004).

85 Ha-Joon Chang highlights the active role of the state in British economic development: *Kicking Away the Ladder* (London, 2003), esp. pp. 19–24; see also J.V.C. Nye, *War, Wine, and Taxes: The Political Economy of Anglo-French Trade, 1689–1900* (Princeton, 2007). My argument in this section is indebted to Alan Carling's suggestion that late mediaeval and early modern geopolitical competition in Europe can be seen as a process of natural selection promoting the emergence of

capitalist states: see, for example, *Social Division* (London, 1992), Part I, and 'Analytical Marxism and Historical Materialism', *Science and Society*, 57 (1993).

4 AGES OF IMPERIALISM

1   R. Brenner, 'What is, and What is Not, Imperialism?', *Historical Materialism*, 14/4 (2006): 90.
2   H. Arendt [1951], *The Origins of Totalitarianism* (London, 1986), p. 143, quoted in D. Harvey, *The New Imperialism* (Oxford, 2003), p. 34.
3   Chris Harman has written an excellent analytical history of imperialism that in many respects parallels mine: 'Analysing Imperialism', *International Socialism*, 2/99 (2003).
4   E.M. Wood, 'A Reply to Critics', *Historical Materialism*, 15/3 (2007): 151–2, commenting on F. Chesnais, 'The Economic Foundations of Contemporary Imperialism', ibid.
5   Influential explorations of the different models of contemporary capitalism include M. Albert, *Capitalism against Capitalism* (Hoboken, NJ, 1992), and P. Hall and D. Soskice, eds, *Varieties of Capitalism* (Oxford, 2001).
6   Wood, 'A Reply to Critics', p. 162.
7   R. Brenner and M. Glick, 'The Regulation Approach: Theory and History', *New Left Review*, I/188 (1991): 111.
8   See, for more extended discussions of the issue of periodization, A. Callinicos, 'Periodizing Capitalism and Analysing Imperialism', in R. Albritton et al., eds, *Phases of Capitalist Development*, (Basingstoke, 2001), and 'Epoch and Conjuncture in Marxist Political Economy', *International Politics*, 42 (2005), and, for a brief appreciation of Harvey's work, id., 'David Harvey and Marxism', in N. Castree and D. Gregory, eds, *David Harvey: A Critical Reader* (Oxford, 2006). Very briefly put, my disagreement with Harvey is that, as part of his broader, and in many ways very productive project of loosening and opening out Marx's categories, he tends to rewrite the theory of the tendency of the rate of profit to fall as a theory of over-accumulation: for example, 'Marx's falling rate of profit argument does convincingly demonstrate that the capitalists' necessary passion for surplus-value-producing technological change, when coupled with the social imperative "accumulation for accumulation's sake", produces a surplus of capital

relative to opportunities to employ that capital,' *The Limits to Capital* (Oxford, 1982), p. 192. But the sense in which this constitutes an *over*-accumulation of capital is surely with reference to profitability – i.e., there is a surplus of capital relative to opportunities for its *profitable* employment. Over-accumulation, in other words, is the other face of a major fall in the rate of profit. This implies the need for a theory explaining why capitalism is prone to generate such falls in profitability. In the absence of such a theory (which need not be Marx's but could, for example, be that developed by Brenner or the kind of wage-squeeze theory championed by Andrew Glyn among others: see the references in n.122 below), then an over-accumulation theory is likely to collapse into a manifestly inadequate disproportionality or under-consumptionist explanation of crises. (This criticism is also relevant, incidentally, to the emphases Simon Clarke tends to make in *Marx's Theory of Crisis* [London, 1994].) By reframing crisis theory in terms of over-accumulation, Harvey tends to shift the focus of explanation away from profitability to what he calls the 'second' and 'third cut' theories of crisis – respectively, financial markets and the 'spatial fix' (the geographical displacement of investment as a means of surplus-absorption). This shift in focus has undeniably had fruitful consequences, but it needs to be more firmly situated within a theory of the tendency of the rate of profit to fall. The dangers involved in not doing so are indicated by Harvey's recent propensity to rewrite the entire history of capitalism as a succession of attempts to solve the problem of surplus capital, a process he dates back to the sixteenth century, when 'the failure to absorb these surpluses [generated by colonial pillage] merely produced the grand European inflation,' 'In What Ways is "The New Imperialism" Really New?', *Historical Materialism*, 15/3 (2007): 61–5 (quotation from p. 61). Wood is entirely right to protest that this involves stretching the concept of capitalism till it loses any specificity: 'A Reply to Critics', pp. 144–7.

9   E.O. Wright, 'Giddens's Critique of Marxism', *New Left Review*, I/138 (1983): 26.

10 The irreducible historical role of contingency is one of the main themes of James McPherson's superb history of the American Civil War, *Battle Cry of Freedom* (New York, 1988). See, on the Second World War, R.J. Overy, *Why the Allies Won* (London, 1995), and, on the Cuban missile crisis, E.R. May

and P. Zelikow, eds, *The Kennedy Tapes* (Cambridge, MA, 1997), and M. Dobbs, *One Minute to Midnight: Kennedy, Khrushchev, and Castro on the Brink of Nuclear War* (London, 2008).

11   J. Darwin, *After Tamerlane* (London, 2007), p. 485. See also P.K. O'Brien, 'The Pax Britannica and American Hegemony: Precedent, Antecedent, or Just Another History?', and J.M. Hobson, 'Two Hegemonies or One?', both in O'Brien and A. Cleese, eds, *Two Hegemonies: Britain 1846–1914 and the United States 1941–2001* (Aldershot, 2002), R.S. Nye, *Bound to Lead* (New York, 1991), esp. chs 1 and 2, and W.C. Wolforth, 'The Stability of a Unipolar World', *International Security*, 24 (1999).

12   B. Porter, *Empire and Superempire* (New Haven, 2006).

13   G. Arrighi, *The Long Twentieth Century* (London, 1994), pp. 27, 28. Compare A. Gramsci, *Selections from the Prison Notebooks* (London, 1971), pp. 56–8, and, in mainstream International Relations, the theory of hegemonic stability – e.g., R. Gilpin, *War and Change in World Politics* (Cambridge, 1981) and R.O. Keohane, *After Hegemony* (Princeton, 1984).

14   G. Arrighi and B. Silver, Introduction, Arrighi, Silver et al., *Chaos and Governance in the Modern World System* (Minneapolis, 1999), p. 27.

15   Ibid., p. 34. Hardt and Negri criticize Arrighi in *Empire* (Cambridge, MA, 2000), pp. 237–9 (quotation from p. 239). Arrighi's most extended response to this criticism is *Adam Smith in Beijing* (London, 2007), pp. 235–49.

16   Arrighi, *Adam Smith in Beijing*, p. 241.

17   C. Wilson, *Profit and Power* (London, 1957), p. 146.

18   J. de Vries and A. van der Woude, *The First Modern Economy* (Cambridge, 1997), pp. 117ff. Herman Schwartz offers an interesting take on the economic dimension of hegemony: 'Hegemonic countries' high levels of productivity and income means they usually constitute a sizeable portion of world import markets,' thereby encouraging other states 'to align around the hegemon' by exporting to it, *States versus Markets: The Emergence of a Global Economy* (2nd edn; Houndmills, 2000), pp. 72, 73. But even if Holland was able to play this role in the still underdeveloped world economy of the seventeenth century, the argument in the text that it was unable to perform the geopolitical functions of hegemony still stands.

Immanuel Wallerstein argues, much more tentatively than Arrighi, that the United Provinces held the position of hegemon 'least plausibly' by comparison with Britain and the US 'because it was least of all the military giant of its era', and that its 'momentary summit' spanned 1625–75, giving way to 'a time of unbroken Anglo-French rivalry' culminating in 'the definitive triumph of England' in 1763: *The Modern World-System II* (New York, 1980), pp. 38, 39, 245.

19   E.J. Hobsbawm, *The Age of Capital 1848–1875* (London, 1975), ch. 3 (quotations from pp. 82, 77). See, for a sophisticated historical overview of the process of industrialization, C. Freeman and F. Louçã, *As Time Goes By* (Oxford, 2001), and, on the Industrial Revolution's impact on the world economy, R. Findlay and K.H. O'Rourke, *Power and Plenty* (Princeton, 2007), ch. 7.

20   S.B. Saul, *Studies in British Overseas Trade 1870–1914* (Liverpool, 1960), p. 112.

21   Ibid., pp. 44, 114, 115.

22   Though it is couched as part of a mistaken critique of Marxian value theory, there is an illuminating discussion of the relationship between gold and other forms of money and economic policy regimes in A. Cutler et al., *Marx's 'Capital' and Capitalism Today* (2 vols, London, 1977, 1978), II, ch. 3.

23   M. Davis, *Late Victorian Holocausts* (London, 2001), esp. Part IV; figures from table P1, p. 7.

24   E.J. Hobsbawm, *The Age of Empire 1875–1914* (London, 1987), p. 51.

25   W.H. McNeill, *The Pursuit of Power* (Oxford, 1982), chs 7 and 8, and P.M. Kennedy, *The Rise of the Anglo-German Antagonism 1860–1914* (London, 1980).

26   John M. Hobson argues that the late nineteenth-century shift to protection was motivated by domestic fiscal and external geopolitical considerations, though this says nothing about the economic effects of these policies: *The Wealth of States* (Cambridge, 1997).

27   See G. Ingham, *Capitalism Divided?* (Basingstoke, 1984), and P.J. Cain and A.G. Hopkins, *British Imperialism: Innovation and Expansion 1688–1914* (London, 1997), for studies that, while overstating the significance of their findings for the interpretation of British history, provide much useful analysis and evidence on the global role of the City in the nineteenth and early twentieth centuries.

28 G. Arrighi et al., 'The Transformation of Business Enterprise', in Arrighi, Silver et al., *Chaos and Governance in the World System*, p. 127.

29 S. Roskill, *Naval Policy between the Wars*, I (London, 1968), p. 500.

30 A. Gamble, *Britain in Decline* (London, 1981), p. 58. A good discussion of strategic decision-making by the British political elite at the beginning of the twentieth century is provided in A. Friedberg, *The Weary Titan* (Princeton, 1988).

31 B. Adams [1900], *America's Economic Supremacy* (New York, 1947), pp. 104–5. Brooks Adams and his more reflective brother Henry both figure in Gore Vidal's fine historical novel, set in *fin-de-siècle* Washington, *Empire* (London, 1987).

32 See, for example, respectively M.E. Brown et al., eds, *Debating the Democratic Peace* (Cambridge, MA, 1996) and K. van der Pijl, *Global Rivalries from the Cold War to Iraq* (London, 2006); quotation from p. xi.

33 F. Zakaria, *From Wealth to Power* (Princeton, 1998), pp. 82. An example of the view criticized by Zakaria is G.F. Kennan, *American Diplomacy 1900–1950* (Chicago, 1951), p. 5.

34 K. Bourne, *Britain and the Balance of Power in North America* (Berkeley and Los Angeles, 1967), quotation from p. viii.

35 H. Münkler, *Empires* (Cambridge, 2007), p. 93; see also ibid., pp. 196–7 n.49.

36 R. Blackburn, *The Overthrow of Colonial Slavery 1776–1848* (London, 1988), p. 542.

37 M. Aglietta, *A Theory of Capitalist Regulation* (London, 1979), p. 77.

38 Bourne, *Britain and the Balance of Power in North America*, pp. 236–7. Henry Adams, who served in the US legation in London during the Civil War, paints a vivid picture of the hostility of the British upper class to the North: [1907] *The Education of Henry Adams* (Oxford, 1999), pp. 99ff.

39 Quoted in Zakaria, *From Wealth to Power*, p. 149.

40 Quoted in A. Roberts, *Lord Salisbury* (London, 1999), p. 617.

41 Adams, *The Education of Henry Adams*, p. 303; Bourne, *Britain and the Balance of Power in North America*, chs 9 and 10, and Friedberg, *The Weary Titan*, ch. 4. See, on the subtle interplay between US and British interests in the making of the Monroe Doctrine, S.F. Bemis, *John Quincy Adams and the Foundations of American Foreign Policy* (New York, 1956), chs XVIII and XIX.

42 F. Zakaria, *The Post-American World* (London, 2008), p. 177.

43 Quoted in W.R. Louis, *British Strategy in the Far East 1919–1939* (Oxford, 1971), pp. 53, 54.

44 R.L. Craigie, 'Outstanding Problems affecting Anglo-American Relations', 12 November 1928, in W.N. Medlicott et al., eds, *Documents on British Foreign Policy 1919–1939*, Series 1A, V (London, 1973), p. 860. Much helpful background on Anglo-American relations in the 1920s will be found in M.J. Hogan [1977], *Informal Entente* (Chicago, 1991), and F. Costigliola, *Awkward Dominion* (Ithaca, 1984), the first more stressing cooperation; the second conflict, between London and Washington.

45 L.D. Trotsky, *Europe and America* (New York, 1971), p. 22.

46 V.I. Lenin, *Collected Works*, XXII (Moscow, 1965), p. 255.

47 M. Barratt Brown, *The Economics of Imperialism* (Harmondsworth, 1974), ch. 8. See V.G. Kiernan's fine study of the military dimension, *European Empires from Conquest to Collapse, 1815–1960* (Glasgow, 1982), and, on the partition of the Middle East, D. Fromkin, *A Peace to End All Peace* (London, 1991).

48 G. Stedman Jones, 'The History of US Imperialism', in R. Blackburn, ed., *Ideology in Social Science* (London, 1972), pp. 216–17. The 'aggressive territorial expansionism' of the early US is one of the main themes of Robert Kagan's *Dangerous Nation: America and the World 1600–1898* (London, 2006); quotation from p. 4. As Stedman Jones notes, the case of the US is the most powerful single counter-example to Joseph Schumpeter's theory of imperialism as an archaic phenomenon reflecting the interests and ideology of pre-capitalist landed aristocracies: [1919] *Imperialism and Social Classes* (New York, 1955); for a critique of the theory, see A. Callinicos, 'Marxism and Imperialism Today', *International Socialism*, 2/50 (1991): 9–12.

49 J. Gallagher and D. Robinson, 'The Imperialism of Free Trade', *Economic History Review*, 2/VI (1953).

50 Saul, *Studies in British Overseas Trade 1870–1914*, p. 228.

51 Gramsci, *Selections from the Prison Notebooks*, p. 68.

52 Arrighi, *Adam Smith in Beijing*, pp. 116–20.

53 C. Harman, *Explaining the Crisis* (London, 1984), pp. 51–4.

54 Schwarz, *States versus Markets*, pp. 152–9 (quotation from p. 153).

55 Cain and Hopkins, *British Imperialism: Innovation and Expansion 1688–1914*, pp. 173–6, which reviews historiographical controversies about the figures.

56 Saul, *Studies in British Overseas Trade 1870–1914*, p. 61.
57 Hobsbawm, *The Age of Empire*, pp. 73–4. See also E.A. Preo-brazhensky [1931], *The Decline of Capitalism* (Armonk, NY, 1985), pp. 17–19.
58 Wood, 'A Reply to Critics', p. 162. See also id., *Empire of Capital* (London, 2003), pp. 110–17.
59 Harvey, 'In What Ways is "The New Imperialism" Really New?', p. 62.
60 See Ranajit Guha's classic study of the ideology informing the Permanent Settlement [1963], *A Rule of Property for Bengal* (Durham, NC, 1996), and, on the origins of British power in India, C.A. Bayly, *Indian Society and the Making of the British Empire* (Cambridge, 1990) and N.B. Dirks, *The Scandal of Empire: India and the Creation of Imperial Britain* (Cambridge MA, 2006).
61 R.P. Dutt, *India Today* (London, 1940), ch. VII.
62 I. Habib, *Essays in Indian History* (New Delhi, 1995), p. 319.
63 Cain and Hopkins, *British Imperialism: Innovation and Expansion 1688–1914*, p. 334.
64 I.M. Drummond, *British Economic Policy and the Empire 1919–1939* (London, 1972), ch. 4.
65 K. Sugihara, ed., *Japan, China, and the Growth of the Asian International Economy, 1850–1949* (Oxford, 2005).
66 Saul, *Studies in British Overseas Trade 1870–1914*, pp. 203–4. See also Mike Davis's brilliant discussion: *Late Victorian Holocausts*, ch. 9.
67 There is an excellent summary of these debates in V.R. Berghahn, 'German Big Business and the Quest for a European Economic Empire in the Twentieth Century', in id., ed., *Quest for Economic Empire* (Providence, 1996); quotation from p. 10. Hobsbawm offers a brilliant overview of the causes of the First World War in *The Age of Empire*, ch. 13.
68 A. Offer, *The First World War: An Agrarian Interpretation* (Oxford, 1989).
69 P.J. Cain and A.G. Hopkins, *British Imperialism: Crisis and Deconstruction 1914–1990* (London, 1993), esp. chs 7 and 10 (quotation from p. 170).
70 A. Tooze, *The Wages of Destruction* (London, 2006), ch. 1. Tooze's study of National Socialist economic policy is enlightening, but his suggestion that Stresemann's strategy could have been successfully continued in the conditions of the Great

Depression seems like an implausible backward projection of the contemporary neoliberal *pensée unique*.

71 Harman, *Explaining the Crisis*, ch. 2, C. Kindleberger [1973], *The World in Depression 1929–1939* (rev. edn, Harmondsworth, 1987), H. James, *The End of Globalization* (Cambridge, 2001), and, on the Ottawa Conference (where Britain got significantly less than it sought), Drummond, *British Economic Policy and the Empire 1919–1939*, ch. 3.

72 N.I. Bukharin, *Selected Writings on the State and the Transition to Socialism* (Nottingham, 1982), p. 19.

73 See Tony Cliff's classic [1948], 'The Nature of Stalinist Russia', in id., *Marxist Theory after Trotsky* (London, 2003).

74 A.S. Milward [1977], *War, Economy, and Society 1939–1945* (Harmondsworth, 1987).

75 Tooze, *The Wages of Destruction*, and chs 6, 7, 9, 13, 14 (quotation from pp. 197, 459, 479).

76 R. Overy, *Goering* (London, 1984).

77 Berghahn, 'German Big Business and the Quest for an Economic Empire in the Twentieth Century, pp. 16, 17.

78 H.G. Schrötter, 'Europe in the Strategies of Germany's Electrical Engineering and Chemicals Trusts, 1919–1939', P. Hayes, 'The European Strategies of I.G. Farben, 1925–1945', and S. Reich, 'Fascism and the Structure of German Capitalism: The Case of the Automotive Industry', in Berghahn, ed., *Quest for Economic Empire*. I discuss the relationship between capitalism and National Socialism in 'Plumbing the Depths: Marxism and the Holocaust', *The Yale Journal of Criticism*, 14 (2001).

79 Quoted in D. Yergin, *The Prize* (London, 1993), p. 319; see the excellent synthesis in W.G. Beasley, *Japanese Imperialism 1894–1945* (Oxford, 1987).

80 J.W. Dower, *War without Mercy: Race and Power in the Pacific War* (New York, 1986).

81 Quoted in W.R. Louis, *Imperialism at Bay 1941–1945* (Oxford, 1977), p. 170.

82 J.H. Elliott, *Empires of the Atlantic World* (New Haven, 2006), p. 55.

83 T. Jefferson, *Writings*, ed. M.D. Peterson (New York, 1984), p. 19.

84 B.F. Fields, 'Slavery, Race and Ideology in the United States of America', *New Left Review*, I/181 (1990): 114. See also R, Blackburn, *The Making of New World Slavery* (London, 1997), esp. chs VI and VIII.

85   P. Fryer, *Staying Power* (London, 1984), p. 134.

86   For example, R. Holfstadter, *Social Darwinism in American Thought* (Boston, 1955).

87   Schwartz, *States versus Markets*, ch. 5; on the South African case, see the historical research summarized in B. Worden, *The Making of Modern South Africa* (Oxford, 1994) and W. Beinart and S. Dubow, eds, *Segregation and Apartheid in 20th Century South Africa* (London, 1995), and studies stressing the formative role of British imperialism, for example, S. Dubow, *Racial Segregation and the Origins of Apartheid in South Africa, 1919–1939* (Basingstoke, 1989), J. Krikler, *Revolution from Above, Rebellion from Below* (Oxford, 1993), and T. Keegan, *Colonial South Africa and the Origins of the Racial Order* (Cape Town, 1996).

88   Schwartz, *States versus Markets*, pp. 118–19; see also Hobsbawm, *The Age of Capital*, ch. 11. The argument of this subsection draws heavily on A. Callinicos, *Race and Class* (London, 1993).

89   Berghahn, 'German Big Business and the Quest for a European Economic Empire in the Twentieth Century', p. 25.

90   W.A. Williams [1959], *The Tragedy of American Diplomacy* (New York, 1972), pp. 50, 51.

91   N. Smith, *American Empire: Roosevelt's Geographer and the Prelude to Globalization* (Berkeley and Los Angeles, 2003), pp. 141–2. Julian Go offers a lucid account of America's early twentieth-century colonial experiments in 'Imperial Power and its Limits', in C. Calhoun et al., eds, *Lessons of Empire* (New York, 2006).

92   G. Arrighi et al., 'Geopolitics and High Finance', and 'The Transformation of Business Enterprise', in Arrighi, Silver et al., *Chaos and Governance in the World System*.

93   For a sympathetic diagnosis of Wilson's failure, see G.J. Ikenberry, *After Victory* (Princeton, 2001), ch. 5.

94   M.J. Hogan, *The Marshall Plan* (Cambridge, 1987), p. 3. See, on US efforts to reconstruct Europe in the 1920s, in addition to Hogan, *Informal Entente*, and Costigliola, *Awkward Dominion*, C.S. Maier, *Recasting Bourgeois Europe* (Princeton, 1975), id., 'The Two Postwar Eras and the Conditions for Stability in Twentieth-Century Europe', *American Historical Review*, 86 (1981), and P.O. Cohrs, *The Unfinished Peace after World War I* (Cambridge, 2006). Two valuable studies of the longer-term project of reshaping Europe in America's image

are K. van der Pijl, *The Making of an Atlantic Ruling Class* (London, 1984) and V. de Grazia, *Irresistible Empire* (Cambridge, 2005).

95   Hogan, *Informal Entente*, p. 226. The extensive evidence of growing friction between London and Washington during the late 1920s, in significant part over Britain's increasing difficulty in maintaining competitiveness after sterling's return to the gold standard at an overvalued exchange rate in April 1925 (a decision strongly disputed within the British establishment and made under American pressure), does not support Arrighi's contention that, in the interwar years, 'Wall Street and the Federal Reserve of New York simply joined the City of London and the Bank of England in maintaining and enforcing the international gold standard, whose main beneficiary was and remained Britain,' *The Long Twentieth Century*, p. 272. Compare Hogan, *Informal Entente*, pp. 208–27, Costigliola, *Awkward Dominion*, chs 4 and 7, and R. Skidelsky, *John Maynard Keynes*, II (London, 1992), ch. 6.

96   Van der Pijl, *The Making of an Atlantic Ruling Class*, ch. 4 (quotation from p. 91).

97   Hogan, *The Marshall Plan*, p. 13. Hogan's and Van der Pijl's accounts bear a family resemblance to John Ruggie's conception of 'embedded liberalism', which he defines as 'the conjunction of multilateralism and safeguarding domestic stability': 'International Regimes, Transactions, and Change', *International Organization*, 36 (1982), quotation from p. 396.

98   Kindleberger, *The World in Depression 1929–1939*, p. 271.

99   Quoted in Gamble, *Britain in Decline*, p. 256 n.21.

100 D. Reynolds, *The Creation of the Anglo-American Alliance 1937–1941* (London, 1981), pp. 261, 5, 78. Randall Schweller has written an interesting realist interpretation of the origins of the Second World War, *Deadly Imbalances* (New York, 1998), that suffers from two major defects: first, using a measure of state capabilities that excludes the contribution made by the Empire, and especially India, to British power, he treats Britain as a 'Lesser Great Power', in a tripolar system of the USSR, the US and Germany, an analysis that, while correct about the trend, overstates Britain's decline in the interwar period; secondly, because, in typical realist fashion, economics only figures in Schweller's account through its impact on state capabilities, he portrays the US in the 1930s as indifferent to the status quo, ignoring its interest in securing a global Open Door.

101 See, in addition to Reynolds's outstanding study and Gabriel Kolko's path-breaking *The Politics of War* (New York, 1970), C. Thorne, *Allies of a Kind* (Oxford, 1979), Louis, *Imperialism at Bay 1941–1945*, C. Layne, *The Peace of Illusions* (Ithaca, 2006), ch. 2, and P. Clarke, *The Last Thousand Days of the British Empire* (London, 2007).

102 R. Skidelsky, *John Maynard Keynes*, III (London, 2000), chs 6–13 (quotation from p. 468).

103 M.P. Leffler, *A Preponderance of Power: National Security, the Truman Administration, and the Cold War* (Stanford, 1992), p. 35.

104 Id., 'The American Conception of National Security and the Beginnings of the Cold War', in G.J. Ikenberry, ed., *American Foreign Policy* (4th edn; New York, 2002), and Louis, *Imperialism at Bay 1941–1945*, chs 16 and 23.

105 Quoted in Leffler, *A Preponderance of Power*, p. 446. Kennan's telegram is available at ⟨www.gwu.edu/~nsarchiv/coldwar/documents/episode–1/kennan.htm⟩. It was followed by his anonymous 'X-article', 'The Sources of Soviet Conduct', *Foreign Affairs*, July 1947. Kennan subsequently claimed that he had been misunderstood as advocating the military containment of the Soviet Union: *Memoirs 1925–1950* (London, 1967), ch. 15.

106 D. Acheson, *Present at the Creation* (New York, 1969), p. 375; T.S. Borden, *The Pacific Alliance* (Madison, 1984), p. 22.

107 Borden, *The Pacific Alliance*, pp. 7–8; figures from p. 23.

108 Ibid., p. 8.

109 See John Dower's great study of the Occupation, *Embracing Defeat* (London, 1999).

110 A.S. Milward, *The Reconstruction of Western Europe 1945–51* (London, 1984), pp. 59, 44. Both Milward and Hogan, *The Marshall Plan*, offer compelling accounts of the highly conflictual processes of bargaining between the US and the Western European states, particularly Britain, in the second half of the 1940s. Peter Burnham's incisive Marxist study documents the determined pursuit of an independent economic policy by British state managers during this period: *The Political Economy of Postwar Reconstruction* (Basingstoke, 1990). The 1947 sterling crisis is also explored in detail in B. Pimlott, *Hugh Dalton* (London, 1985), chs XXVI–XXIX.

111 Layne, *The Peace of Illusions*, ch. 4; quotations from pp. 81, 82.

112 Quoted in Layne, *The Peace of Illusions*, p. 87. The beginnings of European integration are very well covered in Milward, *The Reconstruction of Western Europe, 1945–51*, chs XI–XIV.
113 Quoted in H. Kissinger, *Diplomacy* (New York, 1994), p. 547.
114 Quoted in T.G. Ash, *In the Name of Europe* (London, 1994), p. 87. The role of national interests in the early process of European construction is the main theme of Milward's *The European Rescue of the Nation State* (London, 1994).
115 Milward, *The European Rescue of the Nation State*, pp. 374–5, 427–8.
116 'NSC 68: United States Objective and Programmes for National Security', 14 April 1950, sections VI and IX, available at ⟨http://www.fas.org/irp/offdocs/nsc–hst/nsc–68.htm⟩. See the excellent critical discussion in J.L. Gaddis, *Strategies of Containment* (Oxford, 1982), ch. 4, as well as Acheson, *Present at the Creation*, ch. 41, D. Callahan, *Dangerous Capabilities: Paul Nitze and the Cold War* (New York, 1990), ch. 4, and J. Chace, *Acheson* (New York, 1998), chs 24 and 25.
117 Borden, *The Pacific Alliance*, p. 56; quotation on p. 146.
118 Harman, *Explaining the Crisis*, pp. 75–90; figures and quotation from p. 80. See also M. Kidron, 'A Permanent Arms Economy', *International Socialism*, 1/28 (1967), available at ⟨www.marxists.org⟩, and *Western Capitalism since the War* (Harmondsworth, 1970), and T. Cliff [1957], 'Perspectives on the Permanent Arms Economy', in id., *Marxist Theory after Trotsky*.
119 See, for the first formulation of this idea, A. Callinicos, 'Imperialism, Capitalism, and the State Today', *International Socialism*, 2/35 (1987): 87.
120 Findlay and O'Rourke, *Power and Plenty*, ch. 9.
121 The growing importance of self-financing in the interwar years was noted by Franz Neumann: *Behemoth* (New York, 1944), pp. 318–19; see, for the postwar period, M. Kidron, 'Imperialism: Highest Stage but One' and [1965] 'International Capitalism', in id., *Capitalism and Theory* (London, 1974), pp. 129, 151–2.
122 Harman, *Explaining the Crisis*, pp. 90–102. For an alternative interpretation, that also explains the 'long downturn' as a crisis of profitability but locates the latter in the uneven economic development of the major capitalist centres, see R. Brenner, 'The Economics of Global Turbulence', *New Left Review*, I/229 (1998), and *The Boom and the Bubble* (London, 2002).

In contrast, Andrew Glyn and his co-thinkers explain the crisis as a profit squeeze caused by workers' success during the boom in driving up real wages: P. Armstrong et al., *Capitalism since World War II* (London, 1984) and A. Glyn, *Capitalism Unleashed* (Oxford, 2006), ch. 1. The crisis of the Bretton Woods system is analysed in F. Block, *Origins of International Economic Disorder* (Berkeley/Los Angeles, 1977) and R. Parboni, *The Dollar and its Rivals* (London, 1981; quotation from p. 98).

123 Layne, *Peace of Illusions*, ch. 5, provides detail on how Washington overcame threats to its European hegemony from Gaullism in the 1960s and at the end of the Cold War. Van der Pijl, *Global Rivalries from the Cold War to Iraq*, chs 2–7, traces US efforts to maintain its hegemony across the postwar decades.

124 B. Porter, 'Trying to Make Decolonization Look Good', *London Review of Books*, 2 August 2007: 6.

125 See the excellent discussion of postwar British strategy in D. Reynolds, *Britannia Overruled* (London, 1991), chs 7 and 8, and, on the Malaya, Cyprus and Kenyan 'emergencies', respectively, C.A. Bayly and T. Harper, *Forgotten Wars* (London, 2007), R. Holland, *Britain and the Revolt in Cyprus, 1954–1959* (Oxford, 1998), and D. Anderson, *Histories of the Hanged* (London, 2005).

126 M. Kidron, 'Imperialism', p. 132. In *Foreign Investments in India* (Oxford, 1965), Kidron plots the shift from the network of British management agencies, heavily dependent on state support, that dominated the Indian economy under British rule to the very different pattern of investment by multinational corporations operating in sometimes uneasy partnership with locally controlled capital, both private and state, after independence. I am grateful to Nigel Harris for impressing on me the importance of this study.

127 World Bank, *World Development Report 1985*, p. 126.

128 N. Harris, 'Theories of Unequal Exchange', *International Socialism*, 2/33 (1986): 119–20. See A. Emmanuel, *Unequal Exchange* (London, 1972), and S. Amin, *Unequal Development* (New York, 1976), and, for other critiques, C. Bettelheim, 'Theoretical Comments', appendix to Emmanuel, *Unequal Exchange*, M. Kidron, 'Black Reformism: The Theory of Unequal Exchange', in id., *Capitalism and Theory*, A. Brewer, *Marxist Theories of Imperialism* (2nd edn, London,

1990), ch. 9, and G. Carchedi, *Frontiers of Political Economy* (London, 1991), ch. 6.

129 Kidron, 'Imperialism', pp. 134–7.

130 N. Harris, *India-China: Underdevelopment and Revolution* (New Delhi, 1974), p. 171.

131 Borden, *The Pacific Alliance*, ch. 6.

132 G. Kolko, *Anatomy of a War* (New York, 1985), pp. 111–12.

133 'Annex – Plan for Action in South Vietnam', 24 March 1965, in N. S. Sheehan et al., *The Pentagon Papers* (New York, 1971), p. 432. The same obsession with credibility governed the Nixon administration's efforts to extricate the US from Vietnam: for example, R. Dallek, *Nixon and Kissinger* (London, 2007).

134 Kidron, 'International Capitalism', p. 162, and Harris, *India-China*, pp. 173–4.

135 S. Bromley, *American Hegemony and World Oil* (Cambridge, 1991), p. 86. See also id., 'The United States and Control of World Oil', *Government and Opposition*, 40 (2005), and J. Rees, *Imperialism and Resistance* (London, 2006), ch. 3.

136 Quoted in Yergin, *The Prize*, p. 702. Lawrence Freedman's masterly study of the perplexities of US Middle Eastern policy since the late 1970s elegantly demonstrates how hard it is to be an imperial power: *A Choice of Enemies: America Confronts the Middle East* (London, 2008).

137 M. Mann, 'Globalization and September 11', *New Left Review*, II/12 (2001): 54.

138 For the South African case, see D. Innes, *Anglo American and the Rise of Modern South Africa* (London, 1984), ch. 6, and D. Yudelmann, *The Emergence of Modern South Africa* (Cape Town, 1984).

139 P. Clawson, 'The Development of Capitalism in Egypt', *Khamsin*, 9 (1981), and J. Waterbury, *The Egypt of Nasser and Sadat* (Princeton, 1983). Vivek Chibber's study of the failure of India's state-promoted industrialization is exceptionally important because of the comparative perspective it adopts and its focus on the relationship between the state and capital: *Locked in Place* (Princeton, 2003).

140 N. Harris, *The End of the Third World* (London, 1986), B. Cumings, 'The Origins and Development of the Northeast Asian Political Economy', *International Organization*, 38 (1984), A.H. Amsden, 'Third World Industrialization', *New*

Left Review, I/182 (1990), and Schwartz, *States versus Markets*, ch. 11.

141 Neoliberalism's poor economic record in the South is acknowledged by a World Bank economist in W. Easterley, 'The Lost Decades: Developing Countries' Stagnation in Spite of Policy Reform', *Journal of Economic Change*, 6 (2001).

142 B. Anderson, 'From Miracle to Crash', *London Review of Books*, 16 April 1998. Chibber argues that the support of Japanese capital, which sought to use South Korea's cheap labour and access to the US market, facilitated Seoul's successful adoption of export-led industrialization in the 1960s: *Locked in Place*, ch. 3.

143 I am indebted here to the pioneering analysis of Alexandro Dabat and Luis Lorenzano, *Argentina: The Malvinas and the End of Military Rule* (London, 1984).

144 F. Halliday, *Iran: Dictatorship and Development* (Harmondsworth, 1979), ch. 9; see ibid., pp. 282–4, for a useful discussion of the concept of sub-imperialism, as well as Halliday's earlier treatment in *Arabia without Sultans* (Harmondsworth, 1974), pp. 498ff., where the influence of dependency theory is evident.

145 The theory of regional security complexes developed by Barry Buzan and others can be helpful in understanding the geopolitical dynamics discussed in this and the preceding paragraph: e.g., B. Buzan and O. Waever, *Regions and Powers* (Cambridge, 2003). For a more extended discussion of sub-imperialisms, see Callinicos, 'Marxism and Imperialism Today', pp. 31–9.

146 F. Halliday, *The Making of the Second Cold War* (London, 1983), and *Cold War, Third World* (London, 1989), and, on Afghanistan, J. Cooley, *Unholy Wars* (London, 1999).

147 R.L. Garthoff, *The Great Transition* (Washington, DC, 1994), p. 423 n.24. See, for a detailed account of especially the later stages of the nuclear arms race, in R. Rhodes, *Arsenals of Folly* (London, 2008), and, for broader interpretations, C. Harman, 'The Storm Breaks', *International Socialism*, 2/46 (1990), and A. Callinicos, *The Revenge of History* (Cambridge, 1991).

148 Callinicos, 'Marxism and Imperialism Today', p. 27.

5 IMPERIALISM AND GLOBAL POLITICAL ECONOMY TODAY

1 R.H. Wade, 'The Invisible Hand of the American Empire', *Ethics and International Affairs*, 17 (2003): 77.

2   Ibid., pp. 78, 80, 81–2.

3   R. Brenner, 'What is, and What is Not, Imperialism?', *Historical Materialism*, 14/4 (2006): 90.

4   Id., 'Imperialism and Neoliberalism', paper given at *Historical Materialism* conference, London, 10 November 2007.

5   S. Bromley, 'The United States and Control of World Oil', *Government and Opposition*, 40 (2005): 253–4.

6   G.J. Ikenberry, *After Victory* (Princeton, 2001), p. 255.

7   P. Gowan, *The Global Gamble* (London, 1999). See also R. Parboni, *The Dollar and its Rivals* (London, 1981), ch. 1.

8   R.H. Wade and F. Veneroso, 'The East Asian Crisis: The High Debt Model versus the Wall Street-Treasury-IMF Complex', *New Left Review*, I/228 (1998).

9   There was considerable subsequent dispute among the participants over whether such a promise was part of the final agreement on German unification: M.R. Gordon, 'Anatomy of a Misunderstanding', *New York Times*, 25 May 1997. But the semi-official American history of the negotiations makes it amply clear that even the membership of a Federal Republic incorporating East Germany in NATO was extremely hard for Gorbachev and his team to swallow: P. Zelikow and C. Rice, *Germany Unified and Europe Transformed* (Cambridge, MA, 1997).

10 Z. Brzezinski, *The Grand Chessboard* (New York, 1998), pp. 74, 79.

11 S.F. Cohen, 'The New American Cold War', *The Nation*, 10 July 2006 (online edition), ⟨www.thenation.com⟩. See also G. Achcar, 'Rasputin Plays at Chess: How the West Blundered into a New Cold War', and P. Gowan, 'The Euro-Atlantic Origins of NATO's Attack on Yugoslavia', in T. Ali, ed., *Masters of the Universe?* (London, 2000).

12 Quoted in T.S. Borden, *The Pacific Alliance* (Madison, 1984), p. 240 n.29.

13 G. Arrighi, *The Long Twentieth Century* (London, 1994), p. 5.

14 Id., *Adam Smith in Beijing* (London, 2007), pp. 133, 160. Arrighi rightly stresses that a major difference between the Great Depression of the late nineteenth century and the 'long downturn' a hundred years later was that in the first case the gold standard emerged, if anything, strengthened, introducing a deflationary bias that may have encouraged the spread of protectionist policies, while in the second the

collapse of the dollar-exchange standard at the start of the 1970s helped to produce the distinctive pattern of stagflation (high and rising unemployment *and* inflation): ibid., pp. 116–20. But he doesn't address the specific combination of going off gold and embracing Imperial Preference that shaped British economic policy in the hinge decades of the 1930s and 1940s.

15 Quoted in D. Fromkin, *A Peace to End All Peace* (London, 1991), p. 500.

16 Quoted in Arrighi, *Adam Smith in Beijing*, p. 136.

17 Quoted in J.L. Gaddis, *Strategies of Containment* (Oxford, 1982), p. 7.

18 See the discussion of purchasing power parity (PPP) calculations in §5.2.3. The rationale for using PPP rather than market exchange rates for Chinese and Russian defence spending is to give a more accurate measure of the resources these states are devoting to the military.

19 P. Anderson, 'The Figures of Descent', *New Left Review*, I/161 (1987): 71–3.

20 On the US role in founding the UN, see S.C. Schlesinger, *Act of Creation* (Boulder, 2003), and P. Gowan, 'US: UN', *New Left Review*, II/24 (2003).

21 B. Buzan, *The United States and the Great Powers* (Cambridge, 2004), p. 136.

22 A. Gramsci, *Further Selections from the Prison Notebooks* (ed. D. Boothman; London, 1995), pp. 429–30.

23 T. Friedman, *The World is Flat* (London, 2005), p. 12.

24 K. Waltz, 'The Emerging Structure of International Politics', *International Security*, 18 (1993): 77.

25 Id., 'Structural Realism after the Cold War', *International Security*, 25 (2000): 27.

26 W. Wolforth, 'The Stability of a Unipolar World', *International Security*, 24 (1999).

27 A. Moravcsik, 'Taking Preferences Seriously: A Liberal Theory of International Politics', *International Organization*, 51 (1997): 535.

28 A. Rugman, 'Globalization and Regional International Production', in J. Ravenhill, ed., *Global Political Economy* (Oxford, 2005), p. 264.

29 I am particularly indebted here to S. Ashman, 'Globalization as Uneven Development' (PhD thesis, University of Birmingham, 2006).

30 C. Giles, 'Warning over Cost Benefits of Emerging Economies', *Financial Times*, 3 October 2006.
31 K. van der Pijl, *Global Rivalries from the Cold War to Iraq* (London, 2006), pp. 283–6.
32 Rugman, 'Globalization and Regional International Production', pp. 269–70.
33 Ibid., pp. 270–84 (quotation from p. 284).
34 K. Bronfenbrenner and S. Luce, 'The Changing Nature of Corporate Global Restructuring', Paper for US–China Economic and Security Review Commission, 14 October 2004, ⟨www.uscc.gov⟩, pp. i, 21.
35 'Textile production moves away from China as taste for fast fashion grows', *Financial Times*, 30 August 2005.
36 P. Bond, *Looting Africa* (London, 2006).
37 C. Brown-Humes, 'A Grown-Up Brady Bunch', *Financial Times*, 2 March 2006.
38 World Bank, *World Development Indicators 2008*, ⟨www.siteresources.worldbank.org⟩, table 2.5a.
39 G. Duménil and D. Lévy, 'Neo-Liberal Income Trends', *New Left Review*, II/30 (2004): 111, 119.
40 M. Brewer et al., *Poverty and Inequality in Britain: 2008*, Institute of Fiscal Studies, June 2008, ⟨www.ifs.org.uk⟩, pp. 27–8.
41 *Globe & Mail*, 9 February 2006. See more generally on poverty and inequality the very helpful discussions in B. Milanovic, *Worlds Apart* (Princeton, 2005), R. Kaplinsky, *Globalization, Poverty and Inequality* (Cambridge, 2005), and R.H. Wade, 'Globalization, Growth, Poverty, Inequality, Resentment, and Imperialism', in J. Ravenhill, ed. *Global Political Economy* (2nd edn, Oxford, 2007).
42 K. Guha et al., 'Middle America Misses Out on Benefits of Growth', *Financial Times*, 1 November 2006.
43 R. Brenner, paper for *Historical Materialism* Conference, 11 November 2007; International Monetary Fund, *World Economic Outlook*, April 2008, ⟨www.imf.org⟩, p. 4. For up-to-date discussions of profitability, see Brenner, *The Economics of Global Turbulence* (London, 2006), C. Harman, 'The Rate of Profit and the World Today', *International Socialism*, 2/115 (2007), and the discussion of the latter article by Jim Kincaid, Chris Harman and Fred Moseley, *International Socialism*, 2/119 (2008). Brenner traces the development of successive bubbles in *The Boom and the Bubble* (London, 2002) and

'New Boom or New Bubble?', *New Left Review*, II/25 (2004); Graham Turner discusses the collapse of the latest in *The Credit Crunch* (London, 2008).

44   This policy shift is lucidly expounded by one of its architects in N. Lawson, (1980) 'The New Conservatism', and (1984), 'The British Experiment', in id., *The View from Number 11* (London, 1992), and at ⟨www.margaretthatcher.org⟩.

45   D. Harvey, *A Short History of Neo–Liberalism* (Oxford, 2005).

46   See C. Hay, 'Globalization's Impact on States', in Ravenhill, ed., *Global Political Economy*, and, for a sceptical take on the claims sometimes made about neoliberalism's effectiveness by Marxist scholars, C. Harman, 'Theorizing Neoliberalism', *International Socialism*, 2/117 (2008).

47   F. Jameson, 'Postmodernism, or The Cultural Logic of Late Capitalism', *New Left Review*, I/146 (1984): 78.

48   Wade, 'Globalization, Growth, Poverty, Inequality, Resentment, and Imperialism', p. 390. See the detailed critique of PPP measures of income in A. Freeman, 'The Inequality of Nations', in Freeman and B. Kagarlitsky, eds, *The Politics of Empire* (London, 2004), and, in defence, A. Maddison, *Contours of the World Economy, 1–2030 AD* (Oxford, 2007), pp. 295–301. Caution in these matters is indicated by recent recalculations that have significantly reduced the size of the Chinese economy as measured by PPP, lowering its share of global GDP in 2005 from 14.39 to 9.58 per cent: see, for example, A. Keidel, 'The Limits of a Smaller, Poorer China', *Financial Times*, 13 November 2007.

49   Arrighi, *Adam Smith in Beijing*, p. 389.

50   For example, R. Walker and D. Buck, 'The Chinese Road', *New Left Review*, II/46 (2007), M. Hart-Landsberg and P. Burkett, *China and Socialism* (New York, 2005), and, for a fascinating study of patterns of working-class resistance, C.K. Lee, *Against the Law: Labour Protests in China's Rustbelt and Sunbelt* (Berkeley and Los Angeles, 2007). My main disagreement with these analyses is that, in my view, China before the introduction of Deng Xiaoping's reforms in 1978 did not represent any form of socialism but rather bureaucratic state capitalism; hence the past generation's transition has been from one form of capitalism to another: see, e.g., N. Harris, *The Mandate of Heaven* (London, 1978), and C. Hore, 'China's Century?', *International Socialism*, 2/103 (2004).

51   G. Dyer, 'Growth in Chinese Forex Reserves Slows', *Financial Times*, 14 July 2008.

52   F. Zakaria, *The Post-American World* (London, 2008), p. 124; M. Dooley et al., 'The Revived Bretton Woods System', *International Journal of Finance and Economics*, 9 (2004).

53   Ho-fung Hung, 'Rise of China and the Global Overaccumulation Crisis', *Review of International Political Economy*, 15 (2008): 170; I am grateful to Kees van der Pijl for this reference. The *Financial Times* has provided excellent coverage of the contradictions of the Chinese boom: especially J. Kynge and D. Roberts, 'Cut-Throat Competitors', *Financial Times*, 4 February 2003, and R. McGregor, 'China's Unbalanced Economy', ibid., 21 May 2007.

54   Wade, 'The Invisible Hand of American Empire', pp. 82–3.

55   H.M. Schwartz, *States versus Markets: The Emergence of a Global Economy* (2nd edn; Basingstoke, 2000), ch. 9, Harman, 'Theorizing Neoliberalism', p. 99, and Brenner, *The Boom and the Bubble*.

56   IMF, *World Economic Outlook*, April 2008, p. 18.

57   Paper at *Historical Materialism* Conference, 10 November 2007; R. Atkins, 'Onwards and Upwards', *Financial Times*, 31 December 2008. See, for a theoretical and historical framework, M. Itoh and C. Lapavitsas, *Political Economy of Money and Finance* (London, 1999).

58   J. Frankel, 'The Euro Could Surpass the Dollar within Ten Years', 18 March 2008, ⟨www.voxeu.org⟩.

59   J. Authers, 'Smiling Dollar', *Financial Times*, 4 September 2008.

60   Buzan, *The United States and the Great Powers*, pp. 68, 69–70, 74, 103.

61   A. Callinicos, 'Imperialism and Global Political Economy', *International Socialism*, 2/108 (2005): 122–3.

62   For example, 'Post-Wolfowitz Planning Begins', *Financial Times*, 19 May 2007. Perry Anderson's splendid polemic is a valuable corrective to the EU's boastful celebrations of its 'soft power' but it overstates Brussels' subordination to Washington: 'European Hypocrisies', *London Review of Books*, 20 September 2007.

63   J. Nye, *The Paradox of American Power* (Oxford, 2002).

64   C. Serfati, *Imperialisme et militarisme* (Lausanne, 2004), chs 8 and 9 (quotation from p. 198); H. Münkler, *Empires* (Cambridge, 2007), p. 167. The EU's geostrategic bifurcation is

reflected in its arms industry, which is dominated by the Franco-German consortium EADS and Britain's BAE Systems, which, though it has successfully campaigned for the status of pre-ferred supplier to the British military, has concentrated in recent years on becoming a major US arms producer.

65 T. Murphy, 'East Asia's Dollars', *New Left Review*, II/40 (2006): 47–9 See also id., 'Japan's Economic Crisis', ibid., II/1 (2000), and G. McCormack, 'Remilitarizing Japan', ibid., II/29 (2004).

66 J. VandeHei et al., 'US, India Seal Nuclear Deal', *Washington Post*, 2 March 2006.

67 M. Haynes, 'The Return of Russian Power?', *International Socialism*, 2/116 (2007).

68 Serfati, *Imperialisme et militarisme*, ch. 7 (quotation from p. 184).

69 Brzezinski, *The Grand Chessboard*, ch. 5.

70 P. Anderson, 'Jottings on the Conjuncture', *New Left Review*, II/48 (2007): 11. On Metternich and Castlereagh, see Henry Kissinger's brilliant doctoral thesis, *A World Restored* (London, 1957). Anderson expresses in a particular sharp and elegant form the views of many other radical scholars, perhaps most notably Leo Panitch and Sam Gindin: see 'Global Capitalism and American Empire', in Panitch and Colin Leys, eds, *The New Imperial Challenge: Socialist Register 2004* (London, 2003), 'Finance and American Empire', in Panitch and Leys, eds, *The Empire Reloaded: Socialist Register 2005* (London, 2004), and 'Superintending Global Capital', *New Left Review*, II/35 (2005). See my exchange with them: Callinicos, 'Imperial-ism and Global Political Economy', Panitch and Gindin, ' "Imperialism and Global Political Economy" – A Reply to Alex Callinicos', *International Socialism*, 2/109 (2006), and Callinicos, 'Making Sense of Imperialism: A Reply to Leo Panitch and Sam Gindin', ibid., 2/110 (2006). Gopal Balakrish-nan raises but fails to answer some interesting questions about the relationship between capitalism and geopolitics today in 'States of War', *New Left Review*, II/36 (2005).

71 *The National Security Strategy of the United States of America*, September 2002, ⟨www.whitehouse.gov⟩, pp. 26, 28.

72 Brzezinski, *The Grand Chessboard*, ch. 6 (on East Asia).

73 R. A. Pape, 'Soft Balancing against the United States', and T.V. Paul, 'Soft Balancing in the Age of US Primacy', *International Security*, 30 (2005).

74   G. Dyer, 'Stirrings in the Suburbs', *Financial Times*, 20 July 2008.

75   Quoted in D. Callahan, *Dangerous Capabilities: Paul Nitze and the Cold War* (New York, 1990), p. 379.

76   Department of Defense, *Quadrennial Defense Review Report*, 6 February 2006, ⟨www.defenselink.mil⟩, pp. 29, 30.

77   Buzan, *The United States and the Great Powers*, p. 115. For surveys of geopolitical rivalries in contemporary Asia, see K. E. Calder, *Asia's Deadly Triangle* (London, 1997), and B. Emmott, *Rivals* (London, 2008). There is an interesting discussion of the debates among US policy intellectuals over alternative strategies for containing China in Arrighi, *Adam Smith in Beijing*, ch. 10.

78   Anderson, 'Jottings on the Conjuncture', p. 11.

79   P.M. Kennedy, *The Rise of the Anglo–German Antagonism 1860–1914* (London, 1980), ch. 15.

80   W.G. Beasley, *Japanese Imperialism 1894–1945* (Oxford, 1987), pp. 126–7.

81   K. Barbieri, *The Liberal Illusion: Does Trade Promote Peace?* (Ann Arbor, 2002).

82   See, on the 1970s, Parboni, *The Dollar and its Rivals*.

83   Anderson, 'Jottings on the Conjuncture', pp. 12–13, 15. See J.J. Mearsheimer and S.M. Walt, 'The Israel Lobby', *London Review of Books*, 23 March 2006, and *The Israel Lobby and US Foreign Policy* (London, 2007).

84   G. Achcar, 'US Imperial Strategy in the Middle East', in id., *Eastern Cauldron* (New York, 2004), quotation from pp. 18–19. See also the admirably clear-headed discussion of the Israel lobby in N. Chomsky and G. Achcar, *Perilous Power: The Middle East and US Foreign Policy* (London, 2007), ch. 3, and, on the elder Bush administration's conflicts with Israel, A. Shlaim, *The Iron Wall* (London, 2001), ch. 12, and L. Freedman, *A Choice of Enemies: America Confronts the Middle East* (London, 2008), ch. 13.

85   G. Friedman, *America's Secret War* (London, 2004), pp. 246.

86   D. Harvey, *The New Imperialism* (Oxford, 2003), p. 19; see also ibid., p. 25.

87   See, on US military doctrine under Clinton, Gilbert Achcar's remarkably prescient 'The Strategic Triad: The United States, Russia, and China', *New Left Review*, I/228 (1995), and, for the militarization of US foreign policy in the 1990s, A.J. Bacevich, *American Empire* (Cambridge, MA, 2002), and D. Priest,

The Mission (New York, 2003). Wolfowitz's geopolitical outlook is outlined in 'Bridging Centuries', *The National Interest*, 47 (1997). James Mann has written an excellent study of the neoconservatives in *Rise of the Vulcans* (New York, 2004). I offer a more detailed interpretation of the origins of the Iraq War in *The New Mandarins of American Power* (Cambridge, 2003), and 'Iraq: Fulcrum of World Politics', *Third World Quarterly*, 26 (2005); see also John Rees's incisive analysis, *Imperialism and Resistance* (London, 2006). The group of radical scholars writing under the name 'Retort' offer some suggestive insights in their book *Afflicted Powers* (London, 2005), but their interpretation of the war as serving the interests of the US 'oil-arms-military-engineering-construction-finance-drugs nexus' (p. 71) is unpersuasive, partly because such a comprehensive list lacks explanatory power, partly because it denies any role to geopolitics.

88 A.J. Bacevich, 'Surge to Nowhere', *Washington Post*, 20 January 2008, and P. Cockburn, 'Who is Whose Enemy?', *London Review of Books*, 6 March 2008, 'Iran v. America', ibid., 19 June 2008, and 'America Concedes', ibid., 18 December 2008. Naomi Klein argues that 'the reconstruction of Iraq . . . has been anything but [a failure] for the disaster capitalism complex' (Halliburton, Blackwater & Co), marking 'the violent birth of a new economy', a neoliberal 'model for privatized war and reconstruction', *The Shock Doctrine* (London, 2007) pp. 381, 382, an analysis that captures part of the truth but that ignores the immense damage the occupation has done to the geopolitical position of the US.

89 Z. Brzezinski, *The Choice: Global Domination or Global Leadership* (New York, 2004), pp. 221, 63.

90 Quoted in H. Cooper, 'Russia Steps Up its Push; West Faces Tough Choices', *New York Times*, 11 August 2008. Friedman offers interesting broader analyses in 'Georgia and Kosovo: A Single Intertwined Crisis', 25 August 2008, and 'The Medvedev Doctrine and American Strategy', 2 September 2008, ⟨www.stratfor.com⟩. I am grateful to Craig Brandist for these references.

91 A. Callinicos, *The Resources of Critique* (Cambridge, 2006), ch. 4.

92 See, on this new convergence, Rees, *Imperialism and Resistance*, ch. 7, and, for much more on the *altermondialiste* movement, A. Callinicos, *An Anti-Capitalist Manifesto* (Cambridge,

2003), and 'The Future of the Anti-Capitalist Movement', in H. Dee, ed., *Anti-Capitalism: Where Now?* (London, 2004), and Callinicos and C. Nineham, 'At an Impasse? Anti-Capitalism and the Social Forums Today', *International Socialism*, 2/115 (2007).

INDEX